P9-BYS-170

BOBBY FLAY
COOKS AMERICAN

Also from Bobby Flay

Bobby Flay's Boy Meets Grill

Bobby Flay's from My Kitchen to Your Table

Bobby Flay's Bold American Food

BOBBY FLAY
COOKS AMERICAN
GREAT REGIONAL RECIPES WITH SIZZLING NEW FLAVORS

BOBBY FLAY WITH JULIA MOSKIN

HYPERION

NEW YORK

Copyright © 2001 Bobby Flay

Photographs copyright © 2001 Gentl & Hyers/Edge

All rights reserved. No part of this book may be used or reproduced in any manner whatsoever without
the written permission of the Publisher. Printed in Singapore. For information address Hyperion,
77 West 66th Street, New York, NY 10023-6298.

Library of Congress Cataloging-in-Publication Data

Flay, Bobby

     Bobby Flay cooks American : great regional recipes

with sizzling new flavors / Bobby Flay with Julia Moskin.—1st ed.

         p.   cm.

    Includes index.

    ISBN 0-7868-6714-0

    1. Cookery, American—Southwestern style. I. Moskin, Julia.

II. Title.

    TX715.2.S69 F5697 2001

    641.5979—dc21   2001016814

First Edition

10 9 8 7 6 5 4 3 2 1

For my daughter Sophie.
        America is such a beautiful place,
        I can't wait to watch you discover it.

Love, Daddy

Contents

The Fourth of July   217

Acknowledgments

I'd like to thank the following people for their help and support of this book:

Julia Moskin
Jane Dystel
Leslie Wells
Gentl & Hyers
Chris Hewitt
Vicki Wells
Katie Brown
My business partners, Jerry Kretchmer, Jeff Bliss, and Laurence Kretchmer
The staff and management of Mesa Grill and Bolo
The staff and management of Food Network
The staff and management of CBS's *The Early Show*

A special thank you to my assistant and friend Stephanie Banyas, whose involvement in this book made it all possible. Thanks for being so incredible.

and of course Mom and Dad.

Introduction

My first cookbook was called *Bold American Food,* and bold is just what it was—from the flavors of the food to the fact that I was writing a cookbook at all. I had recently opened Mesa Grill (a Southwestern restaurant, even though I'd lived my whole life in New York City), and my formal training was in the French culinary tradition. And calling it "American food" may have been the boldest move of all.

In 1991, when Mesa Grill opened, chefs all over America were still figuring out what American food was. The reign of French cooking was over, and American regional chefs like Wolfgang Puck, Alice Waters, and Paul Prudhomme were all presenting their different ideas. In New York, the hottest restaurants were serving food from Louisiana, the South, California, and the Southwest. I loved being part of the movement to define what American cooking could be, and I'm proud that Mesa Grill is still hopping a decade later.

The fad of American regional cooking may have passed—but the fact of American regional cooking is still going strong. I've spent a good chunk of the last two years on the road, and I can tell you that we Americans are prouder than ever of our food. The people who used to worship French cuisine have become barbecue experts instead. Michigan morels have become more prized than Italian truffles. We've realized that we have top-notch ingredients and a world-class culinary tradition right here in America. Even better, we've got farmers and cooks who know those ingredients inside out, and we've got a knack for taking the best of each tradition and making it part of the lively mix.

I knew I was going to have to do a whole book of American recipes after the first time I tasted real red rice in Savannah. There I was, a professional chef with formal training and almost twenty years of restaurant experience—and somehow no one had ever told me about this delicious dish. What else was I missing? I realized that there was still a whole lot of great American food out there waiting for us—and then I went out looking for it.

In the process, I got to watch cooks all over America interpret their own local food. I listened when they told me why they do what they do, and who taught them how. Most of the people I met weren't trained chefs; instead, they were legendary home cooks, or people who proudly run restaurants that serve totally local food—Southern buffets, Chesapeake crab houses, real Texas barbecue joints.

Those cooks made a huge contribution to this book, and you'll find their names and voices in these pages along with mine. I realized from watching them that I did know a lot about American ingredients—but not as much as I thought. There's a lot more you can do with okra than make gumbo, and a lot more to cornmeal than just cornbread. I already knew that the best tortillas are made fresh from cornmeal dough (*masa*)—but I didn't know that you could deep-fry a tortilla until it blows up like a balloon, then fold it in half to make something called a puffy taco, a specialty of San Antonio, Texas. That's what regional ingredients are all about—familiarity breeds creativity. I've worked with Southwestern ingredients for fifteen years, but I had never thought of that!

Everything I learned about American cooking I put to work in this book. When I got back into my own kitchen after each trip, I always found that one or two dishes had stayed with me. I knew I was going to cook them in some way, shape, or form, because I woke up thinking about them and couldn't stop imagining how they'd taste if I made them my own. What if I pulled out those Idaho potatoes and used sweet potatoes instead? What if I used a puree of ancho chiles instead of bottled hot sauce? Wouldn't cilantro taste even better than parsley there?

That's how all these recipes came to be. I went out there looking for the flavors that I've always loved—American classics like corn, shellfish, steak, squash, tamales, fruit cobblers, fried chicken, smoked ham, sweet onions, fresh salmon, chili, and mashed potatoes. Then I made them my own, and as you know, my recipes are all about flavor. This book isn't a history of American food, or a collection of the most authentic recipes for clam chowder and apple pie. It's a cookbook of my recipes, all inspired by the best American dishes—like Split Pea-Green Chile Soup with Chorizo and Toasted Cumin Crema, Vidalia Onion and Jersey Tomato Salad with Blue Ranch Dressing, Smoked Chicken and Caramelized Vegetable Pot Pie with a Sweet Potato Biscuit Crust, and Pistachio Pralines.

This book is like a photo album for me, with each recipe being a snapshot of a time and place in my life. First of all, it's a record of my travels and the dishes that inspired me to explore my own ideas about American food. Two American institutions—steakhouse dinners and summer cookouts at the beach—are powerful influences on the food in this book. You'll spot my first love, the flavors of the Southwest, all over these recipes. There are also some personal favorites, like a variation on my family's corned beef and cabbage and my grandmother's sauerbraten—recipes that weren't always American, but have become classics.

For the first time, I've included menus with recipes for my two favorite holidays in this book. It's not surprising that Thanksgiving and the Fourth of July are my favorites—they're the ones that are about cooking, eating, and hanging out. They're perfect occasions to celebrate the American table. As always, go ahead and add your own ideas and traditions to the mix.

And remember, get out there and eat America—it's waiting for you!

—Bobby Flay, New York City

Basic Techniques and Ingredients

Roasting Peppers

To roast bell peppers or chile peppers like poblanos, preheat the oven to 400°F. Rub the whole peppers with olive oil, place on a baking sheet, and roast, turning once, for about 20 minutes or until softened and blackened. Transfer the peppers to a brown paper bag, close the top, and set aside for 5 minutes (this helps steam the skins loose). Cut the peppers in half, and use your fingers to remove the stems, seeds, and peels. Do not rinse the roasted peppers in water.

Roasting Garlic and Shallots

Preheat the oven or a toaster oven to 300°F. For a whole head of garlic, cut off the top third of the head. For individual garlic cloves or shallots, leave whole (do not peel). Rub with olive oil and wrap tightly in foil. Roast 45 minutes to an hour, until very soft. Squeeze out the pulp from the skins. To squeeze a whole head of garlic, press on the bottom with your thumbs as though you are trying to turn the head inside out; the pulp will slip out of the skins. Pick out any bits of skin and chop or puree in a food processor.

Roasting Corn

Preheat the oven to 350°F. Remove the cornsilk and most of the cornhusks, leaving one layer to cover the corn. Dip in water, place on a sheet pan, and roast for 45 minutes. One ear of corn will yield about ½ cup kernels.

Toasting Spices

Whole spices, such as cumin and fennel seeds, are toasted to release the flavors. Heat a small heavy skillet over medium-low heat, then add the spices. Toss them in the pan until fragrant, about 2 or 3 minutes. Watch them carefully, as they can burn quickly.

Toasting Nuts and Coconut

Nuts are toasted to deepen their flavors. Preheat the oven to 350°F and spread the nuts out on a sheet pan. Toast 6–10 minutes, until fragrant and slightly browned. Check them often, as they can burn quickly. Small amounts can be toasted in a toaster oven.

Making Chipotle Puree

To make chipotle puree, buy canned chipotles in *adobo* (see below) and puree them with the sauce in a blender or food processor. Refrigerated, chipotle puree keeps indefinitely.

Chile Types

Ancho chiles are dried poblanos (see below), very dark red with a spicy raisin flavor. They are fruity, with moderate heat.

Arbol chiles are dried chiles, small, tapered, and very hot.

Cascabel chiles, available dried, offer a great combination of fruity, earthy, and tealike flavors and medium heat.

Chipotle chiles are smoked jalapeños with fiery and smoky tastes. They are available dried or preserved in *adobo,* a vinegar sauce, and a little goes a long way. For chipotle puree, see above.

Habanero chiles are also known as Scotch bonnets. They are among the hottest of all chiles. They are small with a rounded shape and range from light green to orange and red, depending on ripeness.

Jalapeño chiles are about 3 inches long, widely available, and have a pure hot flavor. They can range from green to red, depending on ripeness.

New Mexico chiles are the dried version of a New Mexico green, similar to an Anaheim. They have a deep, roasted flavor.

Pasilla chiles are dried chiles with an earthy flavor and medium heat.

Poblano chiles look like long, flattened dark green bell peppers. They provide medium heat and a lot of fresh pepper flavor.

Serrano chiles are slender, about 2 inches long, and very hot. They can be green or red.

(See Sources, page 231, for places to buy chiles.)

Chicken Stock

Makes 6 cups

2 pounds raw chicken carcasses, or bones with some meat attached
2 celery stalks, coarsely chopped
2 carrots, coarsely chopped
1 onion, coarsely chopped
6 peppercorns
1 bay leaf
8 sprigs parsley
2 quarts cold water

Combine all the ingredients in a large pot. Bring to a boil over high heat, skimming off any scum that rises to the top. Reduce the heat to a simmer and cook, uncovered, for 2 hours. Strain through cheesecloth or a fine strainer, let cool, and remove any fat that has risen to the top. Refrigerate up to 2 days or freeze.

Shrimp Stock

Makes 4–5 cups

2 tablespoons olive oil
3 cups raw shrimp shells and tails
1 large onion, coarsely chopped
1 small carrot, coarsely chopped
½ celery stalk, coarsely chopped
1 cup white wine
1 tomato, coarsely chopped, or ¼ cup canned plum tomatoes
1 bay leaf
6 cups cold water

In a large pot, heat the oil over high heat until almost smoking. Add the shrimp shells, onion, carrot, and celery, and cook, stirring, 5 minutes. Add the remaining ingredients and the cold water and bring to a boil. Reduce the heat to a simmer and cook, partly covered, 40 minutes. Strain through cheesecloth or a fine strainer, let cool, and refrigerate up to 2 days or freeze.

BOBBY FLAY
COOKS AMERICAN

Postcard from Ipswich and Gloucester, Massachusetts

The towns of the North Shore of Massachusetts have been working ports for hundreds and hundreds of years—and they're still hard at it. This isn't quaint New England: This is the reality of people making a living from the Atlantic Ocean, whether they're digging up clams on the beach, baking bread for swordfishermen to take out on the boats, or negotiating deals to bring those fish to cooks all over America. Around here, old New England cooking traditions mix with the imported traditions of the Italian, Greek, and Portuguese communities—so there's *chourico* sausage in the clambakes and clams on the pizza.

Working as a professional chef can be physically grueling, but I've never been so exhausted as I was after a morning of clamming with Charlie Gianakakis, a man in his eighties who's out on the mudflats at low tide almost every day. To find the clams, he looks for a small hole on the surface of the mud, then bends double and whacks the digger into the sand, tossing up about a foot of sand before prying the clam loose from its bed. Charlie does this over and over again, and it looks about as challenging as a game of Candyland. When I tried to do it, I was panting and in pain after ten minutes—and I didn't have a single clam to show for it!

Charlie's bushels of clams, along with most of the other seafood that pours onto the docks in Ipswich and Gloucester, are sold at auction to buyers for the big companies that process and distribute the seafood nationwide. I tagged along behind Louie Linquata, a buyer, as he quickly inspected piles of striped bass, swordfish, cod, scrod (which are just baby cod), clams, and mussels. Scallops and squid are also big New England harvests from the sea. I asked him what he was looking for, and he reeled off the three features of a really fresh fish: firm flesh, clear eyes, and red gills. (Brown gills and clouded eyes are always signs that the fish has been out of water for a while. When you're buying fillets, make sure the flesh is springy and firm, not mushy.) Louie picked out a striped bass for me and later grilled it with a fantastic tomato-garlic-mint relish that I think the Pilgrim fathers would have arrested him for—it was that good.

A little way down the waterfront, I ducked into the warm, welcoming Virgilio's Sicilian Bakery. Even if the sign didn't say Sicilian, I would have known right away from the religious names of the breads. (In Sicily, almost every kind of bread, pastry, and candy is named after a saint, nun, or priest.) Virgilio's specialty is the *scala,* meaning "stairs," a soft loaf that can be broken up into individual rolls—which makes it popular on the fishing boats. For his fantastic

Italian sandwiches, Mr. Virgilio uses a crusty St. Joseph's roll, round with four peaks on the top that make it look like a bishop's hat.

I brought a bag of fresh Virgilio's rolls to a clambake I got myself invited to on the beach at Gloucester. The clambake is a slow cooking method, but a great one. A local expert showed me the method that the Native Americans invented and taught to the settlers: a pit lined with slabs of local granite to hold the heat, and with wood on top burning down to red embers. Wet, salty seaweed is spread on top in a thick bed, topped with potatoes, corn cobs, clams, mussels, oysters, lobsters, and, often, Italian hot sausage or spicy Portuguese *chourico.* The pit is covered to hold the heat and then left alone for a few hours. The combination of baking on a red-hot slab and steaming in salt water reminded me of the method they use for oyster roasts in Savannah, a thousand miles farther south.

Next, I went in search of my very favorite New England dish: clam chowder. Yes, I'm from Manhattan—but even I know that creamy New England chowder is the real thing. A local cook who calls herself the "Chowder Lady" goes one better: She's got eight different chowders, one for each North Shore town. The bare tradition calls for salt pork, potatoes, clams, and cream (though milk, plus flour for thickening, is probably more traditional). Fish chowder is an equally old local tradition, made with the salted cod that many New England fortunes were founded on. Before technology made fresh fish available, salt cod was the first product that the settlers mastered—and they exported it all over the world. As a tribute, Massachusetts still has a fat codfish on its state seal.

Soups
and
Chowders

Mesa Grill's Pumpkin Soup with Cinnamon Cream and Toasted Pumpkin Seeds

Roasted Butternut Squash Soup with Toasted Almond Croutons

Cold Summer Tomato and Spring Onion Soup with Grilled Scallops

Lobster and Green Chile Bisque with Toasted Corn Relish

New England Clam and Sweet Potato Chowder

Roasted Cauliflower and Lobster Soup with Crushed Almonds

Steamed Clams with Coconut Milk and Hot Pepper Flakes

Crawfish and Oyster Bisque

Steamed Mussels in Roasted Tomato–Saffron Broth

Oyster and Caramelized Onion Pan Roast

Bronzed Chicken and Red Bean Soup

Split Pea–Green Chile Soup with Chorizo and Toasted Cumin Crema

Mesa Grill's Pumpkin Soup with Cinnamon Cream and Toasted Pumpkin Seeds

This velvety soup is a Mesa Grill classic, and my most-requested recipe of all time. I used to use squash in this recipe, and saved pumpkin for my favorite pie. But unsweetened pumpkin puree has the perfect texture for this creamy soup. I always add a handful of earthy, roasted pumpkin seeds, because I love crunch in my food, even in a soup. Especially in a soup.

I often use Mexican cinnamon in my cooking at Mesa Grill. It's sweeter and less spicy than the cinnamon we find at our markets. Mexican cinnamon is also known as *canela;* you can find it easily at any Mexican, Asian, or Indian grocery store. Feel free to use canned pumpkin puree (the unflavored kind) in this recipe; I always do. It's one of the few canned products I allow into my kitchens!

Serves 4

3 tablespoons unsalted butter
1 large onion, coarsely chopped
2 cloves garlic, coarsely chopped
2 carrots, peeled and coarsely chopped
2 stalks celery, coarsely chopped
7 cups water
1½ cups canned pumpkin puree (not flavored pie filling)
¼ teaspoon ground cinnamon, Mexican if possible
¼ teaspoon allspice
¼ teaspoon ground ginger
¼ teaspoon freshly grated nutmeg
2 tablespoons honey
2 teaspoons chipotle puree (page xiii)
¾ cup crème fraîche or sour cream
Salt and freshly ground pepper
1 teaspoon ground Mexican cinnamon for garnish
Toasted Pumpkin Seeds (see below)

1. Heat the butter in a large saucepan over medium heat. Add the onion, garlic, carrots, and celery, and cook, stirring occasionally, until soft. Do not brown. Add the water and bring to a boil. Reduce the heat and simmer 20–30 minutes. Strain the stock into a clean medium saucepan. Whisk the pumpkin puree into the stock until smooth. Bring to a simmer and add the spices, honey, and chipotle puree. Cook 15–20 minutes.

Add water if the soup seems too thick. Turn off the heat and whisk in ¼ cup of the crème fraîche. Season with salt and pepper to taste.

2. Mix together the remaining crème fraîche and 1 teaspoon cinnamon until combined. Ladle the soup into bowls, drizzle with cinnamon crème fraîche, and sprinkle with toasted pumpkin seeds. Serve immediately.

Toasted Pumpkin Seeds

2 cups pumpkin seeds, preferably fresh (but raw ones from the market will work)
2 tablespoons vegetable oil
Kosher salt

1. Preheat the oven to 350°F. If using fresh seeds, rinse them in a bowl of water to remove the strings and pulp. Blot dry on paper towels.

2. On a shallow baking pan, toss the seeds with the oil and season with salt to taste. Bake until lightly golden brown and crisp, tossing occasionally, 30–35 minutes. Let cool.

Roasted Butternut Squash Soup with Toasted Almond Croutons

Butternut squash is about as American as you can get. I've found recipes using it from New Mexico to New England. For this seductive soup, I inject some Mediterranean warmth with saffron, almonds, and harissa—a fiery Moroccan chile paste. Smooth squash is great with toasted nuts, texture- and flavor-wise, so I serve this with crunchy almond croutons.

Serves 6

For the vegetable stock:

1 onion, peeled and coarsely chopped
2 stalks celery, coarsely chopped
1 large carrot, coarsely chopped
2 cloves garlic, smashed
6 sprigs parsley
2 sprigs thyme
1 bay leaf
6 black peppercorns
8 cups cold water

For the soup:

1 large butternut squash, halved and seeded
3 tablespoons unsalted butter, softened at room temperature
2 teaspoons olive oil
Pinch of saffron
½ teaspoon ground cinnamon
¼ teaspoon freshly grated nutmeg
Pinch of ground cloves
½ cup crème fraîche
2 teaspoons harissa (available at Middle Eastern and specialty foods markets)
Salt and freshly ground pepper
Toasted Almond Croutons (see page 9)
Finely chopped chives

1. Make the vegetable stock: Combine all the ingredients in a saucepan, bring to a boil, reduce the heat, and simmer uncovered for 1 hour. Strain through a fine strainer to make about 6 cups stock. Discard the vegetables.

2. Meanwhile, begin the soup: Preheat the oven to 450°F. Place the squash in a baking dish and brush the cut side with the softened butter. Season well with salt and pepper. Cover with foil and bake for 25 minutes, then remove the foil and continue baking until tender, 35–40 minutes total. Let cool until comfortable enough to handle.

3. Scoop the squash pulp out of the skin. Place it in a large saucepan and add the 6 cups vegetable stock. Bring to a simmer and cook for 20 minutes. Blend in the pot with a hand blender until smooth, or let cool slightly and puree in batches in a blender or food processor. Pour the pureed soup through a strainer into a medium saucepan and warm over medium heat.

4. Meanwhile, heat the olive oil in a small skillet over medium-high heat. Add the saffron and sauté for 30 seconds, then add ¼ cup hot water and bring to a boil. Add the saffron mixture to the soup, then add the cinnamon, nutmeg, and cloves. Simmer for 10 minutes, adding more stock or water if the soup seems too thick. Remove from the heat and whisk in the crème fraîche and harissa. Season with salt and pepper to taste. Ladle into bowls and float a few croutons on top. Garnish with chives.

For the Toasted Almond Croutons: See next page.

Cold Summer Tomato and Spring Onion Soup with Grilled Scallops

This soup is like a great tomato salad in soup form. On a hot August day, it's the most refreshing lunch there is, made with my favorite ripe Jersey tomatoes, chile heat from fresh poblanos, plus a fat, sweet, crusty grilled scallop on top.

To make it, you definitely want to wait until tomatoes are at their peak; they'll be eaten raw and will form the flavor base for the soup. You get even more flavor and body from blending a savory paste of bread and garlic into the liquid, a trick lifted from the traditional Spanish gazpacho.

Serves 6

4 large tomatoes, preferably beefsteaks, peeled, seeded, and finely diced
1 large red pepper, seeded and finely diced
1 large yellow pepper, seeded and finely diced
1 poblano pepper, seeded and finely diced
1 small red onion, peeled and finely diced
¼ cup red wine vinegar
2 medium cucumbers, peeled, seeded, and finely diced
4 cups canned tomato juice
4 cloves garlic, finely minced
3 slices good-quality white bread, crusts left on, roughly torn
   Salt and freshly ground pepper
¼ cup finely sliced scallions (white and light green parts only)
8 large sea scallops
   Olive oil

1. Combine the tomatoes, peppers, onion, vinegar, half of the cucumbers, and the tomato juice in a large bowl.

2. In a food processor, puree the remaining cucumbers with the garlic and the bread until smooth. Add the bread mixture to the tomato mixture and stir to combine. Season with salt and pepper to taste. Fold in the scallions. Chill until ready to serve.

3. When ready to serve, heat a grill to high or heat a grill pan over high heat. Brush the scallops with oil and season with additional salt and pepper. Grill for approximately 2 minutes per side, until browned and crusty. Ladle the soup into bowls and top each bowl with 2 sea scallops.

Toasted Almond Croutons

1 medium-size French baguette, sliced ¼-inch thick
   Olive oil
   Spanish paprika
¼ cup toasted almonds, coarsely chopped

Preheat the oven to 325°F. Brush the bread slices with olive oil on both sides. Sprinkle lightly with paprika on one side. Transfer to a baking sheet, paprika side up, and bake until lightly golden brown, 5–10 minutes. Immediately remove from the oven and sprinkle with almonds.

Lobster and Green Chile Bisque with Toasted Corn Relish

The first dish I ever ate in New Mexico (where I've had some of the best food of my life) was a lobster and green chile taco. I was still a novice as far as cooking with chiles was concerned, so I was stunned by the sophisticated flavor contrast, putting the sweet rich lobster against the fruity, fiery chile. I've re-created it in this soup, with a nutty toasted-corn relish for contrast.

Serves 6

3 tablespoons unsalted butter

1 medium Spanish onion, coarsely chopped

1 large carrot, coarsely chopped

2 stalks celery, coarsely chopped

3 cloves garlic, finely chopped

2 live 1½-pound lobsters

½ cup dry sherry

2 cups white wine

7 cups water

8 sprigs parsley

8 sprigs cilantro

1 bay leaf

8 white peppercorns

2 plum tomatoes, chopped

2 roasted poblano peppers, peeled, seeded, and pureed

2 tablespoons unsalted butter

2 tablespoons flour

2 cups heavy cream

1 cup milk

¼ cup chopped parsley

2 tablespoons honey

Salt and freshly ground white pepper

Toasted Corn Relish (see below)

1. Heat butter in a large saucepan over medium heat. Add the onions, carrots, celery, and garlic, and cook until soft. Do not allow them to obtain color.

2. Plunge a knife between the eyes of the lobsters to kill them, split them in half lengthwise, and remove the sand sack. Separate into tail, claw, and chest pieces, then add the sections to the vegetables and sauté until the shells turn bright red. Remove the lobster pieces from the pan and, when cool enough to handle, remove the meat from the tails and claws and reserve the meat.

3. Chop all of the shells into smaller pieces and return to the pan. Add the sherry and ignite. When the flames subside, add the wine and reduce by half. Add the water, parsley, cilantro, bay leaf, white peppercorns, tomatoes, poblano puree, and salt to taste, and cook over low heat for 25 minutes. Remove most of the shells and pass the soup through a sieve into a clean medium saucepan and bring to a simmer.

4. Melt the butter in another medium saucepan over medium heat. Whisk in the flour and cook for 3 minutes. Whisk in the hot lobster stock and cook until thickened and until the flour taste has cooked out, about 25 minutes.

5. Place the cream and milk in a small saucepan and reduce by half. Add the cream and reserved lobster meat and cook until just heated through. Add the parsley. Season with honey, salt, and pepper. Ladle into bowls and garnish with toasted corn relish.

Toasted Corn Relish

3 ears fresh corn, silks removed and ears soaked in cold water for 5 minutes

¼ cup red onion, finely diced

1 roasted poblano, peeled, seeded, and finely diced

2 tablespoons fresh lime juice

1 tablespoon olive oil

2 tablespoons fresh tarragon, finely chopped

Salt and freshly ground pepper

Preheat grill to high. Remove ears from water and grill in the husk for 15–20 minutes. Remove corn from the cob and combine in a medium bowl with remaining ingredients. Season with salt and pepper to taste.

New England Clam and Sweet Potato Chowder

You chowder purists will just have to trust me on this one. As a big fan of sweet potatoes, I like to substitute them for white ones in traditional recipes. They make for a great chowder, with a hint of color and a note of sweetness that sets this recipe apart. Smoky bacon pulls all the great flavors—clams, potatoes, and cream—together and cuts through the richness. With a salad and bread, this makes a comforting one-dish meal. Or just serve with crisp oyster crackers.

Serves 8

2 cups white wine
2 cups water
48 littleneck clams, scrubbed
Bottled clam juice (optional)
2 cups heavy cream
2 cups whole milk
¼ pound slab bacon, cut into ¼-inch dice
2 medium onions, chopped
2 stalks celery, cut into ¼-inch dice
2 tablespoons flour
2 large sweet potatoes, peeled and cut into ½-inch dice
Salt and freshly ground white pepper
Hot sauce

1. Bring the wine and water to a boil in a large covered saucepan. Add the clams, cover the pot, and cook, shaking the pan occasionally, until all of the clams have opened. Discard any clams that have not opened. Lift out the clams with a slotted spoon and set aside. Strain the liquid through a fine strainer into a bowl. This should yield about 5 cups liquid; add bottled clam juice to make 6 cups. Remove the clams from their shells and roughly chop the meat.

2. Combine the heavy cream and milk in a medium saucepan and bring to a boil. Reduce heat to low and simmer until reduced by half.

3. Meanwhile, cook the bacon in a large saucepan over medium-high heat, stirring often, until golden brown. Transfer the bacon to a plate and pour off all but 3 tablespoons of the bacon fat. Add the onions and celery to the pan and cook until soft. Add the flour and cook, stirring constantly, for 2 minutes. Add the reserved clam broth, stir well, and bring to a simmer. Add the potatoes and cook until just soft but not mushy.

4. Add the cream mixture to the chowder and heat through over low heat. Add the chopped clams and the bacon, mix well, and season with salt, white pepper, and hot sauce to taste.

Roasted Cauliflower and Lobster Soup with Crushed Almonds

This silky soup has an amazing combination of flavors. Cauliflower is one of the most underappreciated vegetables out there, but when it's cooked right—by which I mean until it's completely soft—and then pureed, it has a delicate flavor and a silky texture that actually makes it elegant. That's why I pair it with lobster in this dish. I also love the rich flavor of almonds; their crunch keeps the creamy soup interesting. The cauliflower can be steamed instead of roasted, but don't boil it, or it will become watery.

Serves 4

For the cauliflower:
1½ pounds cauliflower florets
2 tablespoons olive oil
1 cup water
 Salt and freshly ground white pepper

For the lobster:
2 live lobsters, 1 pound each (or 2 cooked lobsters in the shell)

For the stock:
2 tablespoons olive oil
1 large onion, coarsely chopped
1 large carrot, coarsely chopped
1 celery stalk, coarsely chopped
2 tablespoons tomato paste
1 cup dry white wine
½ cup brandy
8 cups water
8 sprigs parsley
1 bay leaf
 Shells of 2 lobsters (see above)

To finish the soup:
 Salt and freshly ground white pepper
½ cup heavy cream
¼ cup coarsely crushed toasted almonds
 Thinly sliced chives, for garnish

1. Make the cauliflower: Preheat the oven to 350°F. In a medium roasting pan, toss the cauliflower with olive oil and water and season with salt and pepper. Cover and roast until soft, about 25–30 minutes. Set aside about 12 florets for garnish.

2. Make the lobster: Bring a large pot of salted water to a boil. Place the lobsters in the pot, cover, and boil about 12 minutes, until bright red. Remove the meat from the shells and reserve them separately.

3. Make the stock: Heat the olive oil in a large saucepan over high heat. Add the onion, carrot, and celery, and cook, stirring, until softened, about 5–7 minutes. Add the tomato paste and cook for 5 minutes more. Add the wine and brandy and cook until reduced to a glaze. Add the water, parsley, bay leaf, and lobster shells, and bring the mixture to a boil. Reduce the heat and simmer for 40 minutes. Strain the stock into a large saucepan.

4. Add the roasted cauliflower to the stock, season to taste with salt and pepper, and bring to a boil. Reduce the heat and cook for 20 minutes. Using an electric hand blender, or working in batches in a food processor, puree the soup until smooth and return it to the saucepan. Bring to a simmer and add the heavy cream and the lobster meat. Cook 1–2 minutes and adjust seasoning. (If the soup is too thick, add a little water.) Ladle the soup into serving bowls and garnish with reserved cauliflower florets, crushed almonds, and chives.

Steamed Clams with Coconut Milk and Hot Pepper Flakes

On Eastern Long Island, where I hang out in the summer, everyone eats steamers by the bucketful. They're fat, juicy soft-shell clams, made for dunking. When I'm ready for a change from plain melted butter, I brew a rich, spicy coconut broth and shower the clams with chopped cilantro.

Serves 4

2 tablespoons olive oil

1 large onion, finely diced

3 cloves garlic, finely chopped

2 cups bottled clam juice

1 can (13 ounces) unsweetened coconut milk

½ teaspoon hot red pepper flakes, or to taste

48 steamer or other clams, scrubbed

2 tablespoons cold unsalted butter, cut into pieces

Salt

2 tablespoons chopped cilantro

1. Heat the olive oil in a large saucepan over medium heat. Add the onion and garlic, and cook until softened and translucent. Do not brown.

2. Add the clam juice, coconut milk, and red pepper flakes, increase heat to high, and bring the mixture to a boil. Add the clams, cover, and cook, shaking the pan occasionally, until all of the clams have opened, 4–6 minutes. Transfer the clams with a slotted spoon to a large bowl, or to individual serving bowls.

3. Raise the heat to high and cook the broth until reduced by half. Whisk in the butter and season to taste with salt. Pour the hot broth over the clams and sprinkle with chopped cilantro. Serve immediately.

Crawfish and Oyster Bisque

These are two favorite ingredients from one of my favorite places to eat—Louisiana. Sweet crawfish and fat Gulf oysters make a soup so rich, it's sexy. Cream and hot sauce round out the flavors.

Because this soup is so simple, it will be much better if you make the easy stock from scratch, using the shells of the crawfish. Shrimp would be a good substitute if you live far away from crawfish country.

Serves 4

8   small new potatoes, scrubbed and quartered
4   tablespoons olive oil
    Salt and freshly ground pepper
2   tablespoons unsalted butter
1   red onion, finely chopped
3   cloves garlic, finely chopped
3   tablespoons flour
2   cups Shrimp Stock (page xiv)
4–5 cups heavy cream
24 oysters, shucked, with their liquor (your fish market can do this for you)
¾   pound cleaned raw crawfish tails (you can buy these at a fish market) or medium shrimp
    Hot sauce to taste
¼   cup finely chopped parsley

1. Preheat the oven to 375°F. Toss the potatoes in a small roasting pan with 3 tablespoons of the olive oil. Season well with salt and pepper. Roast 12–15 minutes or until just cooked through.

2. Heat the butter and the remaining tablespoon of oil over high heat in a medium skillet with straight sides. Add the onion and garlic, and cook, stirring occasionally, until soft but not browned. Add flour and cook for 2 minutes, stirring constantly. (Reduce heat if necessary.) Add the stock, bring to a boil, and cook until thickened and until flour taste has disappeared, 20–25 minutes. Add water if too thick.

3. In the meantime, place the cream in a small saucepan and cook until reduced by half. Add the cream to the stock mixture and bring to a simmer. Add the oysters and their liquor and the crawfish tails and mix well. Adjust seasoning with salt, pepper, and hot sauce to taste, and cook 2–3 minutes, until the shellfish are just cooked through. Remove from the heat and fold in the parsley. Serve immediately.

Steamed Mussels in Roasted Tomato–Saffron Broth

To bring out all the tastes in this simple dish, I first make a flavorful broth to steam the mussels in. With its roasted tomatoes and aromatic saffron, the savory broth becomes as much a part of the dish as the juicy mussels. Don't forget to put out some crusty bread—everybody loves to dunk when they get to the bottom of the bowl. It makes for a fun, family-style dish.

Serves 4

For the roasted tomatoes:

8 plum tomatoes, halved and seeded

6 cloves garlic, peeled

3 tablespoons olive oil

Salt and freshly ground pepper

For the soup:

2 tablespoons olive oil

1 onion, thinly sliced

1 cup dry white wine

3 cups Shrimp Stock (page xiv) or bottled clam juice

Pinch of saffron

Salt and freshly ground pepper

48 cultivated mussels, scrubbed and debearded

¼ cup chopped flat leaf parsley

1. Make the roasted tomatoes: Preheat the oven to 350°F. Toss the tomatoes and garlic with the 3 tablespoons olive oil in a shallow baking pan. Season with salt and pepper to taste. Roast until very soft, 25–30 minutes or more. Transfer the tomatoes, garlic, and any accumulated juices to a food processor and puree until smooth.

2. Make the soup: Heat the 2 tablespoons olive oil in a large saucepan over high heat. Add the onion and cook, stirring often, until soft. Add the wine and cook until reduced by three-fourths. Add the shrimp stock or clam juice and saffron and bring to a boil. Add the roasted tomato puree, season with salt and pepper, and bring to a boil.

3. Add the mussels, cover the pot, and cook until all the mussels have opened, 3–5 minutes. Discard any mussels that have not opened. Divide the mussels among 4 bowls and keep warm. Raise the heat under the broth to high and cook until reduced by half. Stir in the parsley and ladle the broth over the mussels. Serve immediately.

Oyster and Caramelized Onion Pan Roast

This incredibly savory and rich soup is my favorite first course for winter dinner parties. Slowly browning the onions until they turn golden and sweet is the key to deepening all the flavors.

Oysters used to be so plentiful in New York City that they were given away in bars called "oyster saloons" the way we get free pretzels today. A simple brew of oysters, onions, and cream, usually called a pan roast or oyster stew, was a very popular dish of the time. Make this and you'll see why.

Serves 4

2 tablespoons olive oil
1 tablespoon unsalted butter
3 onions, thinly sliced
1 tablespoon sugar
3 cloves garlic, minced
2 Yukon Gold unpeeled potatoes, cut into ½-inch dice
6 cups bottled clam juice
20 oysters, shucked, with their liquor (your fish market can do this for you)
¼ cup crème fraîche
Salt and freshly ground pepper
2 tablespoons finely chopped fresh tarragon

1. Heat the olive oil and butter in a medium saucepan over medium heat. Add the onions and sugar and cook, stirring often, until the onions are golden brown and caramelized, about 20 minutes. Add the garlic and cook for 2 minutes.

2. Meanwhile, put the potatoes in a medium saucepan and cover with cold salted water. Cover, bring to a boil, and cook until the potatoes are just cooked through, about 5 minutes. Drain the potatoes and set aside.

3. Add the clam juice to the onions and bring to a simmer. Add the oysters and their liquor and the potatoes, and simmer just until the oysters have cooked through, 2–3 minutes. Whisk in the crème fraîche and season with salt and pepper to taste. Remove from the heat and stir in the tarragon.

Bronzed Chicken and Red Bean Soup

I like soups to be light but intense. This is somewhere between a soup, a stew, and a chili, with spiced chicken, soft beans, and a savory broth flecked with herbs all floating in the bowl. The method I use to season the chicken is a cousin of blackening, but I call it "bronzing" instead: Nothing gets burned, your smoke alarm won't go off, and the spices gently permeate the meat.

This is a brothy soup, so remember that when choosing your stock: If your stock doesn't taste good, your soup won't either.

Serves 4–6

For the soup:

¾ pound dried red kidney beans, soaked overnight in cold water

2 tablespoons olive oil

1 large onion, finely diced

1 smoked ham hock

2 stalks celery, diced

2 carrots, diced

3 cloves garlic, finely diced

6 cups Chicken Stock (page xiv) or low-sodium canned stock

2 cups water

1 cup chopped canned plum tomatoes, with their juices

8 sprigs thyme

2 bay leaves

8 sprigs parsley

Salt and freshly ground pepper

Few dashes of hot sauce (optional)

2 teaspoons fresh oregano or fresh thyme

Sour cream or crème fraîche (optional)

For the chicken:

3 tablespoons paprika

½ teaspoon coarsely ground black pepper

1 teaspoon cayenne

1 teaspoon oregano

½ teaspoon garlic powder

½ teaspoon salt

5 boneless, skinless chicken breast halves

Olive oil

1. Make the soup: Drain the beans well and set aside. Warm the oil in a large saucepan over medium-high heat. Add the onion and cook, stirring, until soft. Add the ham hock, celery, and carrots, and cook for 2 minutes. Add the garlic and cook 1 minute more. Add the beans, stock, water, tomatoes, thyme sprigs, bay leaves, and parsley sprigs, and bring to a boil. Reduce heat to medium-low and simmer until the beans are soft, adding more stock or water as needed, 1–1¼ hours.

2. Cook the chicken: Preheat a large heavy skillet over high heat. Mix the spices together in a shallow bowl. Season the chicken on both sides with salt. Dredge the chicken on one side in the seasoning. Brush the pan with olive oil and sear the chicken, spice-side down, until browned. Turn over, reduce heat to medium, and cook until just cooked through (it can be slightly underdone since it will finish cooking in the soup), about 8 minutes total. Transfer to a plate, let rest 5 minutes, and dice into bite-size pieces.

3. When the beans are soft, season the soup to taste with salt, pepper, and hot sauce. Add the chicken and thyme or oregano leaves, and cook for an additional 5 minutes. Ladle into soup bowls and top with a dollop of sour cream or crème fraîche.

Split Pea–Green Chile Soup with Chorizo and Toasted Cumin *Crema*

Split pea soup is a New York favorite (in fact, it was introduced by the original Dutch settlers), but I've been wanting to wake up the flavors ever since I made vats of the stuff at my first cooking job. Green chiles have a real flavor affinity for split peas, and they brighten up all the flavors in the soup. Once I added the green chiles, I couldn't resist taking the soup even further in a Mexican direction, substituting spicy chorizo sausage for the usual ham bone and adding a swirl of sour cream flavored with toasted cumin. The result is filling, satisfying, and totally delicious.

Serves 4–6

For the soup:

- 2 tablespoons olive oil
- 8 ounces Spanish (cooked) chorizo, cut into ½-inch thick cubes
- 1 onion, finely diced
- 2 carrots, peeled and finely diced
- 2 stalks celery, finely diced
- 2 cloves garlic, finely chopped
- 2 Yukon Gold potatoes, peeled and diced into ½-inch cubes
- 2 cups green split peas
- 8 cups vegetable stock (see page 8) or water
- 1 bay leaf
  Salt and freshly ground pepper
- 2 poblano peppers, roasted, peeled, seeded, and sliced into ½-inch dice (page xiii)
- ¼ cup chopped cilantro, for garnish

For the cumin *crema*:

- 1 tablespoon cumin seeds
- 1 cup *crema* (available at Latin markets), crème fraîche, or sour cream thinned with buttermilk
  Salt and freshly ground pepper

1. Make the soup: Heat the oil in a medium saucepan over medium heat. Add the chorizo and cook, stirring, until browned on both sides. Transfer the chorizo with a slotted spoon to a plate lined with paper towels. Pour off all but 2 tablespoons of fat from the pan, add the onion, and cook, stirring, until slightly softened. Add the carrots and celery and cook for 5 minutes. Add the garlic and cook for 1 minute. Add the potatoes, peas, stock or water, and bay leaf, season with salt and pepper, and bring to a simmer. Cook about 45 minutes, until the peas are soft.

2. Make the cumin *crema*: Place the cumin seeds in a small skillet and set over medium heat. Toast, tossing often, until lightly browned and fragrant. Transfer to a small bowl and let cool, then grind to a powder in a spice or coffee grinder. Stir the *crema* and cumin together and season with salt and pepper to taste. If desired, transfer to a squeeze bottle.

3. To finish the soup, add the reserved cooked chorizo and the poblano peppers and cook for 5 minutes. Stir in the cilantro and serve. Drizzle each serving with the cumin *crema*.

Postcard from San Antonio and Austin, Texas

I realized on my last trip to San Antonio and Austin that Texas pride applies to everything about the state—its size, its wealth, its music, its history, its people. And last but definitely not least, its food. Everyone I met assured me that I hadn't tasted barbecue, tamales, steak, or enchiladas until I had tasted them in Texas—and I've got to admit that they were mostly right! The big spirit of Texas cuisine tastes a lot like my own cooking style; I felt right at home with all that ancho chile powder, garlic cumin seed, and oregano.

San Antonio has been described as "the northernmost city in Mexico," and it's where I realized that fusion food is just a very old idea with a new name. French-Japanese fusion may not last forever, but Tex-Mex has been around for a long, long time, and it's not going any-where if I can help it. Mary Trevino's Tex-Mex tamales, along with Janie Mora's menudo and chilaquiles, should be designated national monuments. The Trevinos and the Moras have been cooking in San Antonio for generations, and their food and culture is an irresistible combination of North and South.

On my first day, Janie Mora cooked me a traditional San Antonio breakfast of menudo (tripe stewed with red chile, garlic, oregano, and a little hominy) and my favorite chilaquiles. In addition to the fantastic taste, I love how this dish uses ingredients in a creative way. Pico de gallo (mean-ing "beak of the rooster"; it's supposed to have a little bite!) is a basic raw salsa of chopped toma-toes, onions, and fresh chile. For this dish, the pico de gallo is lightly cooked in oil before you add the eggs, scrambling it all together on the griddle. Then broken pieces of tortilla are added too, which absorb the flavors of the aromatics and add a starchy note with great corn flavor.

Mary Trevino, whose family runs the restaurant El Mirador, is ninety years old—but she still makes a mean tamale. In her family, tamales are a beloved Christmas Eve tradition, with the work being shared by all the women as they catch up on a year's worth of gossip. Diana Trevino made me the best enchiladas ever, stuffing tortillas with cheese, then rolling and bak-ing them (topped with red chile sauce) just like an Italian-American dish of manicotti with tomato sauce. Another twist on tradition she showed me is the "puffy taco," a taco where the tortilla is deep-fried, making it puff up like a pillow. Then the puffed, crisp tortilla is wrapped around the savory filling. I was very impressed by the creative thinking behind the dish, which was traditional and yet fresh and new. I only wish I had thought of it myself!

In San Antonio, the line between Mexican and Tex-Mex (also called "border food") is pretty blurry, but the Texas love of beef comes through loud and clear in dishes like carne guisada (beef stewed with onions, peppers, and tomatoes), grilled steak wrapped in fresh corn tortillas, and of course, chile con carne, the state dish. I try to stay away from the whole chili debate (if you're not from Texas, no one in Texas cares what you think about chili anyway), but I love to eat the stuff. Texas chili is an all-meat dish, with lots of chili heat and not a bean to be seen. I even tasted a chili that had thirty-two ingredients, including salt pork and *masa harina* (corn flour) for thickening—but still no beans.

Austin is the place where I found Texas barbecue of my dreams. In this state, every possible meat, from huge sides of beef cattle to wild quail, is cooked "on the pit." Shawn Newsome, a captain in the Texas state police, is famous as a hunter and barbecue man, and has been cooking the stuff since age eleven. These days, he works his own smokehouse, a huge empty propane tank that he converted to a barbecue pit "courtesy of a blowtorch." His method of slowly smoking at a low temperature (over pecan, hickory, and oak woods) works equally well on a big haunch of venison (14 hours) as it does on tiny whole doves (45 minutes). The meat comes out dark, flavorful, and so juicy you have to lean over the table while you eat.

For a different barbecue experience, I visited with the Mikeskas, one of the first families of Texas barbecue. I thought I knew a lot about cooking with fire, but there's always something to learn from people who come from a long line of cooks. Tim Mikeska told me that the most important ingredient in any spice rub is the salt, because the salt begins to cure and flavor the meat long before it goes on the pit. And he tosses chopped lemons—peels and all—into his famous barbecue sauce, for the flavor and because the citrus acids are natural tenderizers. Having tasted Tim's barbecued leg of lamb, I can tell you that it really works.

Last, I sampled the celebrated chicken-fried steak at Threadgill's. Austin has a huge music scene, and Threadgill's is almost as famous for its blues as for its food. CFS (as the dish is affectionately nicknamed) has nothing to do with chicken, other than the bumpy, crunchy crust on the outside that makes it resemble fried chicken. The steaks are dredged in egg, then flour, then egg again—and then slipped into bubbling oil to brown. The result is an extraordinary crust that the cook described to me as "a blistered seal" around the juicy meat. With peppery gravy, it's a great Texas classic. The only thing I don't understand is how you could want to sing the blues after eating one.

Brunch Dishes, Sandwiches, Tacos

Crab and Salmon Griddle Cakes with Smoked Salmon and Chile-Buttermilk Sauce

Ranch-Style Eggs with Chorizo and Tomato–Red Chile Sauce

Tomatillo Chilaquiles with Scrambled Eggs

Sweet Potato–Chicken Hash and Poached Eggs with Green Chile Hollandaise

Pressed BBQ Reuben Sandwich with Homemade Spicy Pickles

Steak Sandwich on Toasted Garlic Bread with Cheddar, Tomato-Olive Relish, and Skillet Fries

Little Havana–Style Cuban Sandwiches

New Mexico–Style Soft Tacos with Hacked Chicken and Salsa Verde

Tacos of BBQ Pork Loin, Roasted Red Bliss Potatoes, and Tomatillo–Red Pepper Relish

Crab and Salmon Griddle Cakes with Smoked Salmon and Chile-Buttermilk Sauce

There's only one secret to great crab cakes: top-quality crabmeat, and plenty of it. As a contrast to the creamy, sweet crab, I add some untraditional (but totally delicious) freshly poached salmon to this ultimate brunch dish. And since it just isn't brunch without smoked salmon, I use it here as a salty, rich garnish to bring out all the flavors.

I always cook my crab cakes in a well-seasoned cast-iron pan, for the crispiest crust. When the crab cakes are still piping hot, drizzle on the cool, tangy buttermilk-based sauce, with its mild chile after-burn. It's my perfected version of that American favorite, ranch dressing.

Serves 4

For the cakes:

2 salmon fillets, 6 ounces each
1 bay leaf
8 sprigs parsley
3 tablespoons lemon juice
4 black peppercorns
1 tablespoon olive oil
½ cup finely chopped red onion
3 cloves garlic, minced
12 ounces jumbo lump crabmeat, flaked
3 tablespoons mayonnaise
2 tablespoons Dijon mustard
2 tablespoons prepared horseradish, drained
2 egg whites, stiffly beaten
½ cup dry bread crumbs
¼ cup finely chopped parsley
 Salt and freshly ground pepper
2 tablespoons canola oil

To finish the dish:

½ pound smoked salmon, thinly sliced
 Chile-Buttermilk Sauce (see below)
 Chopped chives or cilantro, for garnish
 Finely chopped red bell pepper, for garnish

1. Place the salmon in a small saucepan. Cover with cold water and add the bay leaf, parsley, lemon juice, and black peppercorns. Bring to a simmer and cook 8–10 minutes, until just cooked through. Let cool and flake with a fork. (You can do this up to 2 days in advance and refrigerate.)

2. Heat the olive oil in a small skillet, add the onion and garlic, and cook, stirring, until softened.

3. Combine the flaked salmon and crabmeat in a medium bowl. Add the mayonnaise, mustard, horseradish, cooked onion, and garlic, and mix until combined. Fold in the egg whites, then the bread crumbs and parsley, and season with salt and pepper to taste.

4. When ready to serve, heat 2 tablespoons of canola oil in a large skillet. Add ¼ cup of batter for each cake and flatten slightly (to avoid crowding the pan, you may want to cook the crab cakes in batches). Cook on each side 2–3 minutes or until golden brown.

5. To serve, arrange 2 crab cakes on each serving plate. Top each cake with smoked salmon and drizzle with chilled Chile-Buttermilk Sauce. Garnish with herbs and red-pepper.

Chile-Buttermilk Sauce

1 cup sour cream
¼ cup buttermilk
2 serrano peppers, roasted, peeled, and finely chopped (page xiii)
2 cloves garlic, finely chopped
 Squeeze of lime juice
 Salt and freshly ground pepper

Whisk ingredients together and season with salt and pepper to taste. Refrigerate at least 30 minutes.

Ranch-Style Eggs with Chorizo and Tomato–Red Chile Sauce

A simple dish like *huevos rancheros,* the classic Southwestern breakfast, can be spectacular when it's made right. I like all the elements—scrambled eggs, a chile-based *ranchero* sauce, spiced chorizo sausage, and tortillas—and this is my favorite way to combine them, all stacked up together. The sauce is a nice thick red, the eggs soft, the chorizo browned, the tortillas crisp. Fresh cilantro and cool sour cream on top polish up the dish—it's not just for breakfast anymore! Try it for Sunday brunch or supper, with limeade or fresh margaritas.

Serves 4

For the sauce:
- 2 tablespoons olive oil
- 1 large red onion, coarsely chopped
- 4 cloves garlic, coarsely chopped
- 1 cup dry red wine
- 3 cups canned plum tomatoes and their juices, pureed until smooth, and strained
- 2 tablespoons ancho chile powder
- 1 tablespoon pasilla chile powder
- 2 tablespoons honey
- Salt

For the tortillas:
- Canola oil
- Four 6-inch yellow or white corn tortillas

For the eggs:
- 8 ounces Mexican chorizo sausage, removed from the casings
- 4 tablespoons unsalted butter, cut into tablespoons
- 12 large eggs, lightly beaten with 2 tablespoons water
- Salt and freshly ground pepper

To finish the dish:
- ⅔ cup sour cream
- ¾ cup coarsely grated Monterey Jack cheese
- Chopped cilantro

1. Make the sauce: Heat the oil in a medium saucepan over high heat. Add the onions and cook, stirring, until soft. Add the garlic and cook for 1 minute. Add the wine and cook until completely reduced. Add the pureed tomatoes, chile powders, honey, and salt to taste and cook over medium-high heat until the sauce has thickened, stirring occasionally, 20–30 minutes. Season to taste with salt.

2. Make the tortillas: Over medium-high heat, heat 2 inches of oil in a medium skillet fitted with a deep-frying thermometer to 360°F. Fry the tortillas one at a time, turning once, until lightly golden brown on each side. Drain on paper towels and season immediately with salt.

3. Make the eggs: Heat a large skillet over high heat. Add the chorizo and use a wooden spoon to break it up into small pieces. Cook, stirring, until all the chorizo is lightly browned. Remove with a slotted spoon to a plate lined with paper towels and let cool slightly. Pour off all but 1 tablespoon of the fat in the pan. Add the butter to the pan. When melted, turn the heat to medium-low and add the eggs and cooked sausage. Season with salt and pepper and cook over medium-low heat, stirring frequently with a wooden spoon until the mixture is a mass of soft curds, 10–15 minutes.

4. Assemble the dish: Place a teaspoon of sour cream in each of 4 large shallow bowls to secure the tortillas. Place a tortilla on top of each dab of sour cream. Spread 2 tablespoons of the sour cream over the top of each tortilla. Place equal portions of eggs over the tortillas and ladle the warm tomato–red chile sauce on top. Sprinkle each with about 3 tablespoons of the cheese and garnish with chopped cilantro. Serve immediately.

Tomatillo Chilaquiles with Scrambled Eggs

This dish (pronounced chee-la-*kee*-lace) evolved from two simple ingredients that Mexican-American kitchens are never without: salsa and tortillas. It can be eaten for breakfast, lunch, or dinner (shredded cooked chicken is a good addition). Traditionally, the cook lets the tortillas soften in the salsa, which gets thickened in turn by the cornmeal in the tortillas. But I prefer to combine the two by stacking them in layers, then top the dish off with tender scrambled eggs.

Tomatillos are related to both gooseberries and tomatoes, and they have the tart, juicy qualities of both. They're easy to cook with and I love their lemony, herbal flavor—once I've cooked them to soften that natural acidity.

Serves 4

For the tomatillo sauce:
- 15 tomatillos, husks removed, washed, and halved
- 2 red onions, peeled and quartered
- 5 cloves garlic, peeled
- ¼ cup olive oil
-    Salt and freshly ground pepper
- 2 teaspoons chipotle puree (page xiii)
- ¼ cup lime juice
- ½ cup spinach leaves, blanched 30 seconds in boiling water and drained
- 2 tablespoons honey
- ¼ cup chopped cilantro

For the tortillas:
- 2 cups canola oil
-    Twelve 6-inch blue or yellow corn tortillas

For the eggs:
- 3 tablespoons unsalted butter
- 12 large eggs, lightly beaten with 2 tablespoons of water

To finish the dish:
- 4 teaspoons sour cream
- 1 cup shredded white cheddar cheese
- ¼ cup chopped cilantro

1. Make the sauce: Preheat the oven to 400°F. Toss the tomatillos, onions, and garlic with the oil in a roasting pan and season with salt and pepper. Roast until soft and golden brown, 20–25 minutes.

2. Combine the tomatillos, onions, garlic, chipotle puree, lime juice, and spinach in a food processor and blend until smooth. Add the honey, cilantro, and additional salt and pepper if desired, and pulse a few times to blend.

3. Make the tortillas: Heat the canola oil in a medium saucepan fitted with a deep-frying thermometer to 365°F. Fry the tortillas one at a time, until crispy. Transfer to a plate lined with paper towels and season lightly with salt.

4. Make the eggs: Melt the butter over medium-high heat in a large skillet. Reduce the heat to low, add the eggs, and cook slowly, stirring often, until soft curds form. Season with salt and pepper to taste.

5. To assemble: Reheat the tomatillo sauce if necessary. Place a teaspoon of sour cream in each of 4 large shallow bowls. Place a fried tortilla on top and press down to secure the tortilla. Place one-twelfth of the eggs and cheddar cheese on each tortilla and top with another tortilla. Repeat and top with another tortilla. Top the stacks with the remaining eggs and cheese. Ladle the warm tomatillo sauce over. Garnish with chopped cilantro.

Sweet Potato–Chicken Hash with Poached Eggs and Green Chile Hollandaise

There are a lot of reasons I'm proud to be an American—and brunch is one of them. I love the scale of it: dozens of eggs, mountains of bacon, pitchers of Bloody Marys. And the menu includes some of the tastiest, spiciest, and best dishes I know. This recipe combines two of my favorite brunch dishes: hash and eggs Benedict. I'm no doctor, but it's my personal belief that hollandaise sauce is the best hangover remedy in the world.

Serves 4

2 large sweet potatoes
3 boneless, skinless chicken breast halves, about 6 ounces each
  Salt and freshly ground pepper
3 scallions, thinly sliced
¼ cup coarsely chopped cilantro
1 tablespoon chipotle puree (page xiii)
1 tablespoon honey
2 tablespoons olive oil
3 cups water
1 tablespoon white wine vinegar
4 eggs
  Green Chile Hollandaise (see below)

1. Make the hash: In a medium saucepan, cover the potatoes with cold water and bring to a boil over high heat. Reduce the heat and simmer until tender, 25–30 minutes. Drain the potatoes, peel, and cut into ½-inch cubes.

2. Meanwhile, season the chicken breasts with salt and pepper and place in a saucepan of simmering water. Poach 8–10 minutes or until just cooked through. Cut each breast into ½-inch cubes.

3. Place the potatoes, chicken, scallions, cilantro, chipotle puree, and honey in a large bowl and mix gently until combined, then season with salt and pepper to taste. Form into four patties.

4. Heat the olive oil in a large skillet until just starting to smoke. Preheat the oven to 200°F. Sprinkle the patties with salt and pepper and cook on each side until browned and crisp. Keep warm in the oven.

5. Make the poached eggs: Heat the water and vinegar in a deep skillet until simmering. Break an egg into a teacup and gently slip the egg into the water. Repeat with the remaining eggs. Poach 4–5 minutes, or until the whites have set and the yolk is still a bit jiggly. Remove the eggs from the pan with a slotted spoon.

6. To serve, place the patties on serving plates, place an egg on top of each patty, and serve immediately, drizzled with Green Chile Hollandaise.

Green Chile Hollandaise

3 large egg yolks, lightly beaten
1 tablespoon fresh lemon juice
1 stick (8 tablespoons) unsalted butter, melted
1 large poblano pepper, roasted, peeled, seeded, and finely chopped (page xiii)
¼ teaspoon salt
  Pinch of freshly ground white pepper

1. Combine the egg yolks and lemon juice in a medium stainless steel bowl and set it over a pot of simmering water (do not let the bottom of the bowl touch the water; pour some out if necessary). Whisk the yolks until pale yellow and fluffy, 5–7 minutes. Gradually whisk in the melted butter a tablespoon at a time and whisk until incorporated.

2. Remove from the heat, fold in the chopped poblano pepper, and season with salt and white pepper to taste. Serve immediately or keep warm over barely simmering water until ready to serve. (If the sauce gets too hot, it may separate. If it does, you can try whirling it in a blender or with an electric hand blender.)

Pressed BBQ Reuben Sandwich with Homemade Spicy Pickles

Big American sandwiches are some of my favorite foods. This fantastic pressed Reuben (an NYC deli special of corned beef, cheese, and sauerkraut) is a personal creation that spans Miami and New York, two favorite food towns of mine. In Miami's Little Havana, meaty *Cubano* sandwiches, flattened in a sandwich press, are the local favorite (check out my version, page 38).

I apply that pressing method to my own combination of barbecued brisket, red cabbage slaw, and fontina cheese, weighing down the sandwiches with a cast-iron skillet. The final deli touch is a crunchy pickle spear. Homemade pickles are really easy to make and taste fantastic. Rice wine vinegar has a crisp, clean taste, and the traditional pickling spices—coriander, mustard, peppercorns, and hot peppers—are some of my favorites.

Serves 8

For the brisket:

3 cups barbecue sauce of your choice
5 pounds buffalo or beef brisket
3 tablespoons vegetable oil
Salt and freshly ground pepper
2 carrots, coarsely chopped
2 onions, coarsely chopped
2 stalks celery, coarsely chopped
4 cloves garlic, coarsely chopped
6 cups Chicken Stock (page xiv), or
   low-sodium canned stock
2 cups water

For the slaw:

1 red cabbage, cored and shredded
1½ cups red wine vinegar
4 teaspoons honey
Salt and freshly ground pepper

To finish the dish:

16 thick slices soft sandwich bread, or 8
   lengths of soft French or Italian bread,
   sliced lengthwise
8 slices Fontina, Gruyère, or Swiss cheese
1 stick (8 tablespoons) unsalted butter
   Homemade Spicy Pickles (see page 36)

1. Begin the brisket: Place 2 cups of the barbecue sauce in a large shallow baking dish, add the brisket, and turn to coat. Cover and marinate in the refrigerator at least 4 hours or overnight.

2. Cook the brisket: Preheat the oven to 325°F. Heat the vegetable oil in a large casserole over high heat until smoking. Remove the brisket from the marinade, season with salt and pepper, and sear well on both sides. Transfer to a plate. Add the carrots, onions, celery, and garlic to the pan, and cook, stirring, until soft and golden brown. Return the brisket to the pan and cover with the stock, water, and the remaining 1 cup of barbecue sauce. Bring to a simmer on top of the stove, cover, and place in the oven. Cook 2½–3 hours or until tender (about 2 hours if using beef). Remove from the cooking liquid, let rest for 15 minutes, and then slice thinly against the grain of the meat.

3. Meanwhile, make the slaw: Place the cabbage in a large nonreactive bowl. Bring vinegar, honey, and salt and pepper to a simmer in a medium saucepan. Pour the warm mixture over the cabbage and stir to combine. Cover with plastic wrap and let rest 30 minutes at room temperature.

4. Make the sandwiches: Place 8 slices of bread on a work surface. Top each slice with 4–5 slices of the brisket, a slice of cheese, and some of

the red cabbage slaw. Top off with the remaining bread.

5. Melt half of the butter in a large skillet over high heat. Add 4 of the sandwiches to the pan and place another skillet on top, pressing the sandwiches down. Reduce the heat to medium and cook, turning the sandwiches once, until golden brown on both sides and the cheese has melted. Repeat with the remaining sandwiches. Serve with Spicy Pickles.

Homemade Spicy Pickles

4 cups rice wine vinegar
2 tablespoons honey
½ teaspoon hot red pepper flakes
1 teaspoon whole white peppercorns
1 teaspoon coriander seeds
1 teaspoon mustard seeds
½ teaspoon fennel seeds
½ teaspoon toasted cumin seeds (page xiii)
1 tablespoon kosher salt
2 tablespoons coarsely chopped fresh dill
2 tablespoons coarsely chopped cilantro
2 unpeeled long European cucumbers, washed, cut in half crosswise, then quartered lengthwise

1. Combine the vinegar, honey, pepper flakes, peppercorns, coriander seeds, mustard seeds, fennel seeds, cumin seeds, and salt in a medium nonreactive saucepan over high heat and bring to a boil. Let boil for 2 minutes; remove from the heat and let sit until cooled to room temperature. Add the dill and cilantro.

2. Place the cucumber spears in a medium bowl and pour the cooled vinegar mixture over them. Refrigerate, covered, for 24 hours or up to 4 days.

Steak Sandwich on Toasted Garlic Bread with Cheddar, Tomato-Olive Relish, and Skillet Fries

At Virgilio's Sicilian Bakery in Gloucester, Massachusetts, the proprietor let me in on his secret for a great sandwich: "It's all about the bread." But I was making my favorite sandwiches on garlic sourdough bread even before he told me that! Add melting cheese and my untraditional relish of fresh tomatoes and olives, and you get a great combination of Italian hero and all-American steak sandwich. Serve it with a side of crunchy skillet fries: my favorite version of hash browns, with sweet peppers and plenty of onion.

Serves 4

For the relish:

3 large, ripe tomatoes, seeded and diced
¼ cup pitted and chopped black California olives
2 tablespoons finely sliced fresh basil
2 tablespoons finely diced red onion
2 tablespoons olive oil
2 tablespoons balsamic vinegar
Salt and freshly ground pepper

To finish the dish:

2 New York strip steaks, 10 ounces each
2 tablespoons plus ¼ cup olive oil
Salt and freshly ground black pepper
4 cloves garlic, smashed
8 thick slices sourdough bread
4 thick slices sharp cheddar cheese
Boston lettuce leaves

1. Make the relish: Combine all the ingredients in a bowl, mix well, and set aside.

2. Cook the steak: Heat a grill pan or cast-iron pan over high heat until smoking hot. Brush the steaks on both sides with the 2 tablespoons olive oil and season with salt and pepper. Cook until brown on one side, 4–5 minutes. Turn over, reduce the heat to medium, and continue cooking to medium-rare doneness, 5–6 minutes more. Let rest 10 minutes, then slice ¼-inch thick.

3. Make the garlic bread: Mix together the ¼ cup olive oil and the garlic in a small bowl and let sit at room temperature at least 15 minutes. Preheat the broiler. Brush both sides of the bread with the gar-lic oil, place on a baking sheet, and broil 1–2 minutes on each side, until lightly golden brown. Remove the bread and leave the broiler on.

4. Arrange four slices of the garlic bread on a baking sheet. Place 5–6 slices of steak on each slice of bread and top with a slice of cheddar cheese. Place under the broiler for 30 seconds, until just melted. Place a few leaves of lettuce on top of the cheese and top off with the Tomato-Olive Relish and the remaining garlic bread.

Skillet Fries

6 large unpeeled Yukon Gold potatoes
3 tablespoons olive oil
1 large red onion, thinly sliced
1 large red bell pepper, finely diced
1 large yellow bell pepper, finely diced
2 cloves garlic, finely chopped
Salt and freshly ground pepper
¼ cup finely chopped fresh parsley

1. Parboil the potatoes until almost cooked but still firm. When cool enough to handle, grate coarsely and set aside.

2. Heat the olive oil in a medium skillet (preferably cast-iron or nonstick) over medium-high heat. Add the onion and cook, stirring, until soft. Add the peppers and garlic and cook 3–4 minutes. Add the potatoes and cook, stirring, until golden brown. Season to taste with salt and pepper and garnish with parsley.

Little Havana–Style Cuban Sandwiches

As soon as I land in Miami, I start craving a cup of *café con leche* and a *Cubano* (a sandwich of roast pork, ham, cheese, and pickles on French bread); the longer, the better. I head straight for La Esquina de Terras, a corner café in Little Havana run by the Chamizo family.

The magic ingredient in a *Cubano* isn't an ingredient—it's a machine. The fat, overstuffed sandwich is pressed flat in a hot, heavy hinged griddle, reducing the bread to a thin crust and melting the cheese. It's easy to do at home with a heavy skillet. When buying the ingredients, remember that this is the one time when you don't want a "crusty" French loaf; only a soft loaf will give the right effect.

Serves 2–4

For the pork loin:

- 2 tablespoons olive oil
- One 2-pound boneless pork loin
- Salt and freshly ground pepper
- 1 large onion, peeled and coarsely chopped
- 6 cloves garlic, coarsely chopped
- 3 cups Chicken Stock (page xiv), or low-sodium canned stock

For the sandwiches:

- 1 or 2 soft loaves Cuban or French-style bread (about 2 feet total)
- ¼ cup yellow (not Dijon) mustard
- 24 dill pickle slices
- 6 slices Swiss cheese
- 12 very thin slices boiled ham or Virginia ham
- 2 tablespoons unsalted butter

1. Several hours before you plan to make the sandwiches, cook the pork loin: Preheat the oven to 450°F. Heat the olive oil in a medium casserole over high heat. Season the pork with salt and pepper and sear on all sides until browned. Transfer the pork to a plate. Add the onion to the pot and cook, stirring, until golden brown. Add the garlic and cook, stirring, for 2 minutes. Add the stock and the pork and bring to a simmer. Cover tightly and braise in the oven 20–25 minutes. Remove from the oven and let the pork come to room temperature in the liquid. Slice ¼-inch thick.

2. Cut the bread into two 1-foot lengths. Slice the bread in half lengthwise and open up on a work surface, with the cut sides facing up. On the top half of each split loaf, spread 2 tablespoons of mustard. Place 12 pickles on top of the mustard. Place 3 slices of Swiss cheese on top of the pickles. Fold each slice of ham in half and place evenly on the bottom half of each loaf. On top of the ham, distribute the slices of roast pork. Join both halves of the sandwich together.

3. Heat a sandwich grill (if you have one) or a waffle iron or a wide skillet. Spread the butter on the tops of the sandwiches. Close the grill or waffle iron, or place a piece of foil over the sandwich and rest a heavy cast-iron skillet on top, smashing the sandwich flat. Cook until the cheese is melted and the top of the bread is crisp and golden brown, 4–5 minutes. Remove the sandwich carefully and slice it diagonally, from corner to corner.

New Mexico–Style Soft Tacos with Hacked Chicken and Salsa Verde

The variety of fresh and dried chiles in this recipe—anchos, poblanos, jalapeños, *and* New Mexicos—pegs it to the state of New Mexico. Chiles are practically a religion there, one that I was happy to join. I've been playing with chile combinations ever since my first visit, balancing the smoky, fruity, earthy, green, tealike, and just plain hot flavors of different chiles in my own cooking.

Any cooked chicken (or even leftover Thanksgiving turkey) can be used in the tacos, instead of the hacked chicken.

Serves 6–8

For the chicken:

3 tablespoons olive oil
2 pounds chicken legs and thighs, skin removed
Salt
3 tablespoons ancho chile powder
1 large onion, thinly sliced
4 cloves garlic, thinly sliced
1 poblano chile, coarsely chopped
2 dried New Mexico chiles, coarsely chopped
4 cups Chicken Stock (page xiv), or low-sodium canned stock
6 sprigs cilantro

For the sauce:

2 tablespoons olive oil
1 medium red onion, coarsely chopped
1 jalapeño, coarsely diced
8 tomatillos, husked and coarsely chopped
3 tablespoons fresh lime juice
2 tablespoons honey
¼ cup chopped cilantro leaves
Salt and freshly ground pepper

To finish the dish:

Twelve 6-inch corn tortillas, wrapped in a towel and heated 10 minutes in a 200°F oven
Chopped cilantro

1. Make the chicken: Preheat the oven to 350°F. Heat the oil in a large heavy pot or casserole (with a lid) over medium-high heat. Season the chicken with salt and ancho chile powder. Place the chicken in the oil, skin-side down, and let cook until golden brown. Turn over and brown on the other side. Transfer the chicken to a plate.

2. Add the onion to the pan and cook, stirring, until light golden brown. Add the garlic and cook 1 minute more. Return the chicken to the pot, add the chiles, stock, and cilantro, and bring to a boil. Cover and transfer to the oven. Cook until the chicken easily falls away from the bone, about 40 minutes. Remove the chicken from the pot and strain the cooking liquid into a medium saucepan.

3. When the chicken is cool enough to handle, pull the meat off the bones and cut or shred the meat into bite-sized pieces. Bring the reserved cooking liquid to a simmer. Add the shredded chicken and turn off the heat.

4. Meanwhile, make the sauce: Heat the oil in a large skillet over medium heat. Add the onion and jalapeño and cook, stirring, until soft. Add the tomatillos and cook until soft, 10–15 minutes. Transfer the mixture to a blender, add the lime juice, honey, and cilantro, and blend until smooth. Season with salt and pepper.

5. To serve, reheat the chicken in the liquid, if necessary. Use a slotted spoon to divide the chicken among the warm tortillas. Top with the sauce and sprinkle with cilantro, fold, and serve.

Tacos of BBQ Pork Loin, Roasted Red Bliss Potatoes, and Tomatillo–Red Pepper Relish

The pork taco, in my opinion, is one of the great culinary creations of the Americas. Tender shreds of slow-cooked pork are a basic ingredient in a lot of dishes from the Texas-Mexico border, where some of my favorite food comes from. Pork, potatoes, and tomatillos are an amazing combination I discovered there. When you wrap them in corn tortillas with a red pepper salsa and a little cheese, then melt the cheese and crisp the tortilla in a hot oven or on a grill, it makes a fantastic dish. You could also sear the tacos on both sides in a hot, oiled skillet.

Serves 4

For the pork:

- 2 pork loins (about 1½ pounds each)
  Salt and freshly ground pepper
- 2 cups barbecue sauce of your choice
- 3 cups Chicken Stock (page xiv) or
  low-sodium canned stock

For the relish:

- 2 roasted red peppers (page xiii), peeled, seeded, and coarsely chopped
- 4 tomatillos, husked and coarsely chopped
- ½ red onion, finely diced
- 1 jalapeño, finely diced
- ¼ cup freshly squeezed lime juice
- 2 tablespoons olive oil
- 1 tablespoon honey
  Salt and freshly ground pepper
- ¼ cup coarsely chopped cilantro

For the tacos:

- Eight 6-inch corn tortillas
- ¾ cup finely grated white cheddar cheese
- ¾ cup finely grated Monterey Jack cheese
- ½ red onion, finely sliced
- 4 Red Bliss potatoes or other small potatoes, roasted or boiled until soft and sliced ½-inch thick
- ¼ cup chopped cilantro
  Canola oil

1. Start the pork: Preheat the oven to 325°F. Season the pork with salt and pepper and brush with 1 cup of the barbecue sauce. Place the pork in a saucepan. Pour the stock around the pork and bring to a simmer on top of the stove. Cover and place in the oven to braise for 1 hour, or until cooked through. Remove from the cooking liquid. Bring the cooking liquid to a boil on top of the stove and reduce by half. Reserve.

2. Finish the pork: Heat a grill pan or heavy skillet until almost smoking. Place the pork in the pan, brush with the reserved barbecue sauce, and sear 2–3 minutes on each side, basting with more sauce, until a crust forms. Let rest and slice against the grain of the meat into ¼-inch slices.

3. Make the relish: Combine all the ingredients in a medium bowl. Let rest at room temperature for 30 minutes.

4. Make the tacos: Preheat the oven to 350°F. Lightly oil a sheet pan. Lay the tortillas on a flat surface. Sprinkle 1 tablespoon of each kind of cheese over each tortilla. Place a few slices of onion over the cheese, then 3–4 slices of potatoes. Dip the sliced pork into the cooking liquid to moisten, then place 3–4 slices of pork on top of the cheese. Place a little more of the cheese on top of the pork, then some of the cilantro. Fold the tortilla over and press down slightly. Brush the tops of the tortillas with some of the oil and place on the baking sheet. When all the tacos have been assembled, bake until the tortillas are lightly golden brown and the cheese has melted, 5–7 minutes. Serve topped with relish.

Postcard from Miami, Florida

Every day in Miami is a culinary adventure. The food there is different from anywhere else in the States: an incredible combination of Cuban influence, American tradition, and ingredients from around the Caribbean—from the Bahamas to the Yucatan. Added to that is a layer of international sophistication, a group of ambitious young chefs, and a pleasure-seeking population that keeps the city hopping all year round. I never turn down an invitation to Miami!

Here's a perfect Miami day for me: For breakfast, I pull a stool up to the outdoor counter at La Esquina de Terras, where I like the *pastellitos de guayaba;* little turnovers of cream cheese and guava paste. Guava paste is a tangy-sweet concentrate of orange guava pulp; it can be dessert by itself, and it's also stuffed into pastries all around the Caribbean.

At lunchtime, Café Versailles seems to be the crossroads for all of Little Havana, and chef Tony Piedra helps to keep it that way. He's been the chef there for twenty-two years. Piedra stays true to the Caribbean roots of Cuban cooking, making a traditional *ajiaco,* a chicken soup packed with every starch that grows on that island: pumpkin, corn, yuca, malanga, *ñame,* and a few others that went into the pot too fast for me to spot them. Such a soup could be bland and starchy, but cooks pay lots of attention to taste in this town. The flavoring is started with a savory *sofrito*, a Spanish flavor base of onions, garlic, and tomato. He also adds strips of *tassaco,* dried beef, that give the whole soup a deep smoky taste.

Next, I might polish off a plate of *moros* (short for *Moros y Cristianos,* or "Moors and Christians"), the traditional name for black beans and white rice. The Spanish name refers to the colors of the dish: black beans for Moors (Africans) and white rice for Christians (Europeans). But most often, I can't resist a *Cubano*, a sandwich of roast pork, ham, and cheese, pressed flat and melted in a heavy, hot sandwich press. (You'll find my recipe for home kitchens on page 38.) The Cuban sandwich was invented in Miami, and it's a huge, satisfying mouthful. You can also get a *medianoche*, or "midnight," sandwich, a slimmer version of the *Cubano* that makes a great snack any time of the day.

At dinnertime, I head for Joe's Stone Crab. It's the best place to get your fill of sweet, delicious crabmeat. There's no more beautiful sight to me than a big platter of stone crab claws, with their creamy color and shiny, black tips. Stone crabs have oversized claws (that's what makes them so popular) and are native to Miami's Biscayne Bay. Very few stone crabs make it out of the state of Florida, so it's still one of America's completely regional delicacies.

After my first dinner, I go and have a couple more, checking in with the chefs who have made Miami's restaurants an international destination. I don't care whether they call it "Caribbean rim" or "New World Cuisine" or something else altogether, I love the big-flavored combinations of tart, spicy, sweet, and rich that they come up with. My friend Norman van Aken's food includes American, Bahamian, and Cuban influences, just to name a few; he's been studying the traditions ever since he hitchhiked to Key West a couple of decades ago (he liked it so much that he learned to cook and never left). Norman is the one who taught me to make a traditional Cuban *mojo*, the classic sauce for everything from fried plantains to steak, by pounding garlic, fruity-hot Scotch bonnet chiles, cumin, and salt together in a mortar. Then he wakes up all the flavors by pouring in hot olive oil. The smell of that kitchen is something I will never forget!

Late-night Miami is something I can't begin to describe. The hippest restaurants are the ones that serve far into the night. I like to wind down at the Strand, where my friend Michelle Bernstein, a Miami native, is the chef. Her conch ceviche, strips of fresh conch marinated in lemon, lime, and orange juice, is refreshing, tasty, and full of local flavor. Conch is found off the Keys and around the tip of Florida, and making ceviche with it is a great way to soften that rubbery flesh and show off its fresh flavor. After that, it's time for bed so I can get up in the morning and start all over again!

Salads
and
Appetizers

Caramelized Apple Salad with Maytag Blue, Black Walnuts,
   and Spicy Orange Vinaigrette

Vidalia Onion and Jersey Tomato Salad with Blue Ranch Dressing

Wild Mushroom and Quinoa Salad with Fresh Thyme, Aged Goat
   Cheese, and Shallot Vinaigrette

Crispy Soft-Shell Crab Salad with Yellow Tomatoes and Green Garlic
   Vinaigrette

Grilled Quail Salad with a Citrus Baste and Roasted Jalapeño Dressing

Cured Ham and Sautéed Pear Salad with Aged Sherry Vinaigrette
   and Black Pepper

Beer-Battered Squash Blossoms Filled with Goat Cheese and Roasted
   Garlic

Crab Cocktail with Avocado, Coconut, Fresh Chiles, and Lime

Stone Crab Claws with Red Chile–Mustard Mayonnaise

Key Lime–Red Pepper Shellfish Ceviche with Fried Tortillas

Shrimp and Avocado Salad in Roasted Chayote

Grilled Shrimp on Plantain Tostones with Avocado Cocktail Sauce

Fresh Clam and Garlic Flatbread with Flat-Leaf Parsley Oil

Crisp-Fried Oysters with Chile Vinegar–Black Pepper Sauce

Roasted Oysters in Beer with Homemade Hot Sauce

Wild Rice Tamales with Sage Butter

Smoked Chile Chicken Wings with Blue Cheese–Yogurt Dipping Sauce

Caramelized Apple Salad with Maytag Blue, Black Walnuts, and Spicy Orange Vinaigrette

This hearty salad is a distant cousin of the classic American Waldorf salad. I take the chunks of walnuts and apples, add blue cheese for a creamy tang, and toss all the ingredients with fresh greens in a vinaigrette that's alive with orange and a little spicy with ancho chile powder. This makes a great first course for a fall dinner, especially before a hearty soup or stew.

Lightly caramelizing the apples in vinaigrette brings out their sweetness and takes off that raw edge. Black walnuts, which are native to the United States, are more pungent than the regular kind, which are English walnuts.

Serves 4

Spicy Orange Vinaigrette (see below)
2 Granny Smith apples, peeled, cored, and cut into eighths
2 cups watercress
2 cups frisée or another crisp, bitter green
Salt and freshly ground pepper
¼ cup black walnuts or other walnuts, toasted and coarsely chopped
6 ounces blue cheese (preferably Maytag), crumbled

1. Heat ¾ cup of the vinaigrette in a medium skillet over medium-high heat. Add the apples and cook until golden brown on the bottom, then turn over and sauté until just cooked through, 1–2 minutes more.

2. Place the watercress and frisée in a medium bowl and toss with ¼ cup of the vinaigrette. Season with salt and pepper to taste and divide among four plates. Arrange 4 apple pieces on each plate, garnish with walnuts and blue cheese, and drizzle lightly with remaining vinaigrette.

Spicy Orange Vinaigrette

4 cups orange juice
2 tablespoons red wine vinegar
2 tablespoons coarsely chopped red onion
1 jalapeño pepper, coarsely chopped
2 tablespoons ancho chile powder
¾ cup olive oil
1 tablespoon honey
Salt and freshly ground pepper to taste

Heat the orange juice in a small nonreactive pan over high heat and boil until reduced to ¼ cup. Combine the reduced orange juice, vinegar, onion, jalapeño, and ancho powder in a food processor and blend until smooth. With the motor running, slowly add the olive oil until the dressing is creamy and emulsified. Add the honey and salt and pepper to taste.

Vidalia Onion and Jersey Tomato Salad with Blue Ranch Dressing

New Jersey and Georgia may not have much in common, but this simple salad unites the best of both states. Stacked-up slices of ripe Jersey tomatoes and Vidalia onions make a sweet, juicy, crunchy salad that is my favorite beginning to a summer steak dinner. Vidalia onions are so sweet and mild that they taste great raw. They are in season from late spring through Thanksgiving. If you don't live close enough to New Jersey to taste its August tomatoes, any ripe beefsteaks will do.

Serves 4

Blue Ranch Dressing (see below)

2 cups mixed red and green lettuces, such as watercress, Boston lettuce, red leaf lettuce, arugula, or mesclun, coarsely chopped

1 Vidalia onion, sliced about ¼ inch thick (4 slices total)

2 ripe Jersey tomatoes, sliced about ¼ inch thick (8 slices total)

Finely chopped fresh chives, for garnish

1. Make the dressing and set aside or refrigerate until ready to serve.

2. Divide the greens among 4 plates. Place 4 tomato slices on a work surface and top each with a slice of Vidalia onion. Cover with another slice of tomato. Top each plate of greens with one of the onion-tomato "sandwiches."

3. Drizzle with dressing, sprinkle with chopped chives, and serve immediately.

Blue Ranch Dressing

¾ cup buttermilk

¼ cup sour cream

2 cloves garlic, finely chopped

3 tablespoons chopped red onion

⅛ teaspoon cayenne

1 tablespoon fresh lime juice

½ cup crumbled blue cheese, preferably Maytag or another American blue cheese

Salt

Combine the buttermilk, sour cream, garlic, and onion in a blender and blend until smooth. Add the cayenne, lime juice, blue cheese, and a little salt (remember that the blue cheese is salty), and blend until almost smooth. Leave some lumps of blue cheese for texture. Season with salt to taste.

Wild Mushroom and Quinoa Salad with Fresh Thyme, Aged Goat Cheese, and Shallot Vinaigrette

I love salads that let me show off the flavors of several great ingredients. Wild mushrooms, aged goat cheese, and fresh thyme are even better together than on their own. Tangy goat cheese (you want it to be firm so it will crumble) is pungent enough to stand up to the woodsy flavor of wild mushrooms; feta would also be delicious. My shallot vinaigrette, with a sprinkling of fresh herbs, picks up all the flavors.

This is full of big tastes, so a mild background starch like quinoa, with its pearly white grains and fluffy texture, is perfect here. Quinoa is native to the Americas, and I often use it instead of rice or barley.

Serves 4–6

Shallot Vinaigrette (see below)
1½ cups quinoa
3 tablespoons olive oil
1½ pounds mixed mushrooms, preferably wild (such as oyster, portobello, chanterelles, shiitake, etc.), thinly sliced
Salt and freshly ground pepper
2 shallots, finely diced
2 tablespoons chopped fresh thyme leaves
3 tablespoons chopped flat-leaf parsley, plus extra for garnish
4 ounces aged goat cheese, crumbled
½ pound arugula leaves

1. Make the dressing and set aside or refrigerate until ready to serve.

2. Bring a large pot of salted water to a boil and cook the quinoa until tender, 8–10 minutes. Drain well. Rinse with cold water and drain well again. Transfer to a large bowl.

3. Meanwhile, heat the oil in a large skillet over high heat. Add the mushrooms, season with salt and pepper, and cook, stirring, until mushrooms are lightly browned. Add the shallots and cook for 2 minutes more. Turn off the heat and stir in the thyme and parsley.

4. Add the mushroom mixture and the goat cheese to the quinoa. Toss with ½ cup of vinaigrette and season with salt and pepper to taste. Place the arugula in a medium bowl, toss with a few tablespoons of vinaigrette, and season with salt and pepper to taste.

5. To serve, divide the arugula leaves on 4 serving plates. Mound about ½ cup of the quinoa mixture onto the leaves, drizzle with more of the vinaigrette, and garnish with parsley.

Shallot Vinaigrette

⅓ cup white wine vinegar
1 tablespoon Dijon mustard
1 small shallot, finely diced
Salt and freshly ground pepper
¾ cup olive oil

Whisk together the vinegar, mustard, and shallot in a medium bowl and season with salt and pepper. Slowly whisk in the olive oil until emulsified. Season again with salt and pepper to taste.

Crispy Soft-Shell Crab Salad with Yellow Tomatoes and Green Garlic Vinaigrette

At a crab house in the Chesapeake Bay area, I finally learned why the soft-shell crabs I love to serve in my restaurants are so expensive. It takes a lot of patience to get them that way! Chesapeake Bay producers like the Higgins family, crabbers for four generations, bring in the hard-shell blue crabs they catch and keep them in seawater pens. The growing crabs struggle out of their shells when the shells become too small. The Higginses have just four hours to get the crabs out of the water before the new shells harden. They have to be checked constantly, day and night, to make sure the soft ones come out of the water in time.

The best way to cook soft-shell crabs is crisp-fried; I like a crust so thin that you can see the crab through it, so I use rice flour. Yellow tomatoes, which are delicate and less acidic than red ones, are perfect with the light, crunchy crab and the herbaceous vinaigrette.

Serves 4

Green Garlic Vinaigrette (see below)
Canola oil for frying
1½ cups rice flour or all-purpose flour
Salt and freshly ground pepper
1 cup cold water
4 soft-shell crabs, cleaned (your fish market will do this for you)
6 cups mixed greens, such as watercress, Boston lettuce, red leaf lettuce, arugula, or mesclun
2 yellow tomatoes, cut into ½-inch-thick slices

1. Make the dressing and set aside.
2. Pour 3 inches of oil into a deep, heavy pot fitted with a deep-frying thermometer. Warm the oil over medium-high heat to 375°F.
3. Place the flour in a medium bowl and season with salt and pepper. Whisk the cold water into the flour until just combined into a thin batter (a few lumps are okay). Working in two batches of two crabs each, sprinkle each crab with salt and pepper and dip into the batter. Fry crabs until golden brown on each side, 3–4 minutes per side. Transfer to a plate lined with paper towels and repeat with the remaining crabs.
4. Place the greens in a large bowl and toss with ¼ cup of the vinaigrette. Taste to see if you need more dressing, add more as needed, toss again, and season to taste with salt and pepper.
5. Divide the greens among 4 serving plates and place 4 wedges of tomato around the edge of each plate. Place a crab in the center of each plate and drizzle with more vinaigrette. Serve immediately.

Green Garlic Vinaigrette

2 scallions (white bulb and 3 inches of green), coarsely chopped
¼ cup chopped flat-leaf parsley
¼ cup spinach, watercress, or arugula leaves
6 cloves garlic, coarsely chopped
¼ cup rice wine vinegar
½ cup extra-virgin olive oil
1 tablespoon honey
Salt and freshly ground pepper

Combine the scallions, parsley, spinach or other greens, garlic, and vinegar in a food processor and blend until smooth. With the motor running, slowly add the olive oil until the mixture is creamy and emulsified. Add the honey and season with salt and pepper to taste.

Grilled Quail Salad with a Citrus Baste and Roasted Jalapeño Dressing

No place is prouder of its cooking than Texas, and Capt. Shawn Newsome is a real Texas cook I met outside Austin. How could I tell? For one thing, he hunts most of what he cooks: quail, venison, doves, and a lot of other critters. For another, he cooks it all in the barbecue pit he built from a huge propane tank right in his front yard, smoking the meat over a delicious combination of mesquite and pecan wood. Texas cooks aren't scared of thinking big.

Captain Newsome inserts a whole jalapeño pepper into each quail as it smokes; the peppers roast and grow soft during the cooking. I put roasted chiles in my sauce instead. To serve this dish as a light main course, bake a batch of Sweet Potato Biscuits.

Serves 4

For the baste:

- 2 tablespoons olive oil
- 1 large shallot, coarsely chopped
- 3 cloves garlic, coarsely chopped
- 2 cups fresh orange juice
- 1 cup fresh lemon juice
- 2 cups Chicken Stock (page xiv), or low-sodium canned stock
- ½ cup light brown sugar
   Salt and freshly ground pepper
- 1 orange, quartered
- 1 lemon, quartered

To finish the dish:

   Roasted Jalapeño Dressing (see page 53)
- 8 quail, cleaned, bones in
   Olive oil
- 4 cups peppery greens, such as watercress, frisée, arugula, or mizuna, or a combination
   Salt and freshly ground pepper

1. At least 2 hours before you plan to cook the dish, make the baste: Heat the oil in a medium saucepan over medium-high heat. Add the shallot and garlic and cook, stirring, until soft. Add the juices, stock, and sugar, and cook until reduced by half. Season to taste with salt and pepper. Add the orange and lemon quarters, remove from the heat, and let steep for 1 hour. Remove the fruit.

2. Make the dressing and set aside or refrigerate until ready to serve.

3. Place the quail in a large baking dish and pour 1 cup of the baste over. Turn to coat, cover, and refrigerate for 1 hour. Set aside the remaining baste.

4. When ready to cook, heat a grill to high, or a grill pan over high heat until smoking. Remove the quail from the marinade and season with salt and pepper on both sides. Grill 2–3 minutes per side or until cooked to medium doneness, brushing with the remaining baste.

5. Toss the greens in a few tablespoons of the jalapeño dressing and season with salt and pepper. Divide the greens among 4 dinner plates and arrange 2 of the quail on each plate. Drizzle with more of the vinaigrette.

For the Roasted Jalapeño Dressing: See next page.

Cured Ham and Sautéed Pear Salad with Aged Sherry Vinaigrette and Black Pepper

When you get your hands on some great American country ham, like the ones I tasted in Kentucky, this is a fantastic way to use it. Cooking the ham crisps it slightly and really brings its flavor to life in your mouth.

Every ingredient in this simple salad brings a strong flavor to the mix. The whole dish is built around the ham's salty, meaty taste: I toss it with sautéed pears for sweetness, sherry vinegar for tartness, and plenty of black pepper to balance out the salt.

Serves 4

12 ounces cured ham, such as Smithfield, torn into pieces roughly 1 inch long and ½ inch wide

2 Bosc pears, ripe but not soft, cored, and cut into eighths

1 teaspoon coarsely ground black pepper

¼ cup aged sherry vinegar

2 teaspoons Dijon mustard

½ cup olive oil

Salt and freshly ground pepper

6 cups watercress or arugula

1. Heat a medium skillet over high heat. Add the ham and cook until golden brown and crisp. Remove with a slotted spoon and drain on paper towels. Add the pears to the pan and cook, stirring, until softened but not cooked through. Add the black pepper and mix gently.

2. Whisk the vinegar and mustard together in a medium bowl. Slowly whisk in the olive oil and season with salt and pepper to taste. Toss the greens with a few tablespoons of the vinaigrette, until well seasoned. Divide the greens among 4 serving plates. Arrange 4 pear slices around the greens on each plate. Divide the ham on top of the plates. Drizzle with a little more vinaigrette and serve.

Roasted Jalapeño Dressing

2 jalapeño chiles, roasted, peeled, and coarsely chopped (page xiii)

1 small shallot, coarsely chopped

⅓ cup white wine vinegar

1 tablespoon chopped fresh sage

Salt and freshly ground pepper

½ cup olive oil

1 tablespoon honey

Combine the jalapeño, shallot, vinegar, sage, and salt and pepper in a blender, and blend until smooth. With the motor running, slowly add the olive oil until dressing has emulsified. Transfer to a bowl, add the honey, and adjust seasoning.

Beer-Battered Squash Blossoms Filled with Goat Cheese and Roasted Garlic

Some of the best goat cheese in the world is now being made in America, from upstate New York to the Napa Valley. It's rich and tangy—a natural for stuffing sweet squash blossoms. The delicate flowers can come from any kind of squash, but zucchini are the most common; look for them at farmers' and ethnic markets throughout the summer (especially if you live in an Italian neighborhood). Mozzarella and anchovy are the traditional Italian stuffing for zucchini blossoms, but I also love this California-influenced combination. Squashes were grown in the Americas for thousands of years before they made it over to Italy!

Serves 4

For the filling:

Cloves from 1 head roasted garlic (page xiii), pureed
1 tablespoon olive oil
8 ounces domestic goat cheese
1 tablespoon finely chopped fresh thyme
Salt and freshly ground pepper

For the blossoms:

1 bottle (12 ounces) dark beer
1 large egg, lightly beaten
1 cup all-purpose flour, plus extra
2 tablespoons melted butter
Salt and freshly ground pepper
16 zucchini or other squash blossoms, pistils removed if desired
Vegetable oil for deep-frying

1. Make the filling: Combine garlic, olive oil, goat cheese, and thyme in a small bowl, mix until smooth, and season with salt and pepper to taste.

2. Whisk together the beer and egg. Whisk in 1 cup of the flour and continue adding flour a tablespoon at a time until the mixture reaches the consistency of a thin pancake batter. Whisk in the butter and season with salt and pepper to taste. Let rest 10 minutes.

3. Meanwhile, in a deep heavy pot fitted with a deep-frying thermometer, heat 1 inch of oil to 375°F. Stuff each blossom with a few teaspoons of the goat cheese mixture and press the petals closed.

4. Working quickly in batches of 4, dip the blossoms in batter, coating each one completely, and fry, turning once, 1½–2 minutes, or until golden and crisp. Use a slotted spoon to transfer the fried blossoms to paper towels to drain. Make sure the oil returns to 375° before adding each new batch of blossoms. Sprinkle fried blossoms with salt and serve as soon as possible.

Crab Cocktail with
Avocado, Coconut, Fresh Chiles, and Lime

I love how smooth coconut balances out the heat of chiles and the tartness of lime juice in this recipe. It really explodes in your mouth, with all the different flavors and textures coming to life.

Seafood cocktails always feel elegant to me. I like to serve them in frosted martini glasses, or even coconut halves if I happen to have some around.

Serves 6

2 cans (13-ounce) unsweetened coconut milk
1 large red onion, peeled, halved, and thinly sliced
2 serrano chiles, thinly sliced
1 tablespoon honey
Freshly squeezed juice of 2 limes
Salt and freshly ground pepper
24 ounces jumbo lump crabmeat, picked over for bits of shell and cartilage
2 ripe avocados, peeled and cut into medium dice
¼ cup chopped cilantro

1. Whisk together the coconut milk, onion, chiles, honey, and lime juice in a large bowl and season with salt and pepper. Fold in the crabmeat, cover, and marinate in the refrigerator for 30 minutes.

2. Ten minutes before serving, fold in the avocados. Season to taste with salt and pepper.

3. Just before serving, fold in the cilantro. Use martini or other stemmed glasses and divide mixture among them with a slotted spoon.

Stone Crab Claws with Red Chile–Mustard Mayonnaise

No visit to Miami is complete without a plate of claws at Joe's Stone Crab. Stone crabs are called that because the crabs' bodies look like rocks, but the only part we're really interested in is the big, meaty claw. Since the bodies aren't edible, stone crab fishermen just twist off one claw and toss the crab back into the sea; within two years, the claw grows back.

Frozen cooked stone crab claws come in sizes from medium to colossal, and to my mind you want to go as big as you can, to get the full experience. This tangy sauce would also be great on lobster claws or chilled shrimp.

Serves 4

¼ cup Dijon mustard
3 tablespoons ancho chile powder
1 cup best-quality mayonnaise
1 tablespoon fresh lime juice
  Salt
4 pounds cooked stone crab claws, chilled in
   the shell

1. Whisk together the mustard, ancho powder, mayonnaise, and lime juice. Season to taste with salt and divide among 4 serving bowls.

2. Serve the claws with nutcrackers and bowls of sauce for dipping.

Key Lime–Red Pepper Shellfish Ceviche with Fried Tortillas

Ceviche is relatively new to the American table, but chilled seafood in a tangy sauce isn't —who doesn't love shrimp cocktail? Ceviche (pronounced seh-*vee*-chay) is an old Latin-Caribbean version, where the delicate seafood is actually "cooked" in the acid from citrus fruits.

Serves 4

For the ceviche:
- ½ pound medium-size shrimp, peeled and deveined
- 1 pound squid, cleaned and cut into rings
- ½ pound Calico Bay scallops
- 2 cups fresh or bottled key lime juice, or 1 cup each fresh lime and lemon juices
- 1 cup fresh lemon juice
- ½ cup bottled clam juice
- ¼ cup Smoked Red Pepper Sauce (see below)
- 1 yellow pepper, roasted, peeled, seeded, and finely diced (page xiii)
- 1 poblano pepper, roasted, peeled, seeded, and finely diced (page xiii)
- ¼ cup finely chopped red onion
- 1 small orange, segmented
- 1 lemon, segmented
- 1 key lime or if out of season use Persian lime, segmented
- ¼ cup coarsely chopped cilantro

For the tortillas:
- 2 cups peanut oil
- 2 large flour tortillas, cut into sixths
- Salt

1. Bring a medium saucepan of salted water to a boil. Fill a bowl with ice cubes and cover with cold water. Add the shrimp and squid to the boiling water and blanch (boil) for 30 seconds. Lift out of the boiling water and plunge into the ice water to stop the cooking. When cool, drain well on paper towels.

2. Place the blanched shrimp and squid and the raw scallops in a medium bowl, add the lime and lemon juice, mix well, and refrigerate, covered, for 2 hours.

3. Meanwhile, make the red pepper sauce and set aside.

4. Fry the tortillas: Heat oil to 365°F in a deep medium skillet. Add the tortillas in batches, remove to a plate lined with paper towels, and season with salt.

5. After two hours, remove the fish from the refrigerator and pour off all of the juice. Whisk together the clam juice and red pepper sauce until combined and add to the fish. Add the peppers, onion, citrus sections, and cilantro, and gently mix to combine. Season with salt and pepper to taste. Serve in small individual bowls, with 3 tortilla wedges for each serving.

Smoked Red Pepper Sauce

- 1 red pepper, roasted, peeled, seeded, and diced (page xiii)
- 2 tablespoons chopped red onion
- 1 tablespoon chipotle puree (page xiii)
- 2 tablespoons freshly squeezed lime juice
- ¼ cup olive oil
- 1 tablespoon honey
- Salt and freshly ground pepper

Combine the peppers, onion, chipotle puree, lime juice, and oil in a food processor and blend until smooth. Add the honey and salt and pepper to taste and blend 10 seconds more.

Shrimp and Avocado Salad in Roasted Chayote

The first wave of "California cuisine," in the 1970s, brought avocados to the rest of the country. I remember my first avocado as a cup holding crabmeat salad, and I immediately loved how you could eat a bit of salad and a bit of avocado with each spoonful. Here, I've taken the mayonnaise out of the salad and used the creaminess of the avocado itself as a binder.

As my edible serving cup, I like to use halves of *chayote,* the native name for the Southwestern fruit that Louisianans call *mirliton.* It has a mild, almost cucumberlike flavor and a lightly starchy texture that makes it perfect as a partner for big-flavored salads like this one.

Serves 4

For the chayote:

- 4 chayotes, cut in half lengthwise, and pitted
- 3 tablespoons olive oil
- Salt and freshly ground pepper

For the salad:

- 5 tablespoons olive oil
- ¾ pound small shrimp, 31–40 size, peeled and deveined
- Salt and freshly ground pepper
- 1 large ripe avocado, peeled, pitted, and finely diced
- ½ red onion, peeled and thinly sliced
- 3 tablespoons fresh lime juice
- 3 tablespoons chopped cilantro

1. Make the chayote: Preheat the oven to 400°F. Brush the cut sides of the chayote halves with the olive oil and season with salt and pepper. Place in a roasting pan and roast in the oven until just cooked through, 20–25 minutes. Let cool slightly. Scoop a few tablespoons of roasted flesh out of the hollow of each half, making the hollow deeper. Coarsely chop and reserve to add to the salad. Set the chayote halves aside, intact.

2. Meanwhile, make the shrimp salad: Heat 3 tablespoons of the oil in a large skillet over high heat. Season the shrimp with salt and pepper and cook in 2 batches, tossing over high heat just until lightly browned, about 3 minutes. Remove to a plate lined with paper towels. Let cool slightly.

3. Combine the shrimp, avocado, onion, and chopped chayote in a medium bowl. Add the lime juice, remaining 2 tablespoons olive oil, and cilantro, and gently mix to combine. Fill each chayote half with the salad mixture, 2 halves per serving.

Grilled Shrimp on Plantain Tostones with Avocado Cocktail Sauce

I can never decide what I like most about plantains: the texture or the flavor. I use them green, yellow, brown, and black — at every stage of ripeness — and I like them all. I just use different methods for cooking them. Green plantains fry up starchy and crisp, perfect with tender shellfish and a spicy sauce. I use them as a base for my twist on a traditional shrimp cocktail. Adding buttery avocado balances out the bite in the horseradish and hot pepper sauce.

Cuban restaurants all over America serve *tostones,* usually with a powerful garlic oil dipping sauce. The cooking method is very smart. The starchy fruit is fried first in chunks, to make it soft enough to pound flat; then it's fried again to make it crisp all over.

Serves 4

For the sauces:

2 Haas avocados, peeled, pitted, and finely diced
3 tablespoons finely diced red onion
2 cloves garlic, finely chopped
1 tablespoon prepared horseradish, drained
2 tablespoons coarsely chopped cilantro
3 tablespoons fresh lime juice
Salt and freshly ground pepper
2 tablespoons Worcestershire sauce
2 teaspoons hot sauce of your choice, or to taste

For the shrimp:

2 tablespoons olive oil
12 medium shrimp, peeled and deveined
Salt and pepper

For the tostones:

3 cups peanut or canola oil
3 green plantains, peeled with a knife and cut into 2-inch lengths (4 per plantain)
Kosher salt
Cilantro leaves, for garnish

1. Make the sauces: Combine the avocado, onion, garlic, horseradish, cilantro, lime juice, and salt and pepper to taste in a small bowl and set aside.

2. Mix together the Worcestershire and hot sauce in another bowl and set aside or transfer to a squeeze bottle.

3. Make the shrimp: Heat the olive oil in a large skillet or grill pan over high heat until almost smoking. Season the shrimp with salt and pepper. Sauté the shrimp 1–2 minutes, until pink.

4. Make the tostones: Heat the oil in a heavy frying pan fitted with a deep-frying thermometer to 325°F. Working in 3 batches to avoid crowding the pan, add the plantain pieces and fry until soft, about 2 minutes per side, turning once. Using a slotted spoon, transfer to a paper towel–lined plate to drain.

5. When all the pieces have been cooked once, raise the temperature of the oil to 375°F. Using a tostone maker, tortilla press, meat pounder, or other heavy object, flatten each plantain piece to ⅛ inch thick. Fry the tostones again, working in batches, until crisp and golden brown, about 1 minute per side. Drain on paper towels. Sprinkle immediately with salt.

6. To assemble: Place 3 tostones on each serving plate. Top each one with a dollop of avocado relish and a shrimp. Drizzle the Worcestershire/hot sauce over the shrimp and around the plate. Garnish with cilantro leaves.

Fresh Clam and Garlic Flatbread with Flat-Leaf Parsley Oil

If I had grown up in Ipswich, Massachusetts, with its great soft-shell clams and Italian bakeries, this is what I would be grilling every summer weekend. Fresh flatbread is topped with fat, briny clams, then crisped on the grill. Plenty of garlic, olive oil, and parsley drizzled on top punches up the Italian flavors.

This is a great appetizer for a grilled fish dinner, especially Slow Fire-Roasted Striped Bass with a Fresh Mint and Tomato Relish.

Serves 4

For the flatbread:
1½ cups warm water
½ teaspoon dry yeast
3½–4 cups all-purpose flour
1 teaspoon salt
2 tablespoons olive oil

For the parsley oil:
2 cups loosely packed flat-leaf parsley leaves
¼ cup loosely packed spinach leaves, chopped
1 cup olive oil
Salt and freshly ground pepper

To finish the dish:
Olive oil
Salt and freshly ground pepper
8 cloves garlic, thinly sliced
36 littleneck clams, shucked and coarsely chopped (you can buy shucked clams in tubs at fish stores and many supermarkets)
¼ cup chopped fresh parsley

1. Make the dough: Mix the water and yeast in a medium bowl and let stand 15 minutes. Gradually mix in 2 cups of the flour. Stir about 1 minute. Let stand, covered, for at least 1 hour.

2. Transfer the dough to the bowl of a mixer fitted with a dough hook. Add the salt and the olive oil, then add more flour, ⅓ cup at a time, until a soft dough forms. Transfer to a lightly floured surface and knead until satiny, about 5 minutes. Transfer to a clean oiled bowl and let rise in a warm spot for 1½–2 hours, until doubled in bulk. Divide the dough into 4 balls, cover with a clean cloth, and let rise again 30–40 minutes. Roll out each ball into a rough 10- to 12-inch circle (or another shape, if you prefer).

3. Make the parsley oil: Combine the parsley, spinach, and olive oil in a blender, season with salt and pepper, and blend until smooth. Strain into a small bowl.

4. Preheat a grill to medium-high. Brush the dough circles liberally with olive oil on both sides and season with salt and pepper. Grill until crusty and golden brown on one side, 3–4 minutes. Turn over and grill another 3–4 minutes.

5. Remove flatbreads from the grill and arrange them on a large sheet of aluminum foil. When ready to serve, brush the tops with more oil, sprinkle with garlic, divide the clams among the flatbreads, and season with salt and pepper. Place on the grill, close the cover, and cook for 3–4 minutes. Remove the flatbreads from the grill, immediately drizzle with the parsley oil, and garnish with fresh parsley.

Crisp-Fried Oysters with Chile Vinegar–Black Pepper Sauce

You only need to know a few ways to serve great oysters. Completely naked is one (the oyster, that is). This is another: dredged in cornmeal and quickly fried, then dipped into a savory, peppery sauce. The oyster stays cool and briny inside its crisp, hot cornmeal crust, and the contrast is fantastic. Use medium to large oysters for this recipe: the flavor of small ones could get lost.

Serves 4

For the dipping sauce:
- 1 cup white wine vinegar
- 1 ancho chile, coarsely chopped
- 1 tablespoons honey
- 1 shallot, finely chopped
- 2 teaspoons coarsely ground black pepper
- Salt

For the oysters:
- 32 oysters, shucked and patted dry (you can buy pre-shucked oysters at fish stores and many supermarkets), 16 half-shells reserved for serving
- Salt and freshly ground pepper
- 2 cups yellow cornmeal
- Vegetable or peanut oil

1. At least 1 hour before serving, make the sauce: Bring the vinegar to a boil in a nonreactive medium saucepan. Add the chile, turn off the heat, and let steep for 1 hour. Strain into a clean saucepan and bring to a simmer. Remove from the heat and whisk in the honey, shallot, and pepper, and season with salt to taste. Set aside at room temperature until ready to serve.

2. Make the oysters: Season the oysters on both sides with salt and pepper. Place the cornmeal in a bowl and season with salt and pepper. Dredge each oyster in the cornmeal, turning them to coat completely, and tap off any excess.

3. Heat 1 inch of oil in a large skillet until rippling and just starting to smoke. Arrange 4 oyster half-shells on each of 4 serving plates. Fry the oysters, working in batches to avoid crowding the pan, until golden brown on both sides, about 1 minute on each side. Put 2 fried oysters into each oyster shell and serve as soon as possible with small bowls of dipping sauce.

Roasted Oysters in Beer with Homemade Hot Sauce

I knew I was a lucky guy the day I got invited to a Savannah oyster roast. The oyster roast is to the Atlantic coast down South what the clambake is up North: a great party, a taste of history, and a simple celebration of fresh local ingredients.

The oysters are cooked on a red-hot griddle (which can be as much as 15 feet long) under seawater-soaked burlap sacks. The sacks trap the heat and the salty steam just cooks those plump oysters right in the shell. A bottle each of hot sauce and beer is all you need to complete the dish; I've adapted the method for the home kitchen. The only hard part is buying enough beer to cook with *and* to drink. Plump Atlantic oysters like Blue Points, Pine Islands, and Chincoteagues will yield the best results.

Serves 4

For the hot sauce:

1 cup red wine vinegar
2 tablespoons Dijon mustard
1 tablespoon chipotle puree (page xiii)
1 tablespoon honey
½ teaspoon salt

For the oysters:

Three 12-ounce bottles dark beer
2 clean white dish towels
28 plump Atlantic oysters (see above), scrubbed well
Salt and freshly ground black pepper

1. Make the hot sauce: Whisk together all the ingredients in a small bowl.

2. Make the oysters: Preheat the oven to 450°F and place a deep roasting pan (large enough to hold the oysters in a single layer) in the center of the oven. Let heat 10 minutes.

3. Pour 2 bottles of the beer in a large bowl, add the towels, and soak them until they are completely saturated. Lightly wring out.

4. When the pan is very hot, carefully pour in the remaining bottle of beer. Add the oysters in a single layer, season with salt and pepper, cover with the wet towels, and roast 8–10 minutes, or until all of the oysters have opened, discarding any that do not. Serve with hot sauce.

Wild Rice Tamales with Sage Butter

Wild rice and sage are flavors that are made for each other. When you mix them into a classic corn *masa*, or tamale filling, all the tastes flower into a fantastic winter appetizer. Tamales (corn husks stuffed with *masa* and steamed, then served with a sauce or stew) are a Mexican-American Christmas tradition, and they are comforting, savory, and full of corn flavor. I serve tamales all year round at Mesa Grill, changing the flavorings and additions to suit the season.

A light *masa* is the base of an excellent tamale, and there's no getting around it: you need to add fat to the cornmeal mixture. But is it ever worth it! If you can't find corn husks at a Latin grocery store or on the Internet, wrap the *masa* in 4-inch squares of parchment paper or foil as though you are wrapping a present, then steam.

Serves 8

22 dried corn husks (see Sources, page 231)

For the sage butter:

1 stick (8 tablespoons) unsalted butter, slightly softened at room temperature

8 fresh sage leaves, coarsely chopped
Salt and freshly ground pepper

For the *masa*:

1½ cups corn kernels, preferably fresh but frozen is okay

1 medium onion, coarsely chopped
Cloves from 1 head roasted garlic (page xiii), coarsely chopped

1 tablespoon honey

2 cups Chicken Stock (page xiv), or low-sodium canned stock or water

6 tablespoons unsalted butter, cut into pieces

6 tablespoons vegetable shortening

1½ cups yellow cornmeal

1 cup very well cooked wild rice
Salt and freshly ground pepper

1. About 2 hours before you plan to assemble the tamales, rinse the corn husks under running water. Soak them in a bowl of warm water for 2 hours, or until softened.

2. Make the sage butter: Combine the butter, sage, and salt and pepper to taste in a food processor until smooth. Place a sheet of parchment paper or wax paper on a work surface. Arrange the butter along one long side and form into a roll about 1 inch in diameter, leaving a 1-inch border of paper. Roll up the butter in the paper and refrigerate for at least 30 minutes.

3. Make the *masa*: Puree the corn, onion, roasted garlic cloves, honey, and stock in a food processor. Transfer the mixture to a bowl and lightly stir in the butter and shortening (don't mix until smooth). Using your fingers, mix in the cornmeal, and salt and pepper to taste until the mixture comes together and there are no visible lumps of fat. Fold in the wild rice. The mixture may seem loose and too moist, but when the tamales are steamed, it will dry out.

4. Assemble the tamales: Remove the corn husks from the water and set aside the best 18 husks. Drain and pat dry. Tear the remaining husks into 1-inch-wide strips to be used for tying. Lay 2 husks flat on a work surface, end to end, with the tapered ends facing out and the broad bases overlapping by about 3 inches. Place about ⅓ cup of the *masa* in the center, where the bases overlap. Bring the long sides up and over the *masa*, slightly overlapping, and pat down to close. (If the *masa* drips out a little at the seam, that is

no problem.) Tie off each end of the bundle with a strip of corn husk, pushing the *masa* toward the middle as you tie, so that you have a stuffed center and 2 tied-off ends (a bit like a wrapped Tootsie Roll). Trim the ends to about ½ inch beyond the tie. Repeat with the remaining husks and *masa.*

5. Arrange the tamales in a single layer on a steaming rack, cover tightly with foil, and steam over boiling water for 45 minutes. *(After steaming, the cooked tamales can be refrigerated up to 6 hours, then reheated in a 350°F oven 30–40 minutes.)*

6. To serve, slice a slit on top of each tamale and push both ends of the tamale toward the middle to expose the *masa,* as though cutting a baked potato. Top with a pat of sage butter and serve immediately.

Smoked Chile Chicken Wings with Blue Cheese–Yogurt Dipping Sauce

A platter of these spicy chicken wings plus a few friends equals an instant party. They aren't fancy, but they are fun, quick, and totally delicious, especially with good American lager beer. Fresh ingredients and a real, creamy blue cheese sauce make the difference. My hot sauce includes chipotle puree, made from smoked jalapeños for a deeper flavor.

For the full Buffalo wing experience, as they serve them at The Anchor in Buffalo, New York, add celery sticks to the serving platter.

Serves 4

For the blue cheese sauce:
- 1 pint whole milk yogurt
- ¾ cup crumbled domestic blue cheese
- 2 tablespoons red onion, finely chopped
- 1 tablespoon fresh lime juice
- Salt and freshly ground pepper

For the hot sauce:
- 2 cups red wine vinegar
- 3 tablespoons Dijon mustard
- 2 tablespoons chipotle puree (page xiii)
- 2 tablespoons honey
- 2 tablespoons vegetable oil
- 1 teaspoon kosher salt

For the wings:
- 40 chicken wings
- Peanut oil for frying
- 1 stick (8 tablespoons) unsalted butter
- 1 tablespoon ancho chile powder
- 2 tablespoons honey
- Salt

1. Make the blue cheese sauce: Place the yogurt in a medium strainer lined with cheesecloth and set it over a bowl. Place in the refrigerator and let drain for at least 2 hours or up to 10 hours. Transfer the drained yogurt to a medium bowl, fold in the blue cheese, onion, and lime juice, and season with salt and pepper.

2. Make the hot sauce: Whisk all ingredients together in a medium bowl.

3. Cook the wings: Heat 3 inches of oil in a large skillet to 370°F. Working in batches to avoid crowding the pan, add the wings and fry, turning occasionally, until golden brown, 8–10 minutes per batch. Drain on paper towels.

4. When ready to serve, melt the butter in a large skillet over medium heat. Add the hot sauce and bring to a boil. Whisk in the ancho chile powder and honey until blended. Season with salt. Add the wings and cook, stirring, 2–3 minutes.

5. Serve hot, with blue cheese sauce for dipping (and a lot of napkins).

Postcard from the Smoky Mountains, Tennessee

Picture a gorgeous, clear, spring day in the foothills of the great Smoky Mountains. I'm standing in a burbling stream in hip waders, fly-fishing for the first time in my life. My guide assures me trout are plentiful around here (two thousand fish per mile of river, he claims!), so I confidently draw my arm back, then flick it forward. The hook goes flying right into my guide's face and hooks him in the cheek! The poor guy was perfectly calm, but I was ready to whip out my cell phone and call an ambulance—and then the fish market! You can take the boy out of the city, but I'm not sure you can take the city out of the boy.

Eastern Tennessee is very different from the kinds of places chefs usually go to seek inspiration in the kitchen, and I love that about it. There are no esoteric ingredients or little-known ethnic grocery stores, but the food is fresh, seasonal, simple—and totally local.

I learned the true definition of simple cooking when I visited Olivia Sipe, a proud cook who calls herself the Kitchen Witch. She made the best fried okra I have ever tasted in my life, using nothing more than cornmeal. Not even salt and pepper! My habits as a chef would have told me that the okra would be bland without seasoning, but she knew better: It was delicate and perfect. The same goes for her fried chicken, just dipped into flour without a speck of seasoning and pan-fried. I insisted that there was something she wasn't telling me about her recipe—I'm always sure that the cooks I meet are leaving something out! She assured me that she wouldn't invite me all the way down from New York and then try to trick me...but I don't know, she is a witch after all. Maybe magic is her secret ingredient.

I know that the next cook I met didn't leave anything out. Willadeene Parton, the oldest of Dolly's eleven siblings, was one of the warmest, most welcoming people I've ever met. She says that Dolly's a good cook too! Willadeene's meat loaf and corn pudding, two American classics, were great.

There's a movement among some local chefs to call the local cooking "foothills cuisine," a reference to the area's quiet location in the shadow of the Smoky Mountains. It's not quite the South, not the Midwest, and definitely not the East. But the food reminds me of all three. Chef John Fleer of the Blackberry Farm Inn dredges local rainbow trout in flour and fries them. Sounds traditional — but he uses rice flour and pecans for a crisp crust, and clarified butter to deeply brown the skin. To cook collard greens, traditionally slow-simmered with a ham bone, he quickly sautés them in bacon fat, then deglazes the pan with a little bit of super-flavorful balsamic vinegar.

It's great to see how American cooking is evolving outside the usual trendsetting spots. I feel that I'm always learning where my food comes from.

Corn, Pasta, and Rice

Toasted White Corn Porridge with Wild Mushrooms

Shrimp and Grits with Double-Smoked Bacon

San Antonio–Style Goat Cheese Enchiladas with Ancho Chile Sauce

Red Bean Tamales with Roasted Tomato Salsa

Roasted Squash Ravioli with Fresh Sage and Hazelnut Brown Butter

Ear-Shaped Pasta with Fresh Morels, Green Peas, and Sweet Onions

Crawfish Lasagna

My Favorite Spaghetti and Meatballs

Savannah Red Rice with Roasted Salt-and-Pepper Shrimp

Yellow Pepper Risotto with Grilled Shrimp and Black Olive Vinaigrette

Black-Eyed Pea Risotto with Smoked Bacon and Swiss Chard

Toasted White Corn Porridge with Wild Mushrooms

One of the strangest sights I've seen in my travels around America (other than a woman dressed up as a Vidalia onion) is the Phillips Mushroom Farm outside Philadelphia. It isn't like any farm you've ever seen! Instead of fields, there are rooms full of shelving, each stacked with plastic bags covered with mushrooms. The bags are stuffed with compost, then injected with the mushroom molds, and the mushrooms grow all over the outside of the bags. It looks like an episode of *Star Trek*.

In just the last ten years, the availability of delicious, funky mushrooms like Oyster, Hen-of-the-Woods, Pom-Poms, and Royal Trumpets has exploded. Try to find a variety for this sauté.

Serves 4

For the porridge:

1¼	cup finely ground white cornmeal
2	tablespoons olive oil
1	tablespoon unsalted butter
1	large onion, finely diced
2	cloves garlic, finely chopped
5	cups Chicken Stock (page xiv), or low-sodium canned stock
	Salt and freshly ground pepper
½	cup mascarpone or cream cheese

For the mushrooms:

¼	cup olive oil
1½	pounds assorted mushrooms, such as portobello, cremini, oyster, shiitake, etc., cleaned, trimmed, and thinly sliced
1	ounce dried porcini mushrooms, soaked in hot water and drained
	Salt and freshly ground pepper
½	cup dry white wine
2	cloves garlic, finely chopped
½	cup Chicken Stock (page xiv), or low-sodium canned stock
¼	cup finely chopped parsley, plus extra for garnish
2	tablespoons chopped fresh thyme

1. Make the porridge: Preheat the oven to 325°F. Spread the cornmeal evenly on a baking sheet, and bake until lightly golden brown, 8–10 minutes, shaking the pan once.

2. Heat the oil and butter in a medium saucepan over medium-high heat. Add the onion and garlic and cook until soft. Add the chicken stock and 1 tablespoon of salt and bring to a boil. Gradually whisk in the cornmeal until the mixture is smooth. Reduce heat to low, cover, and let simmer (the mixture will bubble more slowly as it thickens). Every 5 minutes, uncover the pot and stir with a flat-bottomed wooden spoon, scraping the porridge up from the bottom of the pan. When it is almost done, after 35–40 minutes, uncover the pot and allow it to cook an additional 5 minutes. If the mixture appears dry, add a few tablespoons of water. Whisk in the mascarpone and season with salt and pepper to taste.

3. When the porridge is almost done, cook the mushrooms: Heat the oil in a large skillet over high heat until almost smoking. Add the mushrooms, season with salt and pepper, and cook, tossing the mushrooms in the pan, until softened and browned. Add the wine and cook until completely evaporated. Add the garlic and stock, and cook until most of the stock has evaporated but the mixture is slightly moist. Remove from the heat and fold in the parsley and thyme.

4. To serve, pour the porridge onto a serving plate and spoon the mushrooms over. Sprinkle with parsley and serve.

Shrimp and Grits with Double-Smoked Bacon

If there is one dish that makes me want to march down Fifth Avenue waving the American flag, it's shrimp and grits. I'll always be grateful to Martha Nesbit of Savannah for introducing me to this Southern dish. As soon as she poured the sunny yellow cheese grits into a big blue bowl, then topped it with a pile of pink shrimp, browned bacon, and green shreds of spring onion, I knew I was in for something great. It is simple, but so delicious you can't imagine. Martha cooked enough for her family of four, and I ate it all!

Sautéing the shrimp in a little of the bacon fat really marries the flavors.

Serves 4

For the cheese grits:

- 1 tablespoon unsalted butter
- 1 tablespoon olive oil
- 1 large onion, finely diced
- 2 cloves garlic, finely chopped
- 2 cups milk
- 3 cups water
- Salt and freshly ground pepper
- 1 cup grits
- 1½ cups finely grated cheddar cheese

For the shrimp:

- 8 ounces double-smoked bacon, cut into ½-inch dice
- 20 large shrimp, peeled and deveined
- Salt and freshly ground pepper
- ¼ cup coarsely chopped scallions

1. Make the grits: Melt the butter and oil together in a medium saucepan over medium heat. Add the onion and garlic and cook, stirring, until soft. Increase the heat to high, add the milk, water, and 1 tablespoon of salt, and bring to a boil. Slowly whisk in the grits, a few handfuls at a time, and bring to a boil. Reduce the heat to a simmer, and cook, stirring often with a wooden spoon, until the mixture is smooth, thick, and falls easily from a spoon, 15–20 minutes. Add the cheese and stir until completely melted. Season with salt and pepper to taste.

2. Meanwhile, make the shrimp: Heat a large pan over high heat until smoking. Add the bacon and cook, stirring, until golden brown. Remove the bacon with a slotted spoon to a plate lined with paper towels. Remove all but 3 tablespoons of fat, and return the pan to the stove over high heat. Season the shrimp with salt and pepper and toss in the pan until pink and lightly browned, 1½–2 minutes per side.

3. To serve, pour a serving of cheese grits into a soup plate. Top each plate with 5 shrimp. Garnish with bacon and chopped scallions.

San Antonio–Style Goat Cheese Enchiladas with Ancho Chile Sauce

The homestyle restaurants of San Antonio, with their authentic Border flavors, are some of my favorite places to eat. Diana Trevino, who runs one of the best cafés in town, showed me how a simple dish like this one — just tortillas, cheese, and sauce — becomes irresistible when made with good, fresh ingredients. Mexican oregano, more pungent than our Mediterranean oregano, punches up the flavor of the sauce.

I'm always envious of the citizens of San Antonio, who can buy warm tortillas made from fresh *masa,* or corn dough, every day at local tortilla factories. Corn tortillas are one of the oldest American foods, made in the Southwest for thousands of years.

Serves 4–6

For the ancho chile sauce:

2   whole ancho chiles
3   tablespoons vegetable oil
1   large red onion, finely chopped
3   cloves garlic, finely chopped
1   tablespoon ground cumin
1   tablespoon dried Mexican oregano
1   cup dry white wine
    One 16-ounce can plum tomatoes and their
        juices, pureed
2   tablespoons honey
2   cups Chicken Stock (page xiv)
    Salt and freshly ground pepper

For the filling:

1¼   pound goat cheese
3   cloves garlic, coarsely chopped
¼   cup freshly grated Romano cheese
2   tablespoons fresh lime juice
¼   cup finely chopped cilantro

To finish the dish:

12   blue or yellow corn tortillas
8   ounces Monterey Jack cheese, grated
3   tablespoons chopped cilantro

1. Make the sauce: Bring 2 cups of water to a boil in a small saucepan. Add the chiles, remove from the heat, and let sit for 30 minutes. Lift out the chiles and pour ¼ cup of the soaking liquid into a food processor. Remove the stems and seeds from the chiles and puree with the cooking liquid until smooth.

2. Heat the oil in a medium saucepan over medium-high heat. Add the onion and cook, stirring, until soft. Add the garlic and cook for 1 minute. Add the cumin and oregano and cook for 1 minute. Add ancho puree and cook for 2–3 minutes. Add the wine, tomatoes, honey, and stock, and simmer for 25–30 minutes or until slightly thickened. Season with salt and pepper to taste.

3. Make the filling: Combine the goat cheese, garlic, Romano cheese, and lime juice in a food processor and blend until smooth. Season with salt and pepper and fold in the cilantro.

4. Preheat the oven to 375°F. Spread ½ cup of the tomato–chile sauce over the bottom of a casserole that can hold the tortillas snugly in one layer. Dip a tortilla in the chile sauce and place on a work surface to lightly coat both sides. Spoon about 2 tablespoons of the goat cheese filling across the tortilla, roll up, and place in the dish. Repeat with remaining tortillas. Pour about 1½ cups of the remaining sauce over the enchiladas and top with the cheese. Cover and bake 20–30 minutes or until the enchiladas are heated through, removing the cover for the last 10 minutes of cooking. Sprinkle with chopped cilantro before serving.

Red Bean Tamales with Roasted Tomato Salsa

This is the best tamale I've ever had—I just wish I could take full credit for the recipe! Tamales, bundles of mild steamed cornmeal, are usually topped with big-flavored salsas or savory meat stews. Mary Trevino of San Antonio, Texas, taught me the rich mess of red beans she puts on her tamales instead, and the combination is delicious, comforting, and incredibly filling.

Corn and beans are two of the three ingredients (squash is the other) that most people lived on in the Americas before the Europeans arrived.

Serves 8

24 dried corn husks (see Sources, page 231)

For the red bean mixture:

2 tablespoons olive oil

1 red onion, peeled and coarsely chopped

1 stalk celery, coarsely chopped

3 cloves garlic, chopped

12 ounces dried red kidney beans, picked over, soaked overnight, and drained

1 meaty ham bone or smoked ham hock (1½–2 pounds)

6 cups water

2 bay leaves

6 sprigs fresh thyme

6 sprigs fresh parsley

Few dashes hot sauce

½ cup thinly sliced scallion

For the *masa*:

½ cup fresh or frozen corn kernels

1 medium onion, quartered

2 cups Chicken Stock (page xiv), or low-sodium canned stock or water

6 tablespoons unsalted butter, cut into pieces

6 tablespoons vegetable shortening

1½ cups yellow cornmeal

2 tablespoons honey

Salt and freshly ground pepper

Roasted Tomato Salsa (see below)

1. About 2 hours before you plan to assemble the tamales, rinse the corn husks under running water. Soak them in a bowl of warm water for 2 hours, or until softened.

2. Make the red bean mixture: Heat the oil in a large heavy casserole or saucepan over medium heat. Add the onion, celery, and garlic, and cook, stirring, until soft. Add the soaked beans, ham bone, water, bay leaves, thyme, parsley, and hot sauce. Bring to a boil, reduce the heat, and simmer for about 2 hours, or until the beans are very soft, adding more water if needed. Season to taste with salt and remove the bay leaves and thyme and parsley sprigs. Remove the ham bone, shred the meat, and add to the bean mixture, discarding the bone. Mash the beans slightly until the mixture is creamy and fold in the green onion. Set aside.

3. Make the *masa*: Puree the corn, onion, and stock in a food processor. Transfer the mixture to a bowl and lightly stir in the butter and shortening (don't mix until smooth). Using your fingers, mix in the cornmeal, honey, and salt and pepper to taste until the mixture comes together and there are no visible lumps of fat. The mixture may seem loose and too moist, but when the tamales are steamed, it will dry out somewhat.

4. Assemble the tamales: Remove the corn husks from the water and set aside the best 20 husks. Drain and pat dry. Tear the remaining husks into 1-inch-wide strips to be used for tying. Lay 2 husks flat on a work surface, end to end, with the tapered ends facing out and the broad bases overlapping by about 3 inches. Place about ¼ cup of *masa* in the center, where the bases overlap, and place about 3 tablespoons of the red bean mixture on top. Bring the long sides up and over the filling, slightly overlapping, and pat down to close. (If the filling drips out a little at the seam, that is no problem.) Tie off each end of the bundle with a strip of corn husk, pushing the filling toward the middle as you tie, so that you have a stuffed center and 2 tied-off ends (a bit like a wrapped Tootsie Roll). Trim the ends to about ½ inch beyond the tie. Repeat with the remaining husks, *masa,* and bean mixture.

5. Arrange the tamales in a single layer on a steaming rack, cover tightly with foil, and steam over simmering water for 45 minutes. *(After steaming, the cooked tamales can be refrigerated up to 6 hours, and reheated in a 350°F oven 30–40 minutes.)*

6. To serve, slice a slit on top of each tamale and push both ends of the tamale toward the middle to expose the filling, as though cutting a baked potato. Top with Roasted Tomato Salsa and serve immediately.

Roasted Tomato Salsa

8 plum tomatoes, cored and sliced in half
3 tablespoons olive oil
1 small red onion, coarsely chopped
4 cloves garlic, coarsely chopped
1 jalapeño chile, coarsely diced
 Salt and freshly ground pepper
2 tablespoons fresh lime juice
¼ cup chopped cilantro

Heat the oven to 375°F. In a medium baking dish, toss together the tomatoes, olive oil, onion, garlic, and jalapeño. Season with salt and pepper and roast until soft, 15–20 minutes. Remove from the oven and coarsely chop the tomatoes. Transfer all the vegetables to a medium bowl and add the lime juice and cilantro. Mix well and season to taste with salt and pepper.

Roasted Squash Ravioli with Fresh Sage and Hazelnut Brown Butter

I always think of squash as a very American ingredient, so I was surprised, when I happened to be in Italy one autumn, that squash turned up on every single menu—stuffed into ravioli, agnolotti, tortellini, and on and on. This fall classic is one of the best ways I know to use the smooth, sweet flesh of the butternut.

Many Italian groceries sell sheets of frozen or fresh pasta dough. You can also make the ravioli using Chinese wonton wrappers: Mound a scant tablespoon of the mixture in the center of one wrapper, wet the edges, and press another wrapper on top. Excess dough around the edges can be trimmed off with a cookie cutter.

Serves 4

For the ravioli:

1 butternut squash, halved and seeded (do not peel)
¼ teaspoon cinnamon
⅛ teaspoon nutmeg
1 tablespoon finely grated orange zest
2 teaspoons chipotle puree (page xiii)
¼ cup finely chopped parsley
¼ cup finely grated Parmesan cheese
   Salt and freshly ground pepper
4 sheets pasta dough (see above)
2 eggs, beaten with 2 tablespoons water
   Chopped chives, for garnish

For the sauce:

2 sticks (8 ounces) unsalted butter
¼ cup coarsely ground hazelnuts
8 sage leaves, cut crosswise into thin shreds
   Salt and freshly ground pepper

1. Preheat the oven to 450°F. Place the squash on a baking sheet and roast until soft. Scoop out the flesh and run it though a food mill, or puree it in a food processor. Place the puree in a medium saucepan and cook over low heat, stirring, until almost dry. Add the cinnamon, nutmeg, orange zest, chipotle puree, parsley, cheese, and salt and pepper to taste.

2. Lay a sheet of pasta dough on a lightly floured work surface and arrange heaping teaspoons of the filling in rows at least 2 inches apart in each direction. Use your fingertip or a brush to moisten the edges of the pasta with the egg wash. Carefully place a second sheet of pasta on top of the first and press down with your fingertips to separate the rows of filling. Repeat with the remaining ingredients. Using a ravioli cutter or pastry wheel, cut a grid to make ravioli squares. Press the edges closed with your fingertips to seal well.

3. When ready to serve, bring a large pot of salted water to a boil.

4. Make the sauce: Melt the butter in a medium skillet over medium-high heat. Let foam up and cook, swirling occasionally, until golden brown. Remove from the heat and add the hazelnuts and sage. Season with salt and pepper to taste.

5. Meanwhile, cook the ravioli: Carefully drop the ravioli into the boiling water and boil gently for about 5 minutes. Lift out with a slotted spoon and divide among 4 serving bowls. Spoon the butter sauce over and garnish with chives.

Ear-Shaped Pasta with Fresh Morels, Green Peas, and Sweet Onions

Morels, like truffles, are one of the last truly wild ingredients. They are big, fat mushrooms that grow wild in Michigan (and in parts of Europe), but they have never been cultivated successfully. No one knows just why and how they grow, but you can recognize them immediately by their tall caps (different from the flat caps of most mushrooms). The caps are covered with wiggly pleats that give the mushrooms a "brainy" look.

Morels thrive in the rains of springtime, so I like to celebrate the end of winter by serving this toss of morels with tender green peas and sweet onions; it makes a great lunch or light dinner. When those three ingredients appear at your farmers' market, you know it's spring.

Serves 4

3   tablespoons olive oil
1   pound fresh morels, sliced in half if large
    Salt and freshly ground pepper
2   sweet onions, such as Vidalia or Walla Walla,
        peeled, halved, and thinly sliced
1   cup dry white wine
2   cups vegetable stock (page 8)
1   cup fresh or thawed frozen peas
2   tablespoons cold unsalted butter
1   pound ear-shaped pasta, cooked to *al dente*
        (just slightly underdone) and drained
1   cup pasta water reserved
2   tablespoons finely chopped fresh mint
2   tablespoons finely chopped flat-leaf parsley
¼   cup freshly grated Parmesan cheese, plus
        extra for serving

1. Heat the olive oil in a large skillet over high heat. Add the mushrooms, season with salt and pepper, and cook, stirring, until lightly browned. Transfer to a plate. Add the onions to the pan and cook, stirring, until soft. Add the wine and cook until all the liquid evaporates. Add the vegetable stock and cook until reduced by half. Add the peas and cook for 2 minutes. Whisk in the butter and season with salt and pepper.

2. Add the pasta to the pan along with the mushrooms, herbs, and cheese, and stir until combined, adding some of the reserved pasta liquid if needed. Cover and cook over low heat for 2 minutes. Serve with more grated cheese.

Crawfish Lasagna

If you can't grow up in an Italian household, the next best way to fall in love with food is to live next door to one as a kid. Mrs. Giordano, a neighbor, cooked huge suppers for her family every Sunday. I would hang around with her children until they had no choice but to take me home for supper—especially when lasagna was on the menu.

This particular lasagna was inspired by my friend Susan Spicer, chef at Bayona in New Orleans. You can taste Louisiana in the sweet-spicy tomato sauce with a touch of cream, and in the tender, juicy crawfish.

Serves 4–6

For the sauce:
- 2 tablespoons olive oil
- 1 large onion, finely diced
- 2 shallots, finely diced
- 1½ teaspoons cayenne
- One 35-ounce can plum tomatoes, drained and pureed in a blender, juices reserved
- Salt and freshly ground pepper
- 2 cups heavy cream
- ¼ cup chopped flat-leaf parsley
- 2 tablespoons chopped fresh basil

For the filling:
- 16 ounces ricotta cheese
- 1 large egg
- 2 tablespoons finely chopped fresh parsley
- Salt and freshly ground pepper

To assemble:
- 20 dried lasagna noodles
- 2 tablespoons unsalted butter
- 1½ pounds crawfish tails or medium shrimp, cooked and peeled
- 2 tablespoons chopped flat-leaf parsley
- 2 tablespoons chopped fresh basil

1. Make the sauce: Heat the olive oil in a medium saucepan over high heat. Add the onion and shallots and cook, stirring, until soft. Add the cayenne and cook for 1 minute. Add the tomatoes and half of the juices and salt and pepper to taste and cook for 20 minutes, or until slightly thickened. While the sauce is cooking, pour the cream into a small nonreactive saucepan and boil until reduced by half. Add the cream to the sauce and cook for 5 minutes. Remove from the heat and stir in the parsley and basil.

2. Make the ricotta filling: Combine all the ingredients and season with salt and pepper to taste.

3. Bring 5 quarts of water to a boil in a large stockpot, add 2 tablespoons of salt and the noodles, and cook until the noodles are just pliable, 5–6 minutes. Drain well.

4. Preheat the oven to 350°F. Coat the bottom of a 9-by-13-inch baking pan with the butter and ½ cup of the tomato-cream sauce and then place a layer of noodles, touching but not overlapping, on top. Trim any overhanging ends. Cover the noodles with half of the ricotta mixture and ½ cup of the tomato-cream sauce. Place a layer of noodles over the cheese, again touching but not overlapping. Trim any overhanging ends. Cover the noodles with half of the crawfish tails or shrimp, ½ cup of the sauce, and half of the herbs. Make another layer of noodles, ricotta, and sauce. Make another layer of noodles, crawfish, and sauce. End with a layer of noodles, ricotta, and sauce. Top with a final layer of noodles and cover with 2 cups of the sauce.

5. Bake 20–30 minutes, or until the lasagna is bubbling. Let rest for 5 minutes before cutting.

My Favorite Spaghetti and Meatballs

Right here: The perfect dish to eat while watching *The Sopranos.* **Italian restaurants in America have gotten much better and more authentic than when I was a kid, but there are still a few old-time red-sauce dishes that I just love. I learned how to make them because they are real home cooking — it's tough to get great spaghetti and meatballs in a restaurant. When you make the dish at home with good ingredients and cook it right, there's nothing better.**

Serves 4

For the meatballs:

2 tablespoons olive oil
4 cloves garlic, finely chopped
8 ounces ground pork
8 ounces ground veal
8 ounces ground beef
2 large eggs, lightly beaten
¼ cup grated Parmesan cheese
¼ cup dry bread crumbs
¼ cup finely chopped parsley
  Salt and freshly ground pepper
1 cup pure olive oil (not extra-virgin), for frying

For the tomato sauce:

2 tablespoons olive oil
1 large onion, finely chopped
4 cloves garlic, finely chopped
  Two 28-ounce cans whole plum tomatoes
    and their juice, pureed in a blender
1 bay leaf
1 small bunch parsley
  Pinch of red pepper flakes, or more to taste
  Salt and freshly ground pepper
6 basil leaves, shredded

To finish the dish:

1 pound #8 or #9 spaghetti
  Freshly grated Parmesan cheese

1. Make the meatballs: Heat the oil in a small skillet over medium-high heat. Add the garlic and cook, stirring, until softened. Transfer to a medium bowl and add the remaining ingredients (except the frying oil). Mix well and season with salt and pepper. Heat the oil in a large skillet over medium-high heat. Roll the mixture into 1½-inch balls (about the size of a walnut) and fry just until lightly browned all over (the meatballs will finish cooking through in the sauce). Remove with a slotted spoon and drain on a plate lined with paper towels.

2. Make the tomato sauce: Heat the olive oil in a medium saucepan. Add the onions and garlic and cook until soft. Add the pureed tomatoes and juice, bay leaf, parsley, pepper flakes, and salt and pepper and bring to a boil. Reduce the heat, add the meatballs, and let simmer 30–40 minutes, until the sauce has thickened. Remove the bay leaf and parsley. Stir in the basil just before serving.

3. To finish the dish, bring a large pot of salted water to a boil. Add the spaghetti and cook until tender but not mushy. Drain well in a colander, and transfer to a large bowl. Reserving the meatballs, toss the sauce with the pasta. Top with meatballs and Parmesan cheese and serve.

Savannah Red Rice with Roasted Salt-and-Pepper Shrimp

Rice and shrimp make a really fantastic combination, as cooks in Savannah, Georgia, have always known. Rice and shrimp have both been cultivated for centuries in the shallow, salty marshes of the Low Country, the coastal region that stretches from Savannah up to Charleston, South Carolina.

Red rice is a Savannah tradition, reflecting the early Spanish immigrants. The technique of beginning a dish by making a savory *sofrito* (slowly sautéing onions, garlic, tomatoes, and peppers until soft and aromatic) comes straight from Spanish kitchens. This simple, satisfying dish also reminds me of the jambalayas of Louisiana.

Serves 4–6

For the rice:
- 3 tablespoons olive oil
- 1 red bell pepper, finely diced
- 1 poblano pepper, finely diced
- 1 stalk celery, finely diced
- 1 red onion, finely diced
- 2 cloves garlic, finely chopped
- 1½ cups long-grain rice
- 1½ cups canned crushed tomatoes and their juices
- 2 tablespoons tomato paste
- 1 cup water
- 2 teaspoons chipotle puree (page xiii)
- 1 teaspoon honey
- Salt and freshly ground pepper

For the shrimp:
- 24 large shrimp, shells on and deveined
- ¼ cup olive oil
- Kosher salt and coarsely ground black pepper

1. Make the rice: Heat the oil in a large heavy saucepan (with a lid) over medium-high heat. Add the peppers, celery, onion, and garlic, and cook, stirring, until soft, about 5 minutes. Add the rice and stir, coating the rice with the mixture. Stir in the tomatoes, tomato paste, water, chipotle puree, and honey, and season with salt and pepper. Bring to a boil. Immediately cover the pot, reduce the heat to low, and cook until the rice is tender and the liquid is absorbed, 18–20 minutes.

2. Preheat the oven to 450°F and place a baking sheet on the center rack. Toss the shrimp in the oil and season liberally with salt and pepper. Arrange the shrimp in a single layer on the hot baking sheet and roast 4–5 minutes or until just cooked through.

3. To serve, spoon a serving of red rice into a shallow bowl and top with 4–6 shrimp.

Yellow Pepper Risotto with Grilled Shrimp and Black Olive Vinaigrette

This is a most elegant version of shrimp with rice, a favorite combination of mine. I came up with it in Savannah, where the local shrimp are fresh, fat, and sweet. If you're feeling brave, I dare you to eat the shrimp with the heads still on—that's where a lot of the flavor is.

With the rich, creamy risotto and sweet shrimp, I like a sauce with a little bite. A pungent, black olive–infused vinaigrette splashed over the yellow rice and pink shrimp does the trick.

Serves 4

For the risotto:
- 2 yellow peppers, roasted, peeled and seeded (page xiii)
- ¼ cup olive oil
- 5 cups Shrimp Stock (see page xiv)
  Salt and freshly ground pepper
- 2 tablespoons olive oil
- 1 large onion, finely chopped
- 2 cloves garlic, finely chopped
- 2 cups Arborio rice
- 1 cup dry white wine
- ¼ cup chopped fresh flat-leaf parsley, plus extra for garnish

To finish the dish:
- 16 large shrimp, peeled and deveined
- 3 tablespoons olive oil
  Salt and freshly ground pepper
  Black Olive Vinaigrette (see below)

1. Make the risotto: Place the peppers in a blender. Add ½ cup of the shrimp stock, blend until smooth, and season with salt and pepper.

2. Pour the remaining shrimp stock into a saucepan and bring to a simmer over medium-low heat.

3. Heat the olive oil in a large saucepan over medium heat. Add the onion and garlic and cook, stirring, until soft, about 5 minutes. Add the rice and stir to coat with the oil. Increase the heat to high, add the wine, and cook until completely reduced. Reduce the heat to medium and add 1 cup of stock, stirring well. Simmer until almost all the liquid has evaporated, then add another ½ cup of stock. Repeat until the rice is almost cooked through but still very slightly firm in the center (you may not use all the stock). Stir in the yellow pepper puree and cook for 2 minutes more, until the rice is completely tender. Add the parsley and season with salt and pepper to taste.

4. When the rice is almost cooked, make the shrimp: Heat a grill to high or heat a grill pan over high heat. Toss the shrimp in the olive oil and season with salt and pepper to taste. Grill the shrimp on both sides until pink and lightly browned.

5. To serve, spoon the risotto onto a platter. Top with the grilled shrimp, drizzle with Black Olive Vinaigrette, and sprinkle with chopped parsley.

Black Olive Vinaigrette
- ¼ cup red wine vinegar
- ½ cup Niçoise or other brine-cured black olives, pitted and coarsely chopped
- 1 tablespoon Dijon mustard
- 2 cloves garlic, coarsely chopped
- ½ cup olive oil
- 1 tablespoon honey
  Salt and freshly ground pepper

Combine the vinegar, olives, mustard, and garlic in a blender, and puree until smooth. Slowly add the olive oil and blend until emulsified. Season with honey and salt and pepper to taste.

Black-Eyed Pea Risotto with Smoked Bacon and Swiss Chard

I've heard a lot of tall tales about how the traditional New Year's dish of black-eyed peas and rice got the name of Hoppin' John. Black-eyed peas might or might not bring good luck, but they're too good to eat only once a year. This is my version, which makes a great side dish for barbecue and roasts. Round grains of Arborio rice make a great addition to the peas; so do tender shreds of Swiss chard.

Serves 4–6

For the black-eyed peas:

1½ cups black-eyed or pigeon peas, picked over and washed

8 ounces smoked bacon (in one piece), cut in half crosswise

1 onion, peeled and quartered

1 bay leaf

Freshly ground pepper

For the risotto:

6–7 cups Chicken Stock (page xiv), low-sodium canned stock, vegetable stock (page 8), or water

3 tablespoons olive oil

1 large onion, finely diced

2 cloves garlic, finely chopped

Salt and freshly ground pepper

1½ cups Arborio rice

1 cup dry white wine

¾ pound Swiss chard, thinly shredded

2 tablespoons red wine vinegar

Hot sauce (optional)

1. Cook the peas: Place the peas in a large pot with water to cover by 2 inches. Turn the heat to high and bring to a boil; skim off any foam that rises to the top. Add the bacon, onion, bay leaf, and ½ teaspoon of black pepper. Turn the heat to medium-low, partially cover the pot, and let the beans just simmer until very tender, 45–60 minutes, adding more boiling water if the mixture is drying out. Drain the peas if necessary, remove and discard the onion pieces and bay leaf.

2. Cut the simmered bacon into small dice and brown in a small skillet over high heat until golden brown and crispy. Set aside.

3. Make the risotto: Bring the stock or water to a bare simmer in a large saucepan over medium heat.

4. Heat the olive oil in a large saucepan over medium-high heat. Add the onion and cook, stirring, until soft. Add the garlic and cook, stirring, for 1 minute. Season with salt and pepper. Add the rice and stir to coat each grain with the oil. Increase the heat to high, add the wine, and cook until completely reduced. Reduce the heat to medium and add 1 cup of stock, stirring well. Simmer until almost all the liquid has evaporated, then add another ½ cup of stock. Repeat until the rice is completely cooked through in the center (you may not use all the stock). When the rice is almost tender, stir in the black-eyed peas, Swiss chard, and sautéed bacon, and 1 final cup of stock. Cook, stirring, until the chard is completely wilted. Stir in the vinegar and season with hot sauce, salt, and pepper to taste.

Postcard from New York, New York

Where do I start? My hometown is simply the best place to eat. Some people don't think of New York City as really American, but I think it's the most American place there is. The whole city is a bubbling, spicy melting pot that never stops, with new ingredients added to the pot all the time. The only question is, what are you in the mood for?

If it's Greek food, you're in luck: Astoria, Queens, is packed with tavernas, some with a leaning toward spit-roasted meats, others toward expertly grilled fish. At Uncle George's, a popular place with great roast lamb and eggplant, the cook told me his secret: lots of lemon in everything.

If it's Latin American home cooking, you're in luck again: There's a great Colombian restaurant that happens to be run by a Czech-Russian guy and a Greek-American woman. They make killer *batidos,* frothy glasses of milk whipped with fabulous tropical fruits like mango, guava, and papaya (and some I couldn't pick out of a lineup: *lulo, guanabana,* and *mora*). The proper accompaniment to a *batido* is a *bandeja campesina,* the Colombian national dish of rice with avocado, red beans, a slab of bacon, and a fried egg—sometimes with a steak alongside too! And then there are the great dishes you see all around Latin America and the Caribbean: *sancocho,* a stew of chicken with every starch you can think of and some you've never even heard of, including sweet potato, taro, corn, *yuca, malanga,* and *ñame; camarones al ajillo,* shrimp braised in oil and more garlic than you can imagine; and tamales and empanadas. When you order an empanada in New York's Latin restaurants, you might be asked: Mexican, Dominican, or Ecuadoran?

Spin the globe or hop on the subway, and you're in the Middle East, forking up Lebanese tabouli salad flavored with sumac, an ancient spice, at El Manara; savoring the weird but delicious Chinese pork with bitter melon at Golden Monkey; sniffing the vat of sugar syrup at Shaheen Sweets and watching the Indian treats called *jelabi,* pretzel-like cookies flavored with saffron, soak up the sweetness.

The raw materials for all this great stuff come through a single, central, produce market, the Hunts Point Terminal in the Bronx. It's closed to the public and located in a pretty forbidding neighborhood, but once you're in, it's dazzling. Each year 150 million boxes of produce flow in and out of the market and every cook in the city can find what he or she needs here: sugarcane, all kinds of chile peppers, Thai vegetables, lichee nuts from Israel, ginger grown in

Colombia and Hawaii, and tomatoes from every warm spot on the globe. A vendor I talked to told me that when he started, broccoli was considered an exotic Italian vegetable! It reminded me of trying to find fresh cilantro when I was just starting out with Southwestern cooking.

Some of the city's best restaurants, of course, don't even serve vegetables. Manhattan's steakhouses are where I learned to eat, and to this day nothing makes me prouder to be a New Yorker than a rare porterhouse at Peter Luger. It takes nerve to serve a steak the way they do—with a sauce of melted beef fat and butter! And then there are the yellow pepper grits at this little place called Mesa Grill....I can't even begin to talk about all the great chefs in New York, or all the great dishes at the city's fine dining restaurants—there are just too many.

So I'm going to talk about pizza instead. New York City thin-crust pizza is addictive stuff: Once you've grown up on it, you can't eat any other kind. But I do make an exception for the pizza my friend Ciro Verdi makes in his 700-degree pizza oven at Da Ciro. He uses only the finest flour, lets his pizza dough ferment for three days to make it tender and flavorful, then brushes it with extra-virgin olive oil and imported, creamy Italian Robiola cheese. It might be my very favorite dish in New York City—even a little better than a plain slice at the neighborhood pizzeria I love, Mimi's. There's no place like home!

Fish
and
Shellfish

Potato-Parsnip–Crusted Cod with Roasted Tomato Broth and Saffron Aïoli

Slow-Roasted Salmon with a Warm Lemon–Crispy Caper Vinaigrette and Thinly Sliced Potatoes

Pan-Roasted Sea Bass with Yellow Pepper Grits and Roasted Poblano Sauce

Cornmeal-Crusted Catfish with Grilled Red Onion Relish and Green Chile Tartar Sauce

Slow Fire-Roasted Striped Bass with a Fresh Mint and Tomato Relish

Pan-Fried Rainbow Trout with Pecans and Brown Butter

Lobster-Cod Cakes with Red Cabbage Slaw and Fresh Basil Dressing

Whole Cracked Lobster with Sherry Vinegar–Tarragon Butter

Gulf Shrimp with Peanuts, Green Chile Strips, and Dirty Rice

Shrimp and Littleneck Clam Curry on Wild Rice Waffles with Candied Mango Butter

Shellfish and Andouille Gumbo with Blue Corn Muffins

Fulton Fish Market Cioppino

Potato-Parsnip–Crusted Cod with Roasted Tomato Broth and Saffron Aïoli

Cod is a great foil for big flavors like saffron mayonnaise and roasted tomatoes. To give the fish the perfect crisp crust, you'll have to trust me a little bit. I know it's hard, but after you put the fish in the skillet, leave it alone. If you lift it up to make sure it isn't sticking, it will stick. If you leave it alone and let it cook, it will firm up and come away from the pan with a beautiful golden crust.

Serves 4

For the aïoli:

Pinch of saffron

¼ cup white wine vinegar

1 tablespoon honey

1 cup good-quality mayonnaise

Salt and freshly ground pepper

For the tomato broth:

8 plum tomatoes, cored, cut in half vertically, and seeded

4 cloves garlic, coarsely chopped

¼ cup olive oil

1 large onion, coarsely chopped

1 carrot, peeled and coarsely chopped

2 cloves garlic, smashed

8 peppercorns

½ cup dry white wine

1 pound fish bones (from mild white fish, not salmon, mackerel, or other oily fish), coarsely chopped

6 cups water

¼ cup chopped fresh parsley

For the cod:

1 small potato, peeled and finely grated

1 parsnip, peeled and finely grated

Four 6-ounce cod fillets

3 tablespoons olive oil

About 3 cups cooked spinach

Chopped parsley

1. Make the aïoli: Combine the saffron, vinegar, and honey in a small saucepan and bring to a simmer. Remove from the heat and let cool. Place the mayonnaise in a small bowl, add the vinegar mixture, stir well until combined, and season to taste with salt and pepper.

2. Meanwhile, make the tomato broth: Preheat the oven to 350°F. Toss the tomatoes and garlic with the oil and season with salt and pepper. Place on a baking sheet (with sides) and roast until soft, about 30 minutes. Transfer the tomatoes, garlic, and any accumulated juices to a food processor and puree until smooth.

3. Place the onion, carrot, garlic, peppercorns, wine, fish bones, and water in a medium saucepan and bring to a boil. Reduce the heat and simmer for 30 minutes. Strain into a clean saucepan and add the tomato puree. Simmer the broth for 15 minutes, add the parsley, and season with salt and pepper to taste. Set aside.

4. Combine the potato and parsnip in a bowl and season with salt and pepper. Season the fillets on both sides with salt and pepper. Cover the top of each fillet (the side without the skin) with a thin layer of the shredded vegetables, pressing down so it adheres.

5. Heat the oil in a large skillet over medium-high heat until almost smoking. Add the fillets to the pan, potato-side down, and cook *without disturbing* until the crust is golden brown, about 3 minutes. Turn over, reduce the heat slightly, and continue cooking until just cooked through, 3–4 minutes, adjusting the heat to prevent burning.

6. Ladle about ¾ cup of the broth into four shallow bowls, add some spinach, and place a fillet on top. Add the aïoli and garnish with chopped parsley.

Slow-Roasted Salmon with a Warm Lemon–Crispy Caper Vinaigrette and Thinly Sliced Potatoes

When I was in Seattle during Copper River salmon season, I didn't just eat salmon every chance I got. I got so carried away that I picked out twenty of the freshest fish in the Pike Place market and overnighted them to New York, so that my cooks and customers could share the experience! Wild American salmon is just an amazing ingredient, but fortunately, farmed salmon (which is most of what is available) is consistently good too.

I like to contrast rich salmon flesh with tangy ingredients like lemon and capers. Whole capers puff up and flower when you fry them in very hot oil; they become even more delicious, less acidic, and lightly crunchy.

Serves 4

For the vinaigrette:

- 3 cups lemon juice, preferably from Meyer lemons
- ¼ cup sherry vinegar
- 1 tablespoon chopped shallot
- 2 cloves garlic, coarsely chopped
- ¾ cup plus 3 tablespoons olive oil
  Salt and freshly ground pepper
- ¼ cup whole capers, drained and patted dry with paper towels
- 2 tablespoons finely chopped parsley

For the potatoes and salmon:

- 2 Idaho potatoes, peeled and very thinly sliced (⅛-inch thick) with a mandoline or the slicing disk of a food processor
- 3 tablespoons olive oil
  Salt and freshly ground pepper
  Four 6-ounce salmon fillets
  Olive oil
  Chopped flat-leaf parsley, for garnish

1. Make the vinaigrette: Boil the lemon juice in a small nonreactive saucepan until reduced to ¼ cup, then let cool. Combine the cooled lemon juice, sherry vinegar, shallot, and garlic in a blender and puree until smooth. With the motor running, drizzle in ¾ cup of the olive oil and season with salt and pepper. Pour the vinaigrette into a bowl.

2. Heat the remaining 3 tablespoons olive oil in a small saucepan over high heat until almost smoking. Add capers and sauté until "flowered" and lightly golden brown. Fold the capers and parsley into the vinaigrette, discarding the oil in the pan. Set aside (do not refrigerate).

3. Meanwhile, preheat the oven to 350°F. Toss the potatoes with the oil and season generously with salt and pepper. Arrange the potatoes in even layers in the bottom of four small 6-inch-diameter *cazuelas* or shallow baking dishes, or 1 large baking dish. Place in the oven and bake until almost soft, about 35 minutes.

4. Remove the potatoes from the oven and reduce heat to 250°F. Lightly brush the salmon on both sides with olive oil and season with salt and pepper on both sides. Place the salmon on top of the potatoes and return the *cazuelas* to the oven. Bake 12–14 minutes, until cooked through. Remove from oven and immediately drizzle with lemon vinaigrette. Sprinkle with chopped parsley and serve.

Pan-Roasted Sea Bass with Yellow Pepper Grits and Roasted Poblano Sauce

I've always loved the fresh corn flavor of all-American grits, and when I figured out how to add a fresh, sweet puree of yellow peppers to them, a favorite side dish was born. The roasted peppers take grits to a whole new level, but without overwhelming them the way red or green peppers might.

There's a good reason that sea bass has become so popular in recent years: restaurant chefs and home cooks alike appreciate that flaky, luscious texture and light, briny flavor. Sea bass from the Pacific coast of Chile are particularly large and sweet.

Serves 4

For the sauce:

    3   poblano peppers, roasted, peeled, seeded,
        and chopped (page xiii)
    ¼   cup red wine vinegar
    3   tablespoons chopped cilantro
    2   tablespoons honey
        Salt and freshly ground pepper
    ½   cup olive oil

To finish the dish:

    Four 6-ounce sea bass fillets, preferably
        Chilean, skin on
    2   tablespoons olive oil
        Salt and freshly ground pepper
        Yellow Pepper Grits (see below)

1. Make the sauce: Combine the peppers, vinegar, cilantro, and honey in a blender and season with salt and pepper. Blend until smooth. With the motor running, slowly add the olive oil until emulsified. Salt and pepper to taste and set aside.

2. Cook the fish: Brush the fish with olive oil on both sides and season with salt and pepper. Heat a heavy skillet or grill pan over high heat until smoking. Cook, skin-side down, 3–4 minutes or until browned. Turn over and continue cooking 2–3 minutes more for medium-well doneness. Place a heaping mound of Yellow Pepper Grits on four dinner plates. Place a fillet on top of each mound and drizzle with the poblano sauce.

Yellow Pepper Grits

    3   yellow peppers, roasted, peeled, and
        seeded (page xiii)
        Two 16-ounce cans hominy (pozole), drained
    2   tablespoons olive oil
    1   tablespoon unsalted butter
    1   large onion, finely chopped
        Salt and freshly ground pepper
    3   gloves garlic, finely chopped
    1   cup heavy cream

1. Place 2 of the roasted peppers in a food processor and puree until smooth. Cut the remaining pepper into fine dice and set aside.

2. Place the hominy in a food processor and puree until smooth. Heat the oil and butter in a medium saucepan over medium heat. Add the onion, season with salt and pepper, and cook, stirring, until soft. Add the garlic and cook for 2 minutes more. Add the hominy, yellow pepper puree, and heavy cream, and season with salt and pepper. Cook for 10 minutes more, fold in the diced yellow peppers, and serve.

Cornmeal-Crusted Catfish with Grilled Red Onion Relish and Green Chile Tartar Sauce

There's no getting around it: The catfish is one ugly fish. But hey—under the skin, a fillet is a fillet. The catfish produces white, firm, sweet fillets perfect for frying. I love the Southern tradition of frying fish in a crunchy cornmeal crust.

I could eat this green chile tartar sauce with a spoon; that's how good it is. The roasted chiles add a great element of heat and sweetness. Juicy, lightly charred sweet onions complete the dish, which is perfect for a casual summer dinner with plenty of fresh corn.

Serves 4

For the tartar sauce:
- 1 poblano chile, roasted, peeled and coarsely chopped (page xiii)
- ¼ cup rice wine vinegar
- 2 tablespoons olive oil
- 1 tablespoon honey
- Salt and freshly ground pepper
- 1 cup best-quality mayonnaise
- ¼ cup finely chopped red onion
- ¼ cup finely diced dill pickles
- 2 tablespoons chopped capers
- 3 tablespoons finely chopped flat-leaf parsley

For the catfish:
- Vegetable oil or peanut oil
- 4 catfish fillets, 6 ounces each
- Salt and freshly ground pepper
- 1½ cups cornmeal
- Lemon wedges
- Grilled Red Onion Relish (see below)

1. Place the poblano, vinegar, and oil in a blender and puree until smooth. Season with honey and salt and pepper, then fold into the mayonnaise until combined. Add the onion, pickles, capers, and parsley, and taste for salt and pepper. Refrigerate for at least 30 minutes before serving.

2. Heat 2 inches of oil in a large, deep pot to 375°F.

3. While the oil is heating, season the catfish on both sides with salt and pepper. Place the cornmeal in a plastic bag and season with salt and pepper. Place the fillets, two at a time, in the bag and shake until they are evenly coated with the cornmeal. Shake off the excess and fry until golden brown on both sides, about 8 minutes. Remove and drain on a plate lined with paper towels. Serve with tartar sauce, lemon wedges, and Grilled Red Onion Relish.

Grilled Red Onion Relish

- 2 red onions, peeled and sliced ¼-inch thick
- Olive oil
- Salt and freshly ground pepper
- 3 tablespoons balsamic vinegar
- 2 tablespoons chopped cilantro

Heat a grill or grill pan until smoking over high heat. Brush the onions with olive oil and season on both sides with salt and pepper. Grill 3–4 minutes on each side, until just cooked through. Transfer to a cutting board and coarsely chop. Transfer to a medium bowl, stir in the vinegar and cilantro, and taste for salt.

Slow Fire-Roasted Striped Bass with a Fresh Mint and Tomato Relish

The blend of superfresh seafood and Italian-American tradition makes the North Shore of Massachusetts a great place to eat. I was expecting Yankee cooking, but found myself eating fresh bread from Virgilio's Sicilian Bakery while watching Louie Linquata, a seafood buyer, roasting wild striped bass topped with an Italian tomato relish. We were right on the beach, and the smoke from his grill mixed with the tomato, garlic, and mint smells — and the sea air too. Wild striped bass is larger than farmed, making for better fillets.

Serves 4

For the relish:

- 8 ripe plum tomatoes, halved, seeded, and diced
- 1 large shallot, thinly sliced
- 2 tablespoons red wine vinegar
- 4 tablespoons olive oil
- ¼ cup chopped fresh mint leaves
  Salt and freshly ground pepper

For the fish:

- Four 6-ounce wild striped bass fillets
  Olive oil
  Salt and freshly ground pepper

1. At least 1 hour in advance, make the relish: Combine the tomatoes, shallot, vinegar, olive oil, and mint in a bowl and season with salt and pepper. Set aside at room temperature.

2. Preheat a grill to medium. Brush the fish with olive oil on both sides and season with salt and pepper. Place the fish on the grill, flesh-side down (if the fillets still have the skin), and let cook undisturbed just until browned. Turn the fillets over, close the lid of the grill, and continue cooking until cooked through, 12–15 minutes total. For the last 5 minutes of cooking, spoon the relish on top of the fillets. Close the grill again and let the relish warm through.

Pan-Fried Rainbow Trout with Pecans and Brown Butter

Based on my recent fly-fishing experience, I have one piece of cooking advice for my readers: Get the number of a good fish store before you go! The only thing I hooked was my fishing guide (sorry, Greg).

My uncle used to take me fishing for brook trout in the Adirondacks; that's when I developed my respect for the cast-iron skillet, the only cooking implement we brought. We'd gut and flour the trout we caught, and fry them in plenty of butter. In this recipe, I brown the butter until it takes on a nutty flavor. Fresh brook trout actually has its own nutty flavor; that's why it's often paired with nuts in classic preparations like trout *amandine,* with slivered almonds.

Serves 4

For the trout:
- 2 cups rice flour or all-purpose flour
  Salt and freshly ground pepper
- 3 large eggs
- 3 tablespoons milk
- 2 cups cornmeal, preferably white
- 8 whole trout (8 to 10 ounces each), scaled and gutted, preferably wild rainbow trout but farmed is okay
- 6 tablespoons vegetable or peanut oil

For the brown butter:
- 2 sticks (8 ounces) unsalted butter
  Grated zest and freshly squeezed juice of 2 lemons
- ½ cup finely chopped pecans
- ¼ cup finely chopped flat-leaf parsley

1. Place the flour in a medium bowl and season with salt and pepper. Whisk the eggs and milk together in a large bowl and season with salt and pepper. Place the cornmeal in a medium bowl and season with salt and pepper.

2. Preheat the oven to 375°F. Slit each trout open along the bottom and gently open it flat, using the spine as a hinge. Cut each fish diagonally into two pieces. Season both the flesh and skin sides with salt and pepper to taste. One at a time, dip each piece into rice flour, then in the egg mixture, then in the cornmeal. Set aside on a rack. Repeat with remaining trout.

3. Heat 3 tablespoons of the oil in a large skillet until almost smoking. Working in batches to avoid crowding the pan, cook the trout just until golden brown on both sides (it will finish cooking later in the recipe). When half of the pieces have been cooked, add the remaining oil to the pan and heat it to almost smoking before continuing. As the pieces are browned, transfer them to a large baking sheet. When all the pieces are browned, place the baking sheet in the oven and bake 5–6 minutes, until just cooked through.

4. While the trout is baking, make the brown butter: Melt the butter in a nonstick skillet over medium-high heat. Watching carefully and lowering the heat if necessary, let the butter foam up and turn golden brown. When the white milk solids brown and the butter smells nutty, immediately stir in the lemon juice, zest, and salt and pepper to taste. Stir in the pecans and parsley.

5. To serve, place the trout on serving plates and pour the hot brown butter over. Serve immediately.

Lobster-Cod Cakes with
Red Cabbage Slaw and Fresh Basil Dressing

Massachusetts fishing towns like Ipswich and Gloucester are where I go for the best chowders and crisp, fresh fish cakes. Those towns were built by men who fished the huge schools of cod and the lobsters that flourished in the North Atlantic. Local lobster used to be so plentiful that bars gave it away free with a beer! That would be my kind of bar.

Together, lobster and cod make a moist, flaky cake with incredible flavor. Light bread crumbs from Japan, called *panko,* make the best thin crust you've ever tasted. I always like to have a cool fresh vegetable with hot, crisp-fried food, so here's a favorite coleslaw recipe. The sweet lobster is great with the fresh basil dressing.

Serves 4

For the poaching liquid:

- 2 cups cold water
- ½ cup dry white wine
- 1 onion, coarsely chopped
- 1 stalk celery, coarsely chopped
- 4 black peppercorns
- 4 sprigs parsley
- 1 pound fresh skinless cod fillet
  Salt and freshly ground pepper

For the cakes:

- 6 tablespoons olive oil
- 1 red onion, finely diced
- 2 cloves garlic, finely chopped
- 1 jalapeño chile, finely diced
- ½ cup best-quality mayonnaise
- 2 tablespoons Dijon mustard
- 2 tablespoons prepared horseradish, drained
- 1 pound cooked lobster meat or lump crabmeat, shredded
- ½ cup Japanese bread crumbs (*panko*) (see Sources, p. 231)
- ¼ cup finely chopped flat-leaf parsley
  Salt and freshly ground pepper
- 2 cups Wondra or cake flour
  Red Cabbage Slaw (see below)

1. Poach the cod: Bring the water, wine, onion, celery, peppercorns, and parsley sprigs to a boil in a medium saucepan. Reduce the heat to a simmer, season the cod with salt and pepper, and poach until just cooked through, 8–10 minutes. Line a plate with paper towels; transfer the cod to the plate to drain. When cool enough to handle, shred the cod into pieces with a fork.

2. While the cod is poaching, heat 2 tablespoons of the olive oil in a small skillet. Add the onion, garlic, and jalapeño, and cook, stirring, until soft. Season with salt and pepper to taste. Let cool slightly.

3. Mix the mayonnaise, mustard, and horseradish together in a large bowl. Add the lobster, cod, and onion mixture, and stir until combined. Fold in the bread crumbs and parsley and season with salt and pepper to taste. Form the mixture into eight cakes, place on a baking sheet, and refrigerate for 1 hour.

4. Place the flour in a shallow medium bowl and season with salt and pepper. Dredge the cakes in the flour and tap off any excess.

5. Heat the remaining 4 tablespoons oil in a large skillet until almost smoking. Cook the cakes over medium-high heat until golden brown on both sides, 3–4 minutes per side. Serve with Red Cabbage Slaw and Fresh Basil Dressing.

Red Cabbage Slaw with Fresh Basil Dressing

½ cup red wine vinegar

3 tablespoons chopped red onion

2 cloves garlic, finely chopped

2 tablespoons best-quality mayonnaise

1 tablespoon Dijon mustard

¼ cup packed chopped fresh basil leaves

¾ cup olive oil

   Salt and freshly ground pepper

1 small head red cabbage, finely shredded

2 carrots, finely shredded

1. Place vinegar, onion, garlic, mayonnaise, mustard, and basil in a blender and mix until smooth. With the motor running, slowly add the olive oil until emulsified. Season with salt and pepper to taste.

2. Combine the cabbage and carrots in a large bowl. Pour the vinaigrette over and mix to combine. Season with salt and pepper and let sit at least 10 minutes before serving.

Whole Cracked Lobster with Sherry Vinegar–Tarragon Butter

As the summer wears on, I get more and more creative with lobster — my favorite outdoor dinner. Plain boiled lobster with melted butter is pretty heavenly, but melted butter perfumed with tarragon—the classic French herb for shellfish — is even more luxurious. I also add a nip of aged sherry vinegar to the rich sauce; I love its tanginess and aroma. The dish is very simple but elegant — the perfect dinner party entrée at summer's end. Serve it with my Roasted Corn and Poblano Pudding.

Serves 4

2 shallots, peeled and finely diced
1 cup aged sherry vinegar
2 sticks (8 ounces) very cold butter, cut into pieces
2 tablespoons finely chopped fresh tarragon
   Salt and freshly ground pepper
   Four 2-pound live lobsters

1. Combine the shallots and sherry vinegar in a small saucepan and reduce over high heat to 2 tablespoons, until very thick and syrupy. Whisk in the butter, piece by piece. Whisk in the tarragon and season with salt and pepper to taste. Keep warm over low heat by resting the small saucepan inside a larger saucepan half-filled with barely simmering water.

2. Meanwhile, bring a large pot of salted water to a boil over high heat. Boil 2 lobsters at a time until cooked through, approximately 12 minutes.

3. Crack the claws and tail of the lobsters (if you want to) and serve each person a lobster with a small bowl of sauce for dipping.

Gulf Shrimp with Peanuts, Green Chile Strips, and Dirty Rice

Shrimp from the Gulf of Mexico are so fat and sweet that they only need a few minutes of cooking, so I devised this last-minute toss of chiles, garlic, lime, and cilantro around them. It's like a Southern-style stir-fry—easy, satisfying, and totally delicious. Chopped peanuts make an unusual but wonderful crunchy garnish.

Dirty rice sounds like something you might not want to eat, but don't be fooled: what makes it dirty is bold seasonings like garlic, peppers, onions, herbs, and most of all, chicken livers.

Serves 4

2 tablespoons olive oil
24 medium shrimp, preferably Gulf shrimp, peeled and deveined
Salt and freshly ground pepper
1 poblano chile, quartered and thinly sliced
3 cloves garlic, finely chopped
3 cups Shrimp Stock (page xiv) or clam juice
2 tablespoons cold unsalted butter
2 tablespoons freshly squeezed lime juice
2 tablespoons freshly chopped cilantro
Dirty Rice (see below)
¼ cup chopped peanuts

1. Heat the olive oil in a large skillet over high heat. Season the shrimp with salt and pepper and sear on both sides until lightly browned, about 1 minute per side. Transfer the shrimp to a plate.

2. Add the poblano chile to the pan and cook, stirring, until softened. Add the garlic and cook for 1 minute more. Add the shrimp stock, bring to a boil, and reduce by half. Add the shrimp back to the pan, stir in the butter, lime juice, and cilantro, and taste for salt and pepper. Spoon onto a platter of Dirty Rice and sprinkle with the peanuts.

Dirty Rice

2 tablespoons olive oil
1 pound chicken livers
Salt and freshly ground pepper
1 large red onion, finely diced
1 yellow pepper, finely diced
1 red pepper, finely diced
1 stalk celery, finely diced
2 cloves garlic, finely chopped
1 serrano chile, finely diced
2 cups long-grain rice, such as Carolina
4½ cups Chicken Stock (page xiv), or low-sodium canned stock
2 tablespoons maple syrup
¼ cup freshly chopped flat-leaf parsley
1 tablespoon finely chopped fresh thyme

1. Heat the olive oil in a medium saucepan over high heat. Season the chicken livers with salt and pepper and sear on both sides just until browned but still pink inside (do not let them cook through, as they will continue cooking in the rice). Using a slotted spoon, transfer the livers to a cutting board to cool.

2. Add the onion to the pan and cook, stirring, over medium-high heat until golden brown. Add the peppers, celery, garlic, and serrano chile to the pan and cook, stirring, about 5 minutes more. Stir in the rice and cook for 2 minutes. Meanwhile, coarsely chop the chicken livers. Add the stock, maple syrup, and chicken livers to the pan and season with salt and pepper. Stir well and bring to a boil. Immediately cover the pan, reduce the heat to low, and cook 14–18 minutes more, until the rice is cooked through. Remove from the heat, sprinkle in the parsley and thyme, and fluff with a fork.

Shrimp and Littleneck Clam Curry on Wild Rice Waffles with Candied Mango Butter

Waffles aren't just for breakfast at my house. A plate of crisp waffles topped with a savory stew or fried chicken is traditional American comfort food, popular at Sunday suppers. I love this for brunch too — especially the way the curry spices perfume the rich, coconut-infused sauce.

Wild rice cooked until very, very tender is the base of my waffle batter; it has a wonderful nutty flavor (wild rice is actually a wild American grass seed, not rice). Candied mango butter brings sweetness and tanginess to the table; it goes with waffles the way a jam would, and goes with curry the way a chutney would.

Serves 4

For the waffles:
2 tablespoons olive oil
1 onion, finely chopped
2 cloves garlic, finely chopped
1½ cups well-cooked wild rice (boil it until very tender, about 45 minutes to 1 hour)
   Salt and freshly ground pepper
1¼ cups all-purpose flour
2 teaspoons baking powder
¼ teaspoon baking soda
1 cup milk
¼ cup buttermilk
2 large eggs
   Salt and freshly ground pepper

For the curry:
1 tablespoon olive oil
12 large shrimp, peeled and deveined
   Salt and freshly ground pepper
3 tablespoons unsalted butter
1 large onion, coarsely chopped
3 cloves garlic, finely chopped
1 large carrot, peeled and coarsely chopped
1 Granny Smith apple, peeled, cored, and coarsely chopped
2 tablespoons Mesa Curry Mix (see below), or a good-quality curry powder of your choice
1 cup white wine
6 cups Shrimp Stock (page xiv)
½ cup heavy cream

½ cup unsweetened coconut milk
2 tablespoons light brown sugar
16 littleneck clams, scrubbed

To serve:
   Candied Mango Butter (see below)
3 tablespoons chopped cilantro

1. Make the waffle batter: Heat the olive oil in a large skillet, preferably nonstick, over medium-high heat. Add the onion and cook, stirring, until lightly browned. Add the garlic and cook for 1 minute more. Add the wild rice and stir just until the mixture is well combined, season well with salt and pepper to taste.

2. In a large bowl, whisk together the flour, baking powder, and baking soda. In another bowl, beat together the milk, buttermilk, and eggs. Pour the liquid ingredients over the dry ingredients and stir together with the whisk until just combined. Stir in the wild rice mixture.

3. Make the curry: Heat the olive oil in a medium skillet over high heat until almost smoking. Season the shrimp with salt and pepper and cook 1–2 minutes on each side, until almost cooked through.

4. Melt the butter in a medium pot. Add the onion, garlic, carrot, apple, and curry powder, and cook, stirring, until soft, 8–10 minutes. Raise the heat to high, add the wine, and cook until

reduced. Add the stock and cook until reduced by half. Reduce the heat to medium, whisk in the cream, coconut milk, and brown sugar, and cook until slightly thickened. Add the shrimp and the clams and cook until the clams open. Season with salt and pepper to taste.

5. To serve: Preheat a waffle iron (preferably Belgian). Lightly grease the surface, if needed. Spoon out 1 cup of batter onto the hot iron. The batter will be thick, so spread it out with a metal spatula. Close the lid and bake until the waffle is golden and crisp. Remove from the iron and cut into quarters. Repeat with remaining batter.

6. Ladle the sauce into serving bowls. Place 3 shrimp and 4 clams in each bowl. Top with 2 waffle quarters and a dollop of the candied mango butter. Sprinkle with cilantro and serve

Mesa Curry Mix

Makes about ½ cup

3 tablespoons ancho chile powder
1 teaspoon cayenne pepper
2 teaspoons cumin seeds, ground
2 teaspoons coriander seeds, ground
2 teaspoons fennel seeds, ground
1 teaspoon ground cardamom
2 teaspoons turmeric
2 teaspoons ground black pepper
1 teaspoon ground cloves

Combine all the ingredients well and store in an airtight container.

Candied Mango Butter

½ cup packed dark brown sugar
2 tablespoons honey
1 large ripe mango, peeled, pitted, and coarsely chopped
2 sticks (8 ounces) unsalted butter, slightly softened
3 tablespoons finely chopped cilantro

Heat the brown sugar and honey in a small saucepan over medium heat until the sugar has melted and is bubbling. Add the mango and cook over medium-low heat until the mango is soft and caramelized (browned). Place in a food processor and process until smooth. Let cool. Add the butter to the bowl of the food processor and whip the mango puree until smooth. Fold in the cilantro, scrape into a ramekin, and refrigerate until firm, at least 1 hour.

Shellfish and Andouille Gumbo with Blue Corn Muffins

I know all my friends in New Orleans are going to call me up, insisting: "That's no gumbo!" The thing is, I like everything about gumbo except the thing that makes it officially gumbo: the okra. (The word gumbo *comes from an African word for okra:* gombo.*)*

The combination of sweet shellfish and spicy sausage, though—I like everything about that. I thicken the liquid with a carefully cooked roux, flour browned in butter, that forms the base of many Louisiana Creole recipes. The roux picks up the flavors of all the vegetables and helps create a tasty broth to cook the shellfish in.

Serves 6

For the broth:

- 2 tablespoons olive oil
- 2 stalks celery, finely chopped
- 2 carrots, finely diced
- 1 large onion, finely diced
- 3 cloves garlic, finely chopped
- 1 stick (8 tablespoons) unsalted butter
- ½ cup flour
- 2 quarts Shrimp Stock (page xiv), or Chicken Stock (page xiv) or low-sodium canned stock
- ½ pound andouille sausage (or another smoked spicy sausage), cut into ½-inch pieces
- 1 teaspoon fresh or dried thyme leaves
  Salt and freshly ground pepper

To finish the dish:

- 4 tablespoons olive oil
- 12 scallops
- 12 large shrimp, peeled and deveined
- 18 littleneck clams, in the shell, cleaned
- 18 oysters, in the shell, cleaned
  Blue Corn Muffins (see below)

1. Heat the olive oil in a medium skillet and cook the celery, carrots, onion, and garlic, stirring, until soft. Melt the butter over medium heat in a large heavy pot. Gradually add the flour, stirring constantly. Cook the mixture (roux) to a light-caramel color, 5–7 minutes, stirring constantly. Add the onion mixture, stir, and cook for about 3 minutes.

2. Meanwhile, bring the stock to a boil in a saucepan. Whisk it into the roux. Bring to a boil, then reduce the heat to a simmer, add the andouille sausage and thyme, and continue simmering for about 20 minutes. Season with salt and pepper to taste.

3. When almost cooked, finish the seafood: Heat 2 tablespoons of the olive oil in a medium skillet over medium-high heat until almost smoking. Season the scallops on one side with salt and pepper and sear the scallops on one side until golden brown, about 2 minutes. Remove and set aside on a plate.

4. Wipe out the skillet and add the remaining olive oil. Heat over medium-high heat until almost smoking. Season the shrimp with salt and pepper and cook until just pink, 3–4 minutes. Remove and set aside with the scallops.

5. Add the scallops, shrimp, clams, and oysters to the broth and continue cooking until the clams and oysters open. Serve with Blue Corn Muffins.

Blue Corn Muffins

  4 tablespoons unsalted butter
¼ cup finely diced red onion
  2 cloves garlic, finely chopped
½ cup milk
  2 large eggs
  1 tablespoon honey
¼ cup finely diced red bell pepper
  1 jalapeño pepper, finely diced
¼ cup fresh or thawed frozen corn
  1 tablespoon finely chopped cilantro
¾ cup blue or yellow cornmeal
½ cup all-purpose flour
1½ teaspoons baking powder
¼ teaspoon baking soda
¼ teaspoon salt

1. Set a rack in the middle of the oven and preheat to 400°F. Grease 6 cups of a muffin pan with nonstick spray.

2. In a small saucepan, melt the butter. Add the onion and garlic and cook, stirring, until soft. In a large mixing bowl, whisk together the milk, eggs, honey, bell pepper, jalapeño, corn, and cilantro. Whisk in the butter mixture.

3. In a separate bowl, stir together the cornmeal, flour, baking powder, soda, and salt. Mix into the liquid mixture. Divide the batter evenly among the muffin cups and bake for 16 minutes, or until set, turning the pan once for even baking.

Fulton Fish Market Cioppino

My favorite thing about San Francisco's cioppino — an Italian-American seafood stew — is that there's a lot of tradition about it, but no rules. The cook just responds to the market, buying whatever fish is the freshest, plumpest, and sweetest. That's how I like to buy fish when I get up early enough to catch the scene at the Fulton Fish Market, Manhattan's wholesale fish market. It's not for the squeamish, or for tourists: It's a real working market with some of the best product anywhere. Any combination of white-flesh fillets and shellfish can go in the pot.

Use good-quality canned tomatoes from Italy here; they really are better in texture and flavor. Don't worry that the fish will get cold while you're reducing the sauce; letting it "relax" after the cooking will make the fish more tender and flaky. And don't forget to toast plenty of sourdough bread to mop up the sauce.

Serves 8

- 3 tablespoons olive oil
- 2 shallots, thinly sliced
- 4 cloves garlic, finely chopped
- 1½ pounds red snapper, cut into 2-inch squares
- 1½ pounds striped bass, cut into 2-inch squares
- 16 large shrimp
  Salt and freshly ground pepper
- 2 cups dry white wine
- 6 cups Shrimp Stock (page xiv) or bottled clam juice
- 2 cups canned Italian plum tomatoes, pureed
- 1 tablespoon honey
  Hot sauce to taste
- 1 bay leaf
- 3 sprigs fresh thyme
- 32 littleneck clams
- 2 cooked lobsters, claws and tails only, tails cut in half (optional)
- 3 tablespoons cold unsalted butter
- ½ cup coarsely chopped fresh parsley

1. Heat the oil in a large heavy pot with a lid over high heat. Add the shallots and garlic and cook, stirring, until soft. Season the red snapper, striped bass, and shrimp with salt and pepper, add to the pot, and cook, stirring, until lightly browned on each side. Add the wine and cook until reduced by three-quarters. Add the stock, tomatoes, honey, a few dashes of hot sauce, bay leaf, and thyme, and bring to a simmer. Add the clams and lobster, cover the pot, and continue cooking until the clams have opened, discarding any that have not opened.

2. Remove the seafood with a slotted spoon and transfer to a large bowl. Bring the cooking liquid to a boil and cook until reduced by half. Whisk in the butter and parsley and season with salt, pepper, and hot sauce to taste. Pour the broth over the seafood and serve.

Postcard from Chesapeake Bay, Maryland

If you could hear crabs laughing, the noise would have been deafening the day I went crabbing on Chesapeake Bay. Wade Murphy, a waterman (that's the local word for fisherman), took me out on his boat one fine spring morning. We were in search of *jimmies* (another local word, this time for adult male crabs). Crab is practically a religion in eastern Maryland, and like a lot of Marylanders (and chefs), I can never get enough fresh crabmeat. So I was on the bay to see where it all begins.

Murphy uses the trotline method for crabbing. You bait a long line at intervals with chicken necks (or cow lips, when you can get them). You slowly pay out the line, which floats on the surface, then sail back to the beginning and start picking up the crabs that have risen to the bait, so to speak. But it's not as easy as it sounds. Leaning out of a moving boat and trying to scoop a 5-inch-wide wiggling crustacean into a net...you've got to be quick and steady. I tried yelling down to the crabs: "Come on up, guys—I've got a great sauce for you!" But they didn't go for it.

When the watermen haul in their lines and head in, the crabs are either sold immediately or dumped into saltwater pens on the edge of the bay. The Higgins family crab company, for example, keeps thousands of crabs—and checks on each one of them every four hours! At least, they do that between April and June, when the crabs shed their hard shells about twenty times—and become, for a few hours at least, soft-shelled crabs. The reason this happens is that the young crab is still growing and needs to get rid of that inflexible shell. If the soft crab isn't removed from the cold water within a few hours, it hardens up again.

A lot of the hard-shell crabs, whether jimmies or *sooks,* females, end up in local crab feasts, fun gatherings for any occasion or no occasion. That's the meal you think of when you think crab house: a newspaper-covered table, a little vinegar, a lot of beer, and a huge pile of boiled crabs speckled with Old Bay seasoning. The hostess of a backyard crab feast I went to told me that the way to catch a Maryland girl is to sprinkle a little Old Bay on your doorstep, and I have to think she's right; all the cooks I met there were addicted to the stuff. It's in the crab cakes, the crab cocktail, the crab imperial, the crab dip, and it is really perfect with rich crabmeat. I don't think any Maryland girl would have me, though...I can't pick crabs nearly fast enough. I gave up after watching a pair of sisters, the local champions, pick a dozen crabs in about a minute. Maybe that's why I love soft-shell crabs so much—you get that great crab flavor, but you just eat the whole thing.

When the locals take a break from eating sweet, blue crabs, they turn to their succulent oysters, like Kent Island, St. George, and Chesapeake Bay, all harvested in the bay. I was lucky enough to go out oystering under sail on a beautiful *skipjack,* or sailboat, built in 1955 and still going strong. There are only about two dozen skipjacks still working the bay. Captained by Ed Farley, we were heading out to dredge oysters, which can't be done in a motorboat. He told me the reason for the plentiful oysters here: The bay is where rivers and the ocean meet, creating warmer, sweeter waters full of vegetation that oysters thrive on.

Dredging for oysters involves lowering a big scoop from the boat and dragging it slowly along the oyster bed. It is a very efficient way for gathering oysters—almost too efficient. Chesapeake oysters have been overharvested, and since it takes each oyster three years to reach a salable size, the oyster population has trouble keeping up with demand. The traditional method of harvesting oysters, tonging, was better for the oysters but worse for the watermen! It is still done, but it's back-breaking work; you use a pair of long tongs to scoop up a few oysters at a time from the ocean floor.

The Maryland state fish (I love states that have a state fish) is striped bass. I like it cooked in the simplest possible way: fried in butter, dredged in a mixture of flour and Old Bay seasoning. That mixture of cayenne, paprika, cloves, ginger, and celery salt, plus some other spices they don't want us to know about, is surely the Maryland state seasoning. I wonder if it really is an aphrodisiac!

Poultry

Blue Corn Fried Chicken with Red Chile Honey

Smoked Chicken and Caramelized Vegetable Pot Pie with a Sweet
  Potato Biscuit Crust

Cumin-Crusted Chicken with Mango-Garlic Sauce and Cilantro Pesto
  Mashed Potatoes

Curry-Fried Chicken with Mango-Yogurt Sauce

Spit-Roasted Chicken with Grilled Lemon and Clementine Sauce

Pan-Roasted Duck Breast with Clementine-Tomatillo Sauce and Wild
  Rice Risotto

Seared Muscovy Duck Breast with Black Pepper–Sweet Mustard Glaze

Sixteen Spice–Rubbed Squab with Aged Goat Cheese, White Chicory,
  and Wild Mushrooms

Blue Corn Fried Chicken with Red Chile Honey

Red chile and blue corn—two of my top ingredients from the Southwestern kitchen— make an excellent addition to Southern fried chicken. Blue cornmeal has the same crispness as yellow, but it's even nuttier and sweeter in flavor.

Dipping fried chicken in honey is Southern tradition. I stir the honey with ancho chile powder to infuse heat and red color into the honey. Serve this with Buttermilk Bacon Smashed Potatoes for a Southern-style feast.

Serves 4

For the chicken:
Peanut oil for frying
1 whole chicken (3–4 pounds), cut up into
    8 pieces
3 cups buttermilk
2 cups all-purpose flour
Salt and freshly ground pepper
4 eggs
2 tablespoons cold water
3 cups blue cornmeal

For the sauce:
1 cup honey
2 tablespoons ancho chile powder

1. Start the chicken: At least 4 hours before you plan to cook it, put the chicken in a large baking dish. Pour in the buttermilk and turn to coat. Cover and place in refrigerator for at least 4 hours and up to 8 hours.

2. Make the sauce: Stir the honey and chile powder together and set aside.

3. Cook the chicken: Heat 1 inch of the oil in a cast-iron skillet to 350°F. Meanwhile, spread the flour out on a plate and season with salt and pepper. Whisk the eggs in a shallow bowl with the cold water. Spread the cornmeal out on a plate and season with salt and pepper.

4. Remove the chicken from the buttermilk, pat dry, and season with salt and pepper. Working in batches to avoid crowding the frying pan, dip each piece of chicken in the flour and shake off any excess. Dip in the egg, then in the cornmeal. Add the chicken pieces to the hot pan, skin-side down. Cover the skillet, reduce the heat to medium-high, and cook for 7 minutes. Remove the cover, turn the chicken over, and cook 6–7 minutes more, until done through and crisp on the outside. Drain on paper towels and repeat process with remaining chicken pieces. Transfer to a platter, drizzle with ancho honey, and serve.

Smoked Chicken and Caramelized Vegetable Pot Pie with a Sweet Potato Biscuit Crust

This savory, comforting dinner is the easiest way I know to make people happy. There's something about pot pies—the creamy filling, the flaky biscuit crust, or the combination—that no one can resist. Smoked chicken adds flavor, but plain chicken breasts will work just as well. This recipe is also a great way to use up cooked chicken, and it shows off my favorite biscuit recipe: The light dough is flavored with sweet potato.

The sauce is enriched with cream, then warmed with chipotle for a perfect flavor balance. Cook the filling and the biscuits separately, then warm them together so you'll have a hot filling and crisp crust.

Serves 4

For the filling:

12 pearl onions, skins removed
2 carrots, peeled and diced
2 parsnips, peeled and diced
16 cremini mushrooms, cleaned and quartered
5 tablespoons olive oil
Salt and freshly ground pepper
4 boneless chicken breast halves, cold smoked (optional; see method, page 148), raw chicken breasts, or 4 cups diced cooked chicken

For the sauce:

2 quarts Chicken Stock (page xiv), or low-sodium canned stock
3 cups heavy cream
1 teaspoon chipotle puree (page xiii)
1 tablespoon honey
1 cup fresh or frozen peas
¼ cup chopped parsley
Salt and freshly ground pepper

To assemble:

Sweet Potato Biscuits (page 166)

1. Make the filling: Preheat the oven to 375°F. In a roasting pan, toss the vegetables in 4 tablespoons of the olive oil and season with salt and pepper. Roast until browned and caramelized, stirring occasionally, 25–30 minutes. Set aside.

2. If using cold smoked or raw chicken, cook the chicken: Heat the remaining 1 tablespoon olive oil in a medium skillet until almost smoking. Season the chicken with salt and pepper on both sides. Cook the breasts on one side until golden brown, about 3 minutes. Turn over, lower the heat, and continue cooking until almost cooked through, about 5 minutes more. Remove the chicken to a cutting board and let sit 5 minutes before cutting into 1-inch cubes.

3. Meanwhile, make the sauce: Pour the chicken stock into a large saucepan, bring to a boil over high heat, and boil until reduced to 3 cups. Pour the cream into a nonreactive saucepan, bring to a simmer over medium-high heat, and simmer until reduced to 1 cup. Add the reduced cream, chipotle puree, and honey to the reduced chicken stock and cook for 2 minutes over medium-low heat. Add the caramelized vegetables, chicken, peas, and parsley, and cook for 2 minutes more. Season with salt and pepper to taste.

4. Assemble the dish: Preheat the oven to 350°F. Place the chicken mixture in a casserole dish and top with the biscuits. Warm through in the oven, about 20 minutes.

Cumin-Crusted Chicken with Mango-Garlic Sauce and Cilantro Pesto Mashed Potatoes

Sweet mango, pungent garlic, and earthy cumin—three of my favorite flavors shine in this easy dish. Cumin, *pepitas* (pumpkin seeds), and *cotija* cheese are common ingredients in Southwestern kitchens. *Cotija* is a sharp, aged grating cheese that firms up when you cook it; it helps the cumin create a fabulous crisp crust for the chicken.

Instead of basil and pine nuts, the ingredients in a classic Italian pesto, I use scallions, cilantro, and *pepitas* to make an aromatic herb paste that swirls through the hot potatoes.

Serves 4

For the sauce:

8 cups Chicken Stock (page xiv)
8 whole black peppercorns
Cloves from 1 head roasted garlic (page xiii), pureed
3 cups red wine vinegar
1 cup white wine vinegar
1½ cups sugar
3 mangoes, peeled, pitted, and pureed
Salt and freshly ground pepper

For the chicken:

5 tablespoons cumin seeds, toasted (page xiii)
1 cup fresh lemon juice
½ cup olive oil
2 tablespoons honey
4 boneless chicken breasts (8 ounces each), skin on
3 tablespoons olive oil
⅓ cup grated *cotija,* Parmesan, or Romano cheese
Salt
Cilantro Pesto Mashed Potatoes (see below)

1. Make the sauce: Combine the chicken stock, peppercorns, and garlic in a medium saucepan and simmer until reduced to 3 cups. Strain into a bowl. Combine the vinegars in a separate medium saucepan and cook until reduced by half. Add the sugar and mango puree to the vinegars and cook until thickened and saucelike. Add the reduced chicken stock and simmer until thickened, about 10 minutes, stirring occasionally. Season to taste with salt and pepper.

2. Make the chicken: Whisk together 2 tablespoons of the cumin seeds, lemon juice, oil, and honey in a medium baking dish. Add the chicken and turn to coat. Cover and refrigerate for 1 hour.

3. Preheat the oven to 400°F. Grind the remaining 3 tablespoons cumin seeds. Combine the ground cumin, *cotija,* and salt and pepper in a shallow bowl.

4. Heat a large ovenproof skillet over medium-high heat. Remove the chicken from the marinade and shake off any excess. Dredge the chicken on the skin side with the spice mixture and place the chicken, skin-side down, in the hot pan. Repeat with remaining chicken and cook on one side until golden brown, 3–4 minutes. Turn the chicken pieces over and transfer the skillet to the oven. Bake 8–10 minutes or until just cooked through. Serve with the mango sauce and Cilantro Pesto Mashed Potatoes.

Cilantro Pesto Mashed Potatoes

2 tablespoons pumpkin seeds
2 cloves garlic
6 spinach leaves
¼ cup chopped cilantro
4 scallions, coarsely chopped
3 tablespoons fresh lime juice
¼ cup olive oil
3 tablespoons grated Parmesan cheese
2 tablespoons honey
  Salt and freshly ground pepper
4 pounds Idaho potatoes, peeled and cut into
    large cubes
1 cup heavy cream
4 tablespoons unsalted butter

1. Combine the pumpkin seeds, garlic, spinach, and cilantro in food processor and puree until smooth. Add the scallions and lime juice and process until smooth. With the motor running, slowly add the oil. Add the Parmesan, honey, and salt and pepper, and pulse several times until combined. Taste for salt and pepper and set aside.

2. Place the potatoes in a large pot of salted water and bring to a boil. Cook until soft, 15–20 minutes. Heat the cream in a saucepan just until bubbles appear around the edges, then turn off the heat and set aside. Drain the potatoes well and run through a food mill into a large bowl or mash in the bowl with a masher until smooth. Stir in the butter and cream and mix until combined. Swirl in the pesto and season to taste with salt and pepper.

Curry-Fried Chicken with Mango-Yogurt Sauce

I know curry powder isn't authentically Indian—but it's been authentically American for hundreds of years. English immigrants long ago brought curry powder to this country and made it part of American cooking, especially in Southern kitchens. (Crab curry is a Charleston classic.)

Curry powder includes some of my favorite spices—toasted cumin, coriander, chile powder, and dry mustard—so I use it to season my coating for Southern fried chicken, for the spice, scent, and color it adds. A cooling, sweet sauce of yogurt and mango tastes great with the hot, spicy chicken, and plays on the Indian theme.

Serves 4

For the sauce:

2 tablespoons olive oil
1 small onion, finely diced
2 cloves garlic, finely chopped
1 large ripe mango, peeled, pitted, and coarsely chopped
2 cups plain yogurt
2 tablespoons fresh lime juice
   Salt and freshly ground pepper
   Honey

For the chicken:

   Vegetable oil, canola oil, or peanut oil for frying
1 whole chicken (3–4 pounds), cut into 8 pieces
   Salt and freshly ground white pepper
2 cups all-purpose flour
1 teaspoon cayenne
2 tablespoons best-quality curry powder
3 large eggs
1 tablespoon cold water

1. Make the sauce: Heat the oil in a small skillet over medium-high heat. Add the onion and cook, stirring, until soft. Add the garlic and mango and cook 1 minute longer. Remove from the heat and let cool to room temperature. Transfer to a food processor, add the yogurt and lime juice, and puree until smooth. Season to taste with salt and pepper. Taste for sweetness and add honey as needed. Refrigerate until ready to serve.

2. Make the chicken: Over high heat, heat 1 inch of oil in a large, deep cast-iron skillet fitted with a deep-frying thermometer to 350°F. Season the chicken all over with salt and pepper. Mix together the flour, 1 tablespoon salt, 2 teaspoons pepper, the cayenne, and the curry powder, and separate into two bowls. Lightly beat together the eggs and the water in another bowl.

3. Dip each piece of chicken in the first bowl of dry ingredients, tap off the excess, and then dip it in the egg mixture. Then dip the chicken into the second bowl of dry ingredients, again tap off the excess, and set aside on a rack until ready to fry.

4. Add the chicken pieces to the hot pan skin-side down, working in 2 batches if necessary to avoid crowding the pan.

5. Cover the skillet, reduce the heat to medium-high (the oil should be bubbling around the chicken), and cook for 7 minutes. Remove the cover, turn the chicken over, and cook, uncovered, 6–7 minutes more, or until golden brown and cooked through. Drain on paper towels and transfer to a platter. Serve with yogurt sauce for dipping.

Spit-Roasted Chicken with Grilled Lemon and Clementine Sauce

Ask any American chef: "What's the most popular dish on your menu?" I'll bet you good money that "roast chicken" is the answer. It's become a modern American classic. Whether you're cooking in New York's fanciest restaurant or hosting a backyard barbecue, cooks agree that the best way to produce juicy meat and a crisp, tender brown crust is to turn it constantly on a spit.

If you don't have a rotisserie for your grill, just have the butcher butterfly the chickens and cut them in half (this will flatten them so that they cook evenly). Grill them over medium-high heat, turning and basting often. Clementines are sweet and not very acidic, but navel oranges can also be used in the recipe.

Serves 4

For the chicken:

3 cups fresh clementine or orange juice
1 cup fresh lemon juice
¼ cup olive oil
6 cloves garlic, coarsely chopped
2 teaspoons coarsely ground black pepper
8 whole cloves
8 sprigs fresh thyme
2 whole small chickens, about 2½ pounds each, rinsed well and patted dry
Salt

For the sauce:

2 clementines or oranges, halved or quartered if large
2 lemons, halved or quartered if large
3 tablespoons olive oil
2 teaspoons fresh thyme leaves
Salt and freshly ground black pepper

1. At least 4 hours before you plan to cook the chicken, whisk together the clementine or orange juice, lemon juice, olive oil, garlic, black pepper, cloves, and thyme in a medium bowl. Place the chickens in a large bowl and pour half of the juice mixture over them. Reserve the remaining marinade. Turn the chickens to coat well. Cover and refrigerate at least 4 hours and up to 8 hours, turning occasionally.

2. Preheat the grill to high and place a drip pan in the center of the grill. Remove the chickens from the marinade (discarding the marinade) and season the chickens with salt. Place on a rotisserie and roast according to the manufacturer's instructions. Every 15 minutes, baste the rotating chickens with the reserved marinade. Continue roasting until the chickens are well browned and reach an internal temperature of 165°F, about 1 hour.

3. During the last 5 minutes of roasting, brush the oranges and lemons with olive oil and sear the cut sides on the grill until browned.

4. When the chickens are done, let rest for 5 minutes before cutting into halves. Make the sauce by squeezing the juice from the grilled fruit into a bowl. Whisk in olive oil to taste, and season with thyme and salt and pepper. If you like, garnish the chicken with the grilled fruit pieces. Drizzle with sauce.

Pan-Roasted Duck Breast with Clementine-Tomatillo Sauce and Wild Rice Risotto

There's just no better flavor pairing for rich, meaty duck than the sweet bite of orange. *Canard à l'orange,* **one of the first French dishes many of us Americans ever tasted, is the classic example. Clementines and tomatillos both have the sweet-sour flavors of orange, and they form the flavor base for this incredible (and definitely un-French) sauce sparked with sharp horseradish and ancho chile.**

Wild rice, a completely American ingredient, and wild ducks are found together in our Great Lakes region, where the wild rice is harvested; they seem to have a natural flavor affinity.

Serves 4

For the sauce:

6 cups Chicken Stock (page xiv), or
   low-sodium canned stock
2½ cups granulated sugar
2 cups rice wine vinegar
3 cups tangerine juice
3 cups orange juice
4 whole black peppercorns
2 tablespoons ancho chile powder
2 tablespoons freshly grated horseradish
½ cup water
2 clementines, quartered and sliced
   ¼ inch thick
2 tomatillos, quartered and sliced
   ¼ inch thick
   Salt and freshly ground pepper

To finish the dish:

1 whole Muscovy duck breast, approximately
   2 pounds (available at gourmet butchers or
   see Sources, page 231), or 2 pounds other
   duck breasts
   Salt and freshly ground pepper
   Wild Rice Risotto (see below)

1. Make the sauce: Pour the chicken stock into a saucepan and boil until reduced by two-thirds, to 2 cups liquid.

2. Meanwhile, combine 2 cups of the sugar and the rice wine vinegar in a saucepan over medium-high heat and cook until the sugar has melted and the mixture becomes syrupy, about 10 minutes. Raise the heat to high and add the orange and tangerine juice and the black peppercorns and cook until reduced to 2 cups. Add the reduced chicken stock. Whisk the ancho powder and horseradish into the sauce until smooth.

3. Meanwhile, pour the remaining ½ cup of sugar and the water into a small saucepan and cook over high heat until the sugar has melted and the mixture is slightly thickened. Add the clementines and cook 1–2 minutes. Add the tomatillos and toss to coat. Add to the sauce, cook 2–3 minutes, and season with salt and pepper to taste. Keep warm.

4. Make the duck: Preheat the oven to 400°F. Heat a medium ovenproof skillet over high heat until almost smoking. Use the tip of a sharp knife to score (cut a grid pattern on) the skin of the duck. Season the duck on both sides with salt and pepper. Place the breast skin-side down in the pan and cook until the skin is golden brown. Drain off the rendered fat. Turn the breast over, place the pan in the oven, and continue cooking to medium doneness, 12–15 minutes. Let rest 10 minutes.

5. To serve, thinly slice the breast against the grain of the meat and spoon the sauce over. Serve with Wild Rice Risotto.

Wild Rice Risotto

    2 tablespoons unsalted butter, slightly softened
    1 teaspoon fresh thyme leaves
6–8 cups Chicken Stock (page xiv), or
         low-sodium canned stock
    2 tablespoons olive oil
    1 red onion, finely chopped
    2 cloves garlic, finely chopped
    2 cups Arborio rice
    1 cup dry white wine
    1 cup wild rice, simmered in water until
         very soft
    ½ cup freshly grated Parmesan cheese
         Salt and freshly ground pepper

1. Mash the butter and thyme leaves together and set aside to infuse the flavor in the butter.

2. Heat the stock to a simmer in a saucepan.

3. Heat the olive oil in a medium saucepan over medium heat. Add the onion and garlic and cook, stirring, until softened. Add the rice and cook, stirring, 1–2 minutes. Add the wine and cook until all the liquid is absorbed. Add 1 cup of hot stock and cook, stirring, until all the liquid is absorbed. Continue cooking, adding stock ½ cup at a time, until the rice is cooked through but not mushy. During the last 2 minutes of cooking, add the cooked wild rice.

4. Stir in the thyme butter and Parmesan cheese and season with salt and pepper to taste.

Seared Muscovy Duck Breast with Black Pepper–Sweet Mustard Glaze

People who like my food are people who aren't afraid of big, intense flavor. For me, the quest for those flavors started at a young age—with mustard, which I slathered onto everything I ate. We tend to take mustard for granted, but it's a bold sauce with a great combination of tartness from vinegar and heat from mustard seeds. This easy recipe really shows the stuff off, with pepper and honey added for even deeper flavor notes.

Mixing smooth and whole-grain mustards together gives you two interesting versions of the same flavor in one dish, plus great texture.

Serves 4

For the glaze:
- ¼ cup Dijon mustard
- 2 tablespoons whole grain mustard
- 2 tablespoons honey
- 2 teaspoons coarsely cracked black pepper
- 2 teaspoons finely chopped fresh thyme
- Salt

For the duck:
- 1 whole Muscovy duck breast, approximately 2 pounds (available at gourmet butchers or see Sources, page 231), or 2 pounds other duck breasts

1. Make the glaze: Combine the mustards, honey, black pepper, and thyme in a medium bowl and season with salt.

2. Make the duck: Preheat the oven to 400°F. Heat a medium ovenproof skillet over high heat until almost smoking. Use the tip of a sharp knife to score (cut a grid pattern on) the skin of the breasts. Season the breasts on both sides with salt and pepper. Place the breast skin-side down in the pan and cook until the skin is golden brown. Drain off the rendered fat. Turn the breast over, place the pan in the oven, and continue cooking to medium doneness, 12–15 minutes.

3. As soon as the duck comes out of the oven, brush it liberally with the mustard glaze. Let rest for 10 minutes, then thinly slice against the grain of the meat and serve immediately.

Sixteen Spice–Rubbed Squab with Aged Goat Cheese, White Chicory, and Wild Mushrooms

Sixteen spices might sound like more than any one dish can handle, but in these proportions they meld into one big, wonderful flavor. To be honest, I'm addicted to this rub, with its earthy, sweet, and spicy tastes, and it took me a long time to perfect it. Chicken thighs would also be good in this aromatic main-course salad, full of crunch and spice. The optional white truffle oil brings out the flavors of the fresh mushrooms.

Serves 4

For the vinaigrette:

3 tablespoons plus ½ cup olive oil

½ pound wild mushrooms (such as oyster, cremini, shiitake), coarsely chopped

Salt and freshly ground pepper

¼ cup white wine vinegar

1 small shallot, finely chopped

2 teaspoons Dijon mustard

1 teaspoon white truffle oil (optional)

To finish the dish:

3 tablespoons olive oil

Salt

4 boneless squab breasts (4–5 ounces), skin on

½ cup Sixteen Spice Rub (see below)

12 ounces white chicory (frisée) or another crisp, peppery green

8 ounces aged goat cheese, crumbled

Finely chopped chives, for garnish

1. Make the vinaigrette: Heat the 3 tablespoons olive oil in a large skillet over high heat. Add the mushrooms, season with salt and pepper, and cook, tossing often, until golden brown.

2. Whisk together the vinegar, shallot, and mustard in a medium bowl. Slowly whisk in the ½ cup olive oil and whisk until emulsified. Whisk in the truffle oil and season with salt and pepper to taste. Fold in the mushrooms and set aside.

3. Cook the squab: Heat the oil in a large skillet over high heat. Season the breasts with salt on both sides. Dredge the skin side of the breasts in the rub and tap off any excess. Place the breasts,

rub-side down, in the hot pan and cook until golden brown, 2–3 minutes. Turn over and cook 2–3 minutes more for medium doneness.

4. Finish the dish: Divide the greens among four plates. Slice the squab on the bias into four slices and arrange on top of the greens. Sprinkle with the goat cheese. Ladle the vinaigrette lightly over the greens and squab and around the plate. Garnish with chives.

Sixteen Spice Rub

3 tablespoons ancho chile powder

1 tablespoon ground fennel seeds

1 tablespoon ground coriander seeds

1 tablespoon light brown sugar

1 tablespoon pasilla chile powder or another pure chile powder

2 teaspoons cinnamon

2 teaspoons chile de arbol powder or another pure chile powder

2 teaspoons chipotle chile powder

2 teaspoons black pepper

2 teaspoons ground ginger

2 teaspoons garlic powder

2 teaspoons onion powder

2 teaspoons allspice

2 teaspoons cumin

1 teaspoon salt

1 teaspoon cloves

Combine all ingredients in a bowl. The rub will keep, stored in an airtight container, for 6 months.

Postcard from Savannah, Georgia

The minute I tasted Martha Nesbit's shrimp and grits, I knew I was going to feel right at home in her town, Savannah, Georgia. Savannah is the southern starting point for a region called the Low Country, the marshy coast that runs up the Atlantic all the way through South Carolina. This part of the South has some great dishes that you just don't see anywhere else, including lots of great local seafood. The unique flavors and ingredients of the Low Country date way back to the eighteenth century, when huge rice plantations covered the Atlantic marshes, and the local population was mostly African, French, and Spanish.

Red rice is to Savannah what pastrami is to New York—you just haven't really been there until you've tasted it. Joe Randall, a great cook, taught me how to transform homegrown "Carolina gold" to red by cooking the rice in a savory brew of tomatoes, onions, peppers, and garlic. I liked it plain, and I loved it after we grilled some local shrimp he'd been marinating in lemon and pepper and put them on top. Simple and delicious: Shrimp and rice is just one of those perfect combinations.

Martha Nesbit is the food editor of the *Savannah Tribune,* but she's also a great home cook. Some people get shy about cooking for chefs, but Martha knows just how good her Low Country specialties are. In a single afternoon, she made fried local flounder, benne wafers, and a big bowl of shrimp and grits that I literally could not stop eating. The combination of creamy cheese grits (she uses handfuls of cheddar cheese and chunks of butter for texture and flavor), and shrimp browned in garlic and a little bacon fat creates just the kind of explosive flavors I love. And some things in life are worth falling off the low-fat wagon for.

Until I went to Savannah, I had never thought of sesame seeds as a particularly American ingredient. But as soon as I got there, suddenly I was seeing these round, thin, toasty-looking cookies everywhere I went. It turns out that sesame seeds aren't only for Asian cooking. Ever since African slaves brought them to this country in the seventeenth century, many dishes in the Southern repertoire have included them. The most popular ones are crisp benne wafers, which can be sweet or savory—both kinds have that strong nutty flavor, but balanced out with butter and either salt or sugar. I have to admit, I found them pretty addictive.

I had a great time at a Low Country oyster roast they threw for me at Fort Jackson, down by the old port. Apparently the first one on record dates from 1566, when Native Americans showed the Spanish explorers how it's done. The method is still pretty simple: Make a big fire, put a griddle on top (the one at Fort Jackson is as big as a barn door), and pile up plenty of local Apalachicola oysters. The experts showed me how to drape wet burlap sacks over the oysters to seal in the heat and keep the oysters from burning. Then you shovel out the hot, juicy oysters onto a table, grab a knife, and start eating. It reminded me a lot of the lobster dinners I like to throw at the beach in the summer: easy, fun, messy, and delicious.

My favorite thing I brought home from Savannah wasn't a recipe for red rice or a tin of benne wafers; it was more of an idea. When I asked Martha Nesbit exactly when she would eat shrimp and grits—breakfast, lunch, or dinner—she looked a little puzzled. "Why, for Sunday supper, of course," she answered. And she told me how she likes to cook on long Sunday afternoons as her family gathers outside in the yard. It reminded me that making great food isn't the only reason for cooking; sometimes just calling friends and family to the table for a meal you've made is the main point. If you can make a weekly tradition out of it, all the better. Sunday supper is an American institution worth keeping up, whatever's on the menu at your house.

Meat

Spice-Rubbed Ribeyes with Pinto Bean Relish

Steak Frites with Red Spice Rub and Blue Cheese Sauce

Nanny Flay's Sauerbraten

Prime Rib with Roasted Corn–Poblano Pudding

Roasted Pork Tenderloin with Sun-Dried Cranberry Stuffing

Molasses-Glazed Pork Roast with Black Pepper Dumplings

Spicy Mango-Glazed Ham with Sweet Potato–Vidalia Onion Salad

Baby Back Pork Ribs with Mustard-Molasses Barbecue Sauce

Smoked Lamb and Goat Cheese Enchiladas with Almond Molé Sauce

Roast Leg of Lamb with Honey, Balsamic Vinegar, and Fresh Mint Baste

Pan-Roasted Lamb Chops with Red Wine–Black Currant Sauce

Caraway-Fennel–Crusted Loin of Lamb with Mustard Sauce and Melted
   Napa Cabbage

Venison–Black Bean Chili with Green Chile *Crema* and White Cornbread

Pan-Roasted Venison with Spicy Cranberry–Mexican Cinnamon Sauce and
   Whipped Sweet Potatoes

Spice-Rubbed Ribeyes with Pinto Bean Relish

A thick, juicy beef rib steak with a savory mess of pinto beans on the side—this robust dish has an Old West spirit. This is a simple and very popular entrée. Ribeye steaks sport a big bone and plenty of marbling in the meat, both of which make for big taste.

Serves 4

For the spice rub:
¼ cup ancho chile powder
1 tablespoon paprika
2 teaspoons freshly ground black pepper
2 teaspoons dry mustard
2 teaspoons ground coriander
2 teaspoons dried oregano
1 teaspoon ground cumin
1 teaspoon arbol chile powder or another pure chile powder
1 teaspoon salt

To finish the dish:
3 tablespoons canola oil
4 ribeye steaks with bone (10–12 ounces each), cut 1½ inches thick
Salt
Pinto Bean Relish (see below)

1. Make the spice rub: Combine all the ingredients in a wide bowl and mix well.

2. Make the steaks: Preheat the oven to 450°F. Heat the oil in a large heavy skillet (preferably cast iron) until smoking. Season each steak with salt and dredge one side well in the spice rub. Sear the steaks spice rub-side down until brown, 4–5 minutes. Turn the steaks over, transfer the pan to the oven, and roast for 6–8 minutes for medium-rare doneness.

3. To serve, spoon a good-sized portion of Pinto Bean Relish onto a plate and top with a steak.

Pinto Bean Relish

¾ pounds dried pinto beans, soaked overnight in water to cover
2 cups water

2 cups Chicken Stock (page xiv), or low-sodium canned stock
2 tablespoons olive oil
1 large red onion, finely diced
3 cloves garlic, finely chopped
2 teaspoons ground cumin
2 plum tomatoes, finely diced
1 roasted red pepper (page xiii), peeled, seeded, and finely diced
1 roasted yellow pepper (page xiii), peeled, seeded, and finely diced
1 poblano pepper, peeled, seeded, and finely diced
2 teaspoons chipotle puree (page xiii)
1 tablespoon honey
2 tablespoons fresh lime juice
Salt and freshly ground pepper
¼ cup coarsely chopped cilantro

1. Drain the beans. In a pot, cover the beans with water and chicken stock. Bring to a simmer and cook until soft, adding more boiling water a little at a time as needed. Drain the beans, reserving 1 cup of the cooking liquid.

2. Heat the olive oil in a large skillet over high heat. Add the onion and cook, stirring, until soft. Add the garlic and cumin and cook 2 minutes more. Add the drained beans, the tomatoes, peppers, chipotle puree, honey, reserved cooking liquid, and lime juice, and cook for 5 minutes or until most of the liquid has evaporated. Season with salt and pepper to taste and fold in the cilantro.

Steak Frites with
Red Spice Rub and Blue Cheese Sauce

After the steak, the best part of a steakhouse dinner (my favorite treat when I was a kid) was always the blue cheese dressing on a wedge of iceberg lettuce. This dish brings that tangy, intense blue cheese flavor right to the steak. Blue brie, a delicious French cheese called Mont-Briac, is like a smoother, creamier blue cheese. If you can't find it, use a combination of three-fourths Brie and one-fourth blue, removing the rind from the Brie.

Serves 4

For the fries:

6 large baking potatoes, such as Idaho or Russet, peeled
   Vegetable or peanut oil for frying
   Salt

For the cheese sauce:

3 tablespoons unsalted butter
3 cups milk
3 tablespoons flour
1¼ cups blue brie cheese, cut into small pieces (see above)
   Pinch of cayenne
   Salt

For the steak:

2 tablespoons ancho chile powder or another pure chile powder
1 tablespoon paprika
1 tablespoon freshly grated black pepper
1 teaspoon ground coriander
2 teaspoons dried thyme
2 teaspoons dry mustard
1 teaspoon kosher salt
   Canola or vegetable oil
4 New York strip steaks (8–10 ounces each), cut about 1 inch thick

1. Start the fries: Cut the potatoes lengthwise into ¼-inch-thick slices, then cut the slices into ¼-inch-thick fries. Place the potatoes in a large bowl of cold water while the oil heats. Pour 3 inches of vegetable oil in a large deep skillet fitted with a deep-frying thermometer and heat to 340°F. Line a sheet pan with paper towels. Drain the potatoes and dry them well. Fry the potatoes in batches 3–4 minutes. Remove to the lined pan to drain. Set aside until ready to serve, reserving the oil in the pot.

2. Make the sauce: Melt the butter in a medium saucepan over medium heat. Heat the milk in a separate medium saucepan. Whisk the flour into the butter and cook, stirring, 3–4 minutes without letting it brown (reduce the heat if necessary). A little bit at a time, whisk the milk into the flour mixture. Whisk the mixture until smooth and thickened. Whisk in the blue brie and cook until completely melted. If the mixture seems too thick, add a little more milk. Season with the cayenne and salt to taste. Keep warm.

3. Cook the steaks: Combine all the ingredients up to (not including) the canola oil in a shallow bowl and toss well. Brush a grill pan or skillet (preferably cast iron) with oil and heat over medium-high heat until almost smoking. Season one side of each steak with salt and dredge the other side in the spice mixture. Place in the hot pan spice-side down and cook until browned, 3–4 minutes. Turn the steaks over and cook 3–4 minutes more for medium-rare doneness. Let rest 5 minutes before serving.

4. Finish the fries: Increase the heat of the oil to 375°F. Line a sheet pan with paper towels. Working in batches to avoid crowding, fry the potatoes again until they turn a deep golden brown. Remove to the lined pan and season immediately with salt.

5. Serve the steaks drizzled with cheese sauce and with fries on the side.

Nanny Flay's Sauerbraten

When my grandmother made her sauerbraten on Sundays, the news would spread from cousin to cousin: "She's making it!" Sauerbraten is a German dish that has long been popular in the States; for me, it was an introduction to what became my favorite combination: sweet and spicy flavors. Serve it with tangy red cabbage and buttered, parslied egg noodles—plus, to make it authentically Nanny Flay's recipe, the best New York seeded rye bread you can find.

Serves 4–6

For the beef:
- 3 tablespoons olive oil
- 1 boneless, rolled beef roast (4–5 pounds), not too lean (look for rump, chuck, bottom, or eye of round)
  Salt and freshly ground pepper
- 2 onions, peeled and diced
- 2 stalks celery, coarsely chopped
- 1 large carrot, peeled and sliced thin
- 3 cloves garlic, coarsely chopped
- 1 cup white wine vinegar
- ½ cup white wine
- 8 cups cold water
- 6 whole cloves
- 8 black peppercorns
- 2 bay leaves
- 8 sprigs parsley
- 6 sprigs fresh thyme

To finish the dish:
- 3 tablespoons unsalted butter
- 3 tablespoons all-purpose flour
- 12 gingersnaps (page 188), crumbled
- 2 tablespoons honey, or to taste
  Braised Red Cabbage (see below)

1. Heat the oil over medium-high heat in a large heavy pot or casserole with a lid. Season the beef all over with salt and pepper and brown the beef in the oil on all sides, about 15 minutes total. Add the remaining beef ingredients and season with salt and pepper. Cover, reduce the heat to a bare simmer, and simmer 1½ hours. Turn the meat over, cover, and simmer 1–1½ hours more, until very tender. Transfer to a large platter, cover with foil, and keep warm. Strain the cooking liquid into a bowl and discard the contents of the strainer. Reserve the liquid.

2. Make the sauce: Melt the butter in a heavy medium saucepan over medium-high heat. When it foams, whisk in the flour and cook, stirring constantly, until golden brown, about 2 minutes. Setting aside ½ cup of the cooking liquid (this is for the cabbage recipe), whisk in the remainder of the cooking liquid, reduce the heat to low, and cook, stirring, until thickened. Mix in the gingersnaps and honey. Season to taste with honey, salt, and pepper.

3. To serve, slice the meat (not too thinly or the slices will crumble). Pass the sauce at the table and serve with Braised Red Cabbage.

Braised Red Cabbage

- 2 tablespoons unsalted butter
- 1 onion, peeled, halved, and thinly sliced
- 3 pounds red cabbage, cored and shredded
- ½ cup reserved cooking liquid from Sauerbraten recipe (above)
- ½ cup white wine
  Salt and freshly ground pepper

Melt the butter in a large skillet (with a lid) over medium heat. Add the onion and cook, stirring, until soft. Add the cabbage, cooking liquid, and wine, and season with salt and pepper to taste. Cover and cook until the cabbage is completely wilted, 15–20 minutes.

Prime Rib with Roasted Corn–Poblano Pudding

The very first restaurant I worked at, Joe Allen's in New York's theater district, was famous for its prime rib. Although I didn't know it then, Joe Allen's was a real, honest American restaurant that served good ingredients, simply cooked. There's definitely nothing better or simpler than a side of American beef! I remember hauling a whole rib roast to the kitchen every day—it must have weighed at least 50 pounds.

Sweet, custardy corn pudding, another American classic, is wonderful with a crusty roast. To help the pudding stand up to the meat, I stud it with roasted green chiles and give it a flavor base of roasted garlic.

Serves 4–6

One 4-rib beef rib roast, about 8 pounds, trimmed of excess fat (but not all fat), at room temperature (remove from the refrigerator at least 1 hour before roasting)
4 cloves garlic, finely sliced
Salt and freshly ground pepper
1 cup white wine
3 cups good-quality beef stock or broth
Roasted Corn–Poblano Pudding (see below)

1. Preheat the oven to 450°F. Using the tip of a small, sharp knife, poke small holes in the meat and insert the garlic slices into them. Season the meat all over with salt and pepper.

2. Place the roast in a large roasting pan, bone-side down. Roast for 15 minutes. Turn the heat down to 350°F and continue to roast for 1¼ hours for medium-rare doneness. Transfer to a carving board and let rest. Place the roasting pan on top of the stove, using two burners, over high heat. Add the wine and cook, stirring and scraping up any brown bits, and reduce completely. Add the stock and reduce by half. Season to taste with salt and pepper. Slice the beef ribs, arrange on plates, and drizzle with some of the jus. Serve with Roasted Corn–Poblano Pudding.

Roasted Corn–Poblano Pudding

2 cups heavy cream
6 cloves roasted garlic, pureed (page xiii)
2 large eggs plus 2 egg yolks
2 ears of corn, charred on the grill or roasted in a 400°F oven, kernels removed (about 2 cups kernels total)
1 poblano pepper, roasted, peeled, and finely diced (page xiii)
Salt and freshly ground pepper

1. Preheat the oven to 300°F. Place the cream in a small saucepan and bring to a simmer. Whisk in the garlic puree and turn off the heat.

2. Whisk the eggs and yolks together in a medium bowl until pale yellow and smooth. Whisking, gradually add the warm cream and whisk until blended. Fold in the corn and poblano pepper, and season to taste with salt and pepper.

3. Fill four well-buttered 6-ounce ramekins with the mixture and place them in a small roasting pan. Pour hot tap water into the roasting pan until it comes halfway up the sides of the ramekins. Bake until the mixture is barely set, about 30 minutes. They can be served unmolded or in the cups.

Roasted Pork Tenderloin with Sun-Dried Cranberry Stuffing

Tenderloin of pork is just as tender and juicy as tenderloin of beef, the piece that filet mignon is cut from. I really love how pork takes on flavor from the aromatics you cook it with; it can even pick up the subtle flavors of different chiles.

This is the perfect recipe for holiday dinners that would be overwhelmed by a whole ham or turkey. It's got those great festive American flavors—clove and cinnamon, cranberries and nuts—but in a manageable size. (You can easily make two for a larger group.)

Serves 4

For the stuffing:
1½ cups dried cranberries
2 tablespoons pine nuts, toasted (page xiii)
2 teaspoons cinnamon
Pinch of ground cloves
2 tablespoons dark brown sugar
1 tablespoon cascabel powder (or another pure chile powder, such as ancho or pasilla)

For the roast:
Salt and freshly ground pepper
2 tablespoons vegetable oil
½ cup flour
1 pork tenderloin (1½–2 pounds)

For the sauce:
2 tablespoons olive oil
1 small onion, finely chopped
1 carrot, finely diced
1 stalk celery, finely diced
2 cloves garlic, finely chopped
6 cups Chicken Stock (page xiv), or low-sodium canned stock
1 cup apple juice
1 teaspoon chipotle puree (page xiii)
1 teaspoon black peppercorns
1 tablespoon cold unsalted butter
Salt

1. Make the stuffing: Bring 2 cups of water to a boil in a medium saucepan. Add the cranberries, remove from the heat, and let rest 1 hour. Drain, reserving the soaking liquid. Place the cranberries in the bowl of a food processor. Add the pine nuts, cinnamon, cloves, brown sugar, cascabel powder, and a few tablespoons of the soaking liquid. Pulse until coarsely chopped.

2. Preheat the oven to 400°F. Place the tenderloin on a work surface. Use a sharp knife to slice the tenderloin horizontally almost in half, leaving the meat connected along one long edge so that you have one long, hinged piece that you can open flat. Season all over with salt and pepper. Spread the stuffing down the center, fold each side over, and tie closed with kitchen twine. Dredge all over in the flour. Heat the oil in an ovenproof skillet over high heat until smoking. Brown the meat on all sides until golden brown. Place in the oven and roast 10–12 minutes, until cooked through.

3. Make the sauce: Heat the oil in a medium saucepan over medium heat. Add the onion, carrot, and celery and cook until soft, 8–10 minutes. Add the garlic and cook for 2 minutes. Add the remaining ingredients, increase heat to high, and cook the sauce until reduced by half, about 8–10 minutes. Strain into a small saucepan and bring to a simmer. Whisk in the butter and season with salt and pepper to taste. Keep warm.

4. Remove the meat from the oven and let rest 10 minutes. Slice into 1-inch pieces. To serve, arrange the slices on serving plates. Pour the hot sauce over and serve.

Molasses-Glazed Pork Roast with Black Pepper Dumplings

These dumplings were inspired by a traditional Pennsylvania Dutch cook in Lancaster County who showed me how to poach dumplings in a savory cooking liquid. I add even more flavor by stirring plenty of black pepper and fresh thyme into the dough. The dumplings are great with a moist pork roast that is glazed with molasses, giving it a rich, sweet edge. Molasses is the common ingredient in a lot of classic American recipes like baked beans, Indian pudding, and shoofly pie.

Serves 6–8

For the roast and sauce:

1½ cups molasses, light or dark
3 tablespoons whole grain mustard
3 tablespoons olive oil
1 pork loin roast (3–4 pounds)
  Salt and freshly ground pepper
1 onion, finely diced
1 large carrot, finely diced
1 stalk celery, finely diced
2 cloves garlic, finely chopped
1 cup dry white wine
6 cups Chicken Stock (page xiv), or low-sodium canned stock
4 sprigs fresh thyme
4 sprigs parsley
  Chopped parsley for garnish

For the dumplings:

2 cups all-purpose flour
1 tablespoon baking powder
2 teaspoons kosher salt
1 tablespoon coarsely ground black pepper
2 tablespoons finely chopped fresh parsley
2 teaspoons finely chopped fresh thyme
4 tablespoons very cold solid vegetable shortening
⅔ cup milk

1. Make the roast: Preheat the oven to 350°F. Combine the molasses and mustard and mix well. Heat the oil in a large heavy casserole over high heat. Season the pork all over with salt and pepper and brown on all sides. Transfer the pot to the oven and roast about 1 hour. Brush the pork liberally with the molasses glaze and continue roasting until the internal temperature reaches 145°F, about 50 minutes. Transfer the roast to a platter (set the roasting pan aside), brush it with more of the glaze, and let rest 15 minutes.

2. While the roast is cooking, make the dumplings: Combine the flour, baking powder, salt, black pepper, parsley, and thyme in a medium mixing bowl. Using your fingertips, work the shortening into the flour mixture until it resembles coarse crumbs. Add the milk, stirring just until the mixture is moistened. Gather the dough into a ball, knead it a few times, and press it out 1 inch thick. Cut into 1-inch chunks and set aside.

3. Cook the dumplings: Remove all but 2 tablespoons of the fat from the roasting pan and place on top of the stove over medium-high heat. Add the onion, carrot, celery, and garlic, and cook, stirring, until soft, 5–7 minutes. Add the wine, increase the heat to high, and cook until liquid is reduced by half. Add the stock and the herbs, bring to a boil, and cook until reduced by one-third. Lower the heat and let the broth simmer. Drop the dumplings into the simmering broth, cover, and simmer until they are puffed and cooked through, 12–15 minutes.

4. Meanwhile, slice the roast and arrange in the center of a serving platter. Cover and keep warm. When the dumplings are done, arrange them around the pork. Spoon the broth and vegetables over the entire dish, sprinkle with parsley, and serve.

Spicy Mango-Glazed Ham with Sweet Potato–Vidalia Onion Salad

I've never met a country ham I didn't like. I tasted a lot of them in my travels around America and liked them all—air-dried, salt-cured, sugar-baked, on biscuits, with eggs, or covered with red-eye gravy. When I get my hands on a whole one, I can't resist giving it the traditional sweet crust, to contrast with the smoky flesh—but I always add fresh and spicy flavor elements like vinegar and habanero (aka Scotch bonnet) chiles.

Sweet potatoes and ham are a natural combination; with Vidalia onions, fresh garlic, and herbs, you've got a lively untraditional potato salad and a great holiday feast.

Serves 4–6

1½ cups red wine vinegar
1½ cups granulated sugar
1 habanero pepper, finely diced
1 cup orange juice
4 ripe mangoes, peeled, seeded, and coarsely chopped
Salt
1 cured and lightly smoked ham (10 pounds), bone in
Sweet Potato–Vidalia Onion Salad (see below)

1. Bring the vinegar and sugar to a boil in a medium nonreactive saucepan over high heat and boil until reduced to ¾ cup. Add the habanero, orange juice, and mangoes, season with salt, and cook until the mangoes are very soft, about 15 minutes. Let cool at least 10 minutes, transfer to a blender, and blend until smooth (or use a hand blender).

2. Roast the ham: Preheat the oven to 350°F. Trim some of the fat off the ham, leaving a layer about ¼-inch thick. Score the surface, using the tip of a sharp knife to cut a diamond pattern into the fat. Place a rack in a roasting pan and add 2 cups of water to the pan. Bake the ham for about 2 hours. During the last 20 minutes of cooking, baste the ham with the glaze every 5 minutes. Remove from the oven and brush with more of the glaze. Let sit for 15 minutes before carving. Slice and serve with Sweet Potato–Vidalia Onion Salad.

Sweet Potato–Vidalia Onion Salad

5 sweet potatoes, sliced into ½-inch-thick slices
½ cup olive oil
Salt and freshly ground pepper
¼ cup balsamic vinegar
2 teaspoons Dijon mustard
2 cloves garlic, finely chopped
2 large Vidalia onions, peeled and thinly sliced
4 scallions, thinly sliced
¼ cup coarsely chopped cilantro

1. Preheat a grill. Brush the potato slices on both sides with ¼ cup of the olive oil, and season with salt and pepper. Grill the potatoes until golden brown and just cooked through. (Or roast the slices until soft in a 400°F oven.)

2. In a medium bowl whisk together the vinegar, mustard, and garlic. Slowly whisk in the remaining ¼ cup oil and season with salt and pepper to taste.

3. Place the potatoes, onions, scallions, and cilantro in a medium bowl, drizzle with the vinaigrette, and toss gently to combine. Season with salt and pepper to taste. Serve at room temperature.

Baby Back Pork Ribs with Mustard-Molasses Barbecue Sauce

It's easy for me to stay out of the big debates about barbecue, because I love every kind: Texas dry rubs, North Carolina vinegar sauces, even Kentucky barbecued mutton. But since mustard is one of my favorite seasonings, I'm especially inclined toward South Carolina's sweet mustard barbecue sauces. I use my variation as a glaze for ribs, stacking up thin layers on the outside of the meat into a caramelized, chewy crust.

I like to keep the meat moist, so instead of grilling pork ribs (the usual solution for home cooks who don't have barbecue pits), I roast them in a hot oven over a panful of seasoned liquid. The rich meat takes on the flavors of the liquid.

Serves 4–6

For the sauce:
- 1 cup cider vinegar
- ½ cup dark brown sugar
- 2 cups molasses
- 1 tablespoon ancho chile powder or another pure chile powder
- ½ cup Dijon mustard
- Salt and freshly ground pepper

For the ribs:
- 3 cups water
- 2 cups soy sauce
- 1 tablespoon whole mustard seeds
- 1 tablespoon fennel seeds
- 6 pounds baby back ribs, cut into 1½-pound slabs
- Salt and freshly ground pepper

1. Make the sauce: Combine the vinegar and sugar in a medium nonreactive saucepan and simmer over medium-high heat until the sugar is completely melted. Remove from the heat and whisk in the molasses, ancho powder, and mustard. Season to taste with salt and pepper. Let cool to room temperature.

2. Make the ribs: Preheat the oven to 400°F. In a saucepan, combine the water, soy sauce, and mustard and fennel seeds, and bring to a boil over medium-high heat. Pour the mixture into the bottom of a roasting pan and place the ribs on a rack over the pan. Bake for 1–1¼ hours, basting with the barbecue sauce every 10 minutes, until cooked through. Cut into single ribs before serving.

Smoked Lamb and Goat Cheese Enchiladas with Almond Molé Sauce

Cold smoking is a great method for infusing meat and vegetables with smoky flavor—without cooking them. (Hot smoking cooks and flavors the food at the same time.) To cold smoke, you wait until the fire is burned almost all the way down—and *then* add the soaked wood. The warm smoke infuses food with its flavor; you end up with raw ingredients that have a smoky taste. Lamb and tomatoes are both great prepared this way, but you can skip the smoking altogether if you prefer.

I like to cook cold-smoked food with other strong flavors, and my favorite molé sauce, with its fascinating combination of cinnamon, nuts, chiles, and spices, certainly fits the bill. Molés, complex Mexican sauces, often have a little unsweetened chocolate added at the end to create a nice finish to the sauce and give it a deep flavor note.

Serves 4–6

2 lamb loins (1½ pounds)
   Salt and freshly ground pepper
6 plum tomatoes
2 tablespoons olive oil
4 scallions, thinly sliced
   Twelve 6-inch flour tortillas
2 cups finely grated Monterey Jack cheese
12 ounces goat cheese, crumbled
½ cup coarsely chopped cilantro
   Almond Molé Sauce (see below)

1. If smoking the lamb and tomatoes (*if not, proceed directly to step 2*): Put two big handfuls of aromatic wood chips (such as oak or hickory) to soak. Make a fire of charcoal or wood in a smoker or Weber grill and let it burn down to embers. Lay the soaked wood chips on the embers. Place the lamb on the grill rack, place the cover on the smoker, and open the top vent slightly. Smoke the lamb for 5 minutes. Meanwhile, rub the tomatoes with olive oil. After 5 minutes, remove the smoker or grill cover, put in the tomatoes, and continue smoking along with the lamb for 10 minutes more.

2. Slice the lamb loins in half lengthwise and then crosswise into ½-inch strips. Dice the tomatoes into ½-inch dice. Heat the olive oil in a large skillet until almost smoking. Add the lamb, season with salt and pepper and toss for 1–2 minutes until just browned. Add the scallions and tomatoes and cook 3–4 minutes, for medium-rare doneness.

3. Make the tacos: Lay the tortillas flat on a surface. Sprinkle ¼ cup of the Monterey Jack on each of the tortillas, place some of the lamb mixture over the cheese, and sprinkle with goat cheese and cilantro. Fold the ends in and roll tightly lengthwise. Ladle the Almond Molé Sauce over and garnish with cilantro.

Almond Molé Sauce

¼ cup plus 2 tablespoons pure olive oil

4 blue corn tortillas, torn in pieces

2 ancho chiles, seeded and stemmed

2 New Mexico chiles, seeded and stemmed

1 pasilla chile, seeded and stemmed

1 red onion, coarsely chopped

½ head roasted garlic, cloves separated

½ cup slivered raw almonds

6 cups Chicken Stock (page xiv)

4 plum tomatoes, peeled, cored, and chopped

¼ cup golden raisins

½ ounce Mexican chocolate, such as Ibarra

2 tablespoons maple syrup

½ teaspoon ground cinnamon

⅛ teaspoon ground cloves

Juice of one lime

Salt and pepper

1. Heat the oil in a large frying pan over medium heat until almost smoking. Fry the tortillas until crisp, 2–3 minutes, and remove to a plate lined with paper towels. Add the chiles to the oil and fry for 10 seconds. Remove to the plate. Discard oil.

2. Heat remaining oil in a medium saucepan over medium heat. Add the onion and cook until soft. Add the roasted garlic and cook for 1 minute. Add the remaining ingredients plus the tortillas and chiles, and cook for 1 hour.

3. Transfer the sauce to a food processor and puree until smooth.

Roast Leg of Lamb with
Honey, Balsamic Vinegar, and Fresh Mint Baste

My favorite roast for a festive dinner is always leg of lamb. I bring out the lamb's natural flavor by roasting it with just salt and pepper; then at the very end, I brush on a glaze of balsamic vinegar and honey. The sugars quickly caramelize to a tangy-sweet crust. Fresh mint has a sweet and peppery quality I like with red meat, and it also reminds me of the mint sauce we used to eat with lamb when I was a kid.

This succulent roast would make a wonderful dinner with my Caramelized Vidalia Onion and Potato Gratin with Fresh Sage.

Serves 6–8

2 cups honey
¾ cup balsamic vinegar
8 mint leaves, finely chopped
   Salt and freshly ground pepper
1 boneless leg of lamb (5–7 pounds), trimmed
      of excess fat
   Salt and freshly ground pepper
   Olive oil

1. Make the baste: Combine the honey, vinegar, and mint in a medium bowl. Whisk together and season with salt and pepper to taste.

2. Roast the lamb: Preheat the oven to 375°F. Season the lamb all over with salt and pepper. Heat the olive oil in a large roasting pan, set over two burners, until smoking. Sear the lamb all over until browned, about 4–5 minutes per side. Transfer to the oven and roast to an internal temperature of 130°F for medium-rare, approximately 1½ hours. During the last 30 minutes of roasting, baste liberally every 10 minutes with the glaze. Remove from the oven and let rest 10 minutes before slicing.

Pan-Roasted Lamb Chops with Red Wine–Black Currant Sauce

Lamb is my favorite meat, and a thick chop cooked right and served with a glass of good red wine is often just what I'm in the mood for—especially on a chilly winter evening. Lamb's definite meaty flavor is what makes it so good with sweet and tangy sides like mint jelly, jalapeño preserves, and cranberry sauce. This sauce has deep, rich flavor from red wine and sweet dried currants, and the wine-simmered vegetables are delicious with the meat.

When it comes to choosing a wine to pour in the pan, the rule is, If you would drink it, you can cook with it. Serve the dish with my Green Garlic Smashed Potatoes.

Serves 4

Eight 1–1¼-inch thick loin, rib, or sirloin lamb chops, trimmed of most fat
Salt and freshly ground black pepper
3 tablespoons olive oil
2 shallots, finely diced
1 large stalk celery, finely diced
1 large carrot, finely diced
2 cups dry red wine
4 cups Chicken Stock (page xiv), or low-sodium canned stock
8 black peppercorns
½ cup dried currants
2 tablespoons cold unsalted butter
2 tablespoons finely chopped tarragon

1. Preheat the oven to 400°F. Season the chops on both sides with salt and pepper. Heat the oil over high heat in a medium roasting pan set on two burners on the stove. Add the chops and cook until browned on one side, 2–3 minutes. Turn over, transfer the pan to the oven, and roast until cooked to medium-rare doneness, 4–5 minutes. Transfer the chops to a plate and loosely cover with foil.

2. Remove all but 2 tablespoons of the fat from the pan. Place the pan on two burners on the stove over high heat. Add the shallots, celery, and carrots, and cook until golden brown, about 10 minutes. Add the wine and cook until completely reduced. Add the stock and cook until reduced to 1 cup. Strain the sauce into a small saucepan, add the peppercorns and currants, and bring to a simmer over medium heat. Whisk in the butter and tarragon and season with salt and pepper to taste. Serve the chops drizzled with the sauce.

Caraway-Fennel–Crusted Loin of Lamb with Mustard Sauce and Melted Napa Cabbage

The combination of being Irish-American and growing up in New York (home of the best delis in the world) means that I ate a lot of corned beef as a kid. I liked our traditional St. Patrick's Day corned beef and cabbage, but I think I liked a corned beef sandwich on rye with mustard even more.

This recipe has some flavor elements of each dish and makes a great dinner entrée. The caraway seeds (from the rye bread) make a crisp and fragrant crust for the lamb loin; mustard comes from the sandwich too. Tender Napa cabbage takes on a soft, luscious texture when you cook it slowly in the oven with honey and vinegar.

Serves 4

3 tablespoons caraway seeds
3 tablespoons fennel seeds
1 lamb loin (2 pounds)
   Salt and freshly ground pepper
3 tablespoons olive oil
1 cup dry red wine
3 cups Chicken Stock (page xiv), or
      low-sodium canned stock
2 tablespoons whole grain mustard
2 tablespoons Dijon mustard
2 tablespoons thinly sliced fresh mint
   Melted Napa Cabbage (see below)

1. Preheat the oven to 400°F. Place both kinds of seeds in a coffee grinder and grind to a powder. Place the mixture on a plate. Season the lamb with salt and pepper to taste and dredge on all sides with the spice mixture. Heat the oil in a medium ovenproof skillet over high heat until almost smoking. Sear the lamb on all sides until browned. Transfer the skillet to the oven and roast lamb 8–10 minutes for medium-rare doneness. Remove and let rest.

2. Wipe all the grease out of the skillet, and place it on top of the stove over high heat. Add the wine and cook until reduced by three-fourths. Add the stock and cook until reduced by half. Whisk in the mustards and season with salt and

pepper to taste. Remove from the heat and stir in the mint.

3. Slice the lamb thinly against the grain of the meat and serve with mustard sauce and Melted Napa Cabbage.

Melted Napa Cabbage

2 pounds Napa cabbage, thinly sliced
1 cup red wine vinegar
2 tablespoons honey
2 cups Chicken Stock (page xiv), or
      low-sodium canned stock
   Salt and freshly ground pepper
2 tablespoons fresh mint, thinly sliced

Preheat the oven to 400°F. Place the cabbage in a roasting pan, stir in the vinegar, honey, and stock, and season with salt and pepper. Cover with foil and bake until the cabage is wilted, about 30 minutes. Remove from the oven and stir in the mint. Serve with a slotted spoon if the mixture is very wet.

Venison–Black Bean Chili with Green Chile Crema and White Cornbread

The big debate over chili—all meat, or meat and beans?—seems pretty simple to me. I never leave out something that tastes good, and black beans definitely qualify. This is one of my favorite winter lunches, whether I make it with farm-raised venison (which is delicious, meaty, and not gamy at all) or lamb or even buffalo.

The interesting thing about chili is *the chiles*. Supermarket "chili powder" is just a mixture of cayenne with other flavorings like onion powder and cumin. You get much deeper flavor from mixing your own spice blend. Anchos are dried poblano peppers, and they have the most spicy, raisiny flavor. I balance anchos with pasillas, which taste earthier and less hot. Chipotles, smoked jalapeño peppers, are marinated in vinegar and lend a tangy, smoky note. Cumin is a signature spice in chili; grinding your own from whole seeds really makes the difference here.

Serves 4–6

For the chili:
- ¼ cup olive oil
- Salt and freshly ground pepper
- 2 pounds venison, lamb, or beef, cut into ½-inch cubes
- 1 large red onion, finely diced
- 4 cloves garlic, finely chopped
- 3 tablespoons ancho chile powder
- 1 tablespoon pasilla chile powder or another pure chile powder
- 1 tablespoon freshly ground cumin
- 1 bottle dark beer, such as Negro Modelo
- One 16-ounce can chopped tomatoes, drained and pureed
- 8 cups Chicken Stock (page xiv) or low-sodium canned stock
- 1 tablespoon chipotle puree (page xiii)
- 1 tablespoon honey
- 2 cups cooked or canned black beans, rinsed and drained
- 2 tablespoons fresh lime juice
- Freshly chopped cilantro
- White Cornbread (see below)

For the *crema*:
- 1 tablespoon olive oil
- 1 large poblano chile, roasted, peeled, seeded, and chopped (page xiii)
- 1 cup Mexican *crema*, crème fraîche, or sour cream thinned with buttermilk
- 1 tablespoon fresh lime juice
- Salt and freshly ground pepper

1. Make the chili: Heat the oil in a large oven-proof pot over high heat. Season the venison with salt and pepper and sauté in batches until browned on all sides. Transfer the meat to a plate and remove all but 3 tablespoons of the fat from the pot.

2. Add the onion to the pot and cook until soft. Add the garlic and cook for 2 minutes. Add the ancho powder, pasilla powder, and cumin, and cook an additional 2 minutes. Add the beer and cook until completely reduced. Return the venison to the pot, add the tomatoes, chicken stock, chipotle puree, and honey, and bring to a boil. Reduce heat to medium, cover the pot, and simmer for 45 minutes. Add the beans and continue cooking for 15 minutes. Remove from the heat, add the lime juice, and adjust seasonings.

3. Meanwhile, make the *crema*: Place the poblano, oil, crème fraîche, and lime juice in a food processor and puree until smooth. Season with salt and pepper to taste.

4. To serve, ladle the chili into bowls and spoon the *crema* on top. Sprinkle with cilantro and serve with White Cornbread.

White Cornbread

2 sticks (8 ounces) unsalted butter, at room temperature
2 cups coarsely ground white cornmeal
2 cups all-purpose flour
2 tablespoons baking powder
2 large eggs, lightly beaten
1 teaspoon salt
2⅔ cups buttermilk
1 tablespoon honey

1. Preheat the oven to 400°F. Butter a 12-inch-square baking pan.

2. In a food processor or mixer, combine the butter, cornmeal, flour, baking powder, eggs, and salt. Process 20–30 seconds, until just mixed. Pour in the buttermilk and honey and process for 20 seconds more. Pour into the prepared pan and bake 10–15 minutes, until firm to the touch and golden. Cut into squares, let cool slightly, and serve.

Pan-Roasted Venison with Spicy Cranberry–Mexican Cinnamon Sauce and Whipped Sweet Potatoes

Juniper berries, the wild purple buds that give gin its piney taste, are perfect for flavoring game meats like venison. These venison steaks are actually quick-marinated in gin, which does some tenderizing as well as adding that great juniper fragrance and flavor. I cut the strength of gin with the fruity sweetness of port, a complex fortified wine that also gives the cinnamon-cranberry sauce its backbone.

Serves 4

For the venison:
- ½ cup gin
- 2 cups ruby port
- 6 sprigs fresh thyme
- 6 juniper berries
- 4 venison steaks, 6 ounces each (or use lamb or buffalo steaks)
- 3 tablespoons olive oil
- Salt and freshly ground pepper

For the sauce:
- 2 tablespoons unsalted butter
- 1 onion, peeled and finely chopped
- 3 cloves garlic, finely chopped
- 2 carrots, finely chopped
- 2 stalks celery, finely chopped
- ½ cup ruby port
- 3 tablespoons dark brown sugar
- ½ cup cranberry juice
- 4 cups Chicken Stock (page xiv), or low-sodium canned stock
- ¼ teaspoon cinnamon, preferably Mexican
- ¼ teaspoon allspice
- ¼ cup fresh cranberries, coarsely chopped
- 2 tablespoons cold unsalted butter
- Salt and freshly ground pepper
- Whipped Sweet Potatoes (see below)

1. Make the marinade: Combine the gin, port, thyme, and juniper berries in a shallow dish. Add the venison and turn to coat. Cover and refrigerate for 30 minutes.

2. Meanwhile, make the sauce: Melt the butter in a medium saucepan over medium-high heat. Add the onion, garlic, carrots, and celery, and cook until soft. Raise heat to high and add the port, cook until dry. Add the remaining ingredients up to the butter and cook until a sauce consistency. Whisk in the cold butter and season with salt and pepper to taste. Keep hot.

3. Cook the meat: Heat the oil in a large ovenproof skillet over high heat until almost smoking. Preheat the oven to 400°F. Remove the venison from the marinade and shake off any excess. Season with salt and pepper to taste. Sear the steaks on one side until brown, 4–5 minutes. Turn them over, place the skillet in the oven, and roast about 6 minutes for medium-rare doneness.

4. Serve with Whipped Sweet Potatoes and sauce.

Whipped Sweet Potatoes
- 4 large sweet potatoes, peeled
- 1 stick (8 tablespoons) unsalted butter
- ½ cup warm milk
- 1 teaspoon chipotle puree (page xiii)
- 2 tablespoons maple syrup
- Salt and freshly ground pepper

Cut the potatoes into large chunks and place in a large saucepan. Cover with water, bring to a boil, and boil until soft. Drain off the water and return to the pan. Shake over medium heat to dry out the potatoes. Add the remaining ingredients and mash until smooth. Season with salt and pepper to taste.

Postcard from Lancaster County, Pennsylvania

I never gave a whole lot of thought to pretzels until I went to check out the food in Lancaster County, Pennsylvania. Lancaster County is the official name of what most of us call "Amish country," where you still see horse-drawn buggies on the roads, boys in those flat-brimmed hats, and girls in long-sleeved dresses and sunbonnets. As I rode along the highway (in a car at first, but then in a buggy), I passed lively groups of these incredibly old-fashioned-looking kids. They were Rollerblading.

That combination of old—with a little bit of a new spark—is what I loved about the food in Lancaster County. Farming is still the main way of life, and you can taste it in everything you eat. Local traditions derive from hearty German farmhouse cooking, so this is the place for fresh, delicious hams and sausages, preserved fruit and vegetables, and piles of dumplings, noodles, pies, and pancakes. Only people who work really hard can eat like this every day, and they certainly do.

I quickly discovered that the favorite local snack is pretzels, which makes sense because most of the local population's ancestors came from Germany. (The "Pennsylvania Dutch" are really *Deutsch*, or German.) There are several local pretzelmakers, some in business for a hundred years or more. When I asked some customers at Hammond's Pretzel Factory how they decide which brand of pretzels to buy, most of them said that they stick with the one their grandparents picked out!

Every single Hammond's pretzel is made by hand. Brian Nicklaus still uses his great-grandfather's original recipe, and the sourdough starter he uses has been going steadily for over seventy years. It's a low-tech system, but totally efficient: The sourdough cultures live in the wooden barrels they use for mixing the dough. After the dough is mixed, the professional rollers go to work: Each one of them can snap off a chunk of dough, roll it into a thin snake, twirl it into that pretzel shape, and put it aside to proof—all in fifteen seconds. Brian tried to teach me to twirl, but it's not as easy as it looks. He was nice about it, though, tactfully saying that he'd use the ones I made in a "variety pack." I'm still waiting to see that.

The pretzels are boiled, then salted, and finally dried out at 600 degrees (the high temperature gives them that nut-brown color). I was surprised to find that they really do taste different when they're fresh: You can taste the yeastiness of the risen dough. And the pretzels taste even better dunked in Hammond's "dipping mustard": You just stick the warm pretzels right into the jar, for a totally authentic Lancaster County snack.

Sausages, another German classic, are big business in Lancaster County. Myron Stolzfus makes the best breakfast sausages I've ever had, but he couldn't (or wouldn't) tell me just what made them so good. Like the pretzel man, he sticks to traditional low-tech equipment and a great old recipe. He also said that the lean hogs he uses give great flavor, but I think he was just trying to get me off the scent. In my experience, the most flavor comes from fat.

Local food experts steered me to the Stroudsburg Inn, where the chef, DeeDee Meyer, grew up in an Amish family. She cooked me some of the true Pennsylvania Dutch dishes, which all had this great farmhouse flavor. Since the Amish don't use electric refrigerators or freezers, they still know how to make summer's fruit and vegetable harvest last the whole winter: Think pickled everything (carrots, beets, even hard-boiled eggs), horseradish, dried apples and apple butter, sauerkraut, and country ham. My favorite dish was something she called *Schnitz und Knepp,* a savory-sweet dish of simmered ham chunks and dried apples, topped with dumplings that steam right in the pot. All the food was homey and comforting, and reminded me that sometimes just salt and pepper can be the perfect seasonings—they don't use a lot of chipotle chiles in Lancaster County.

The weekly farmer's market in Stroudsburg, the county seat, is a big event. Little kids are everywhere, covered with powdered sugar from eating funnel cakes (just like the fried dough I always ate at New York City street fairs), or covered with mustard from eating soft, warm pretzels. I missed the cattle auction—but I did get to eat Ed Schultz's pit beef, an incredibly crusty side of meat that he roasts, slices, and serves up with a hot horseradish mustard I'd kill to get the recipe for. As he said, "That'll make your hair red!"

Sides

Smashed Yukon Gold Potatoes with Green Garlic Butter

Buttermilk-Bacon Smashed Potatoes

Caramelized Vidalia Onion and Potato Gratin with Fresh Sage

Lemon-Glazed Sweet Potatoes

Sweet Potato Biscuits

Cast-Iron Skillet Yellow Cornbread with Maple Butter

Creamed Hominy with Cilantro

Fresh Creamed Corn with Sweet Red Peppers

Roasted Corn on the Cob with *Cotija* Cheese and Fresh Lime Juice

Cornmeal-Fried Okra with Corn Relish

Creamed Kale with Caramelized Baby Onions

Swiss Chard with Red Onions and Serrano Chile Vinegar

Butter Bean and Sweet Onion Succotash

Smashed Yukon Gold Potatoes with Green Garlic Butter

If you are a fan of mashed potatoes (and who isn't?), this dish will blow your mind. I take the warmth and richness of plain mashed potatoes with butter—a delicious dish all by itself—and use it to bring the aromas and flavors of fresh herbs to life. Mashed in with the hot potatoes and melting butter, the herb flavors really blossom.

Any soft herbs like mint, parsley, chives, tarragon, and cilantro would be wonderful in this recipe.

Serves 8

1 stick (8 tablespoons) unsalted butter, slightly softened

6 cloves garlic, finely chopped

¼ cup chopped parsley

¼ cup chopped cilantro
   Salt and freshly ground pepper

5 pounds Yukon Gold potatoes, peeled and cut into large chunks

1 cup heavy cream

1 cup milk
   Salt and freshly ground pepper

1. Place the butter, garlic, and herbs in a food processor and blend until smooth. Season with salt and pepper. Refrigerate until ready to use.

2. Place the potatoes in a large saucepan, cover with cold water, and add 2 tablespoons of salt. Bring to a boil and cook until soft, 10–12 minutes. Drain well and place back in the pan over low heat. Add the cream, milk, and green garlic butter and mash until smooth. Season with salt and pepper to taste.

Buttermilk-Bacon Smashed Potatoes

When you're making *smashed* potatoes, as opposed to mashed potatoes, the goal isn't a smooth texture—it's the most flavor you can get. Tender chunks of potato, thin shreds of red potato skin, nuggets of bacon, and cloves of roasted garlic make for huge flavor, and the buttermilk brings it all together. I could eat this as a meal, but it's really great as a side dish with grilled chicken or barbecued pork.

Serves 8

5 pounds unpeeled Red Bliss potatoes, or other thin-skinned potatoes, quartered

Salt

1 stick (8 tablespoons) unsalted butter, slightly softened at room temperature

1½–2 cups buttermilk

6 cloves roasted garlic (page xiii)

8 slices cooked bacon, crumbled

Salt and freshly ground pepper

1. Place the potatoes in a large saucepan, cover with cold water, and add 2 tablespoons of salt. Bring to a boil and cook until soft, 10–12 minutes. Drain well and place back in the pan over low heat.

2. Add the butter, buttermilk, and roasted garlic, and mash until smooth. Fold in the bacon and season with salt and pepper to taste.

Caramelized Vidalia Onion and Potato Gratin with Fresh Sage

In Vidalia, Georgia, it's all about the onions. For weeks after I got back from that onion-obsessed town, I found myself looking at all my dishes, wondering—how can I slip a little onion in there? The sweet onions they grow in Vidalia are easy to mix with other flavors; they are less aggressive and pungent than regular onions. Their sweetness also means that there is more sugar to caramelize when you brown them. Caramelized Vidalia onions are seriously delicious. That nutty-sweet flavor, sparked with fresh sage, takes your basic potato gratin to a new level.

This dish is very simple, but it is important to have your potatoes sliced really, really thin before you start.

Serves 4

2 tablespoons olive oil
1 tablespoon unsalted butter
3 Vidalia onions, peeled, halved, and very thinly sliced (preferably on a mandoline or the slicing disk of a food processor)
Salt and freshly ground pepper
3 tablespoons finely chopped fresh sage
3 cups heavy cream
6 large Idaho potatoes, peeled and very thinly sliced (preferably on a mandoline)

1. Preheat the oven to 375°F. Heat the oil and butter in a large skillet over medium-high heat until hot but not smoking. Add the onions, season with salt and pepper, and cook, stirring occasionally, until browned and caramelized, 15–20 minutes. Remove from the heat and stir in the sage. Let cool slightly.

2. Make a thin layer of potatoes in a baking dish (about 10 inches square and at least 2 inches deep) and season with salt and pepper. Spread about one-twelfth of the onion mixture over the potatoes and coat with ¼ cup of the cream. Repeat each step to yield 12 thin layers. Press down gently on the layers, cover with foil, place the dish on a sheet pan, and bake for 25 minutes. Remove the cover and bake for another 20–25 minutes, or until the potatoes are tender and golden brown on top. Let rest at room temperature 10 minutes before serving.

Lemon-Glazed Sweet Potatoes

If any sweet potato recipe could persuade you to leave the marshmallows in the cupboard, this is it. A fresh lemon syrup just glazes the tender potato cubes, adding sweetness without drowning out the great flavor. Cutting the potatoes in small pieces gives them plenty of surface to take on the glaze. Try it once: You'll never go back!

Serves 4–6

2 cups fresh lemon juice

2 cups granulated sugar

1 tablespoon finely chopped lemon zest

5 large sweet potatoes, peeled and cut into ½-inch dice

2 tablespoons olive oil
   Salt and freshly ground pepper

1. Combine the juice, sugar, and zest in a small nonreactive pan, bring to a boil, and boil until reduced to ½ cup.

2. Preheat the oven to 375°F. In a large ovenproof skillet, toss the sweet potatoes in the oil and roast until lightly browned and just cooked through, about 20–25 minutes. Transfer the pan to the top of the stove and turn the heat to medium. Pour the glaze over the potatoes and cook, tossing the potatoes often, until glazed and soft.

Sweet Potato Biscuits

These biscuits are both incredibly delicious and incredibly pretty—and it's the sweet potatoes that make them that way. The pale orange color and lightly sweet flavor have kept them in the bread baskets at Mesa Grill for years. They are great on their own or with honey butter, with jalapeño preserves, with fried chicken, in shortcakes, and on top of pot pies. In short: They're my favorite biscuits.

Makes 12

2 cups all-purpose flour
1 tablespoon plus ¼ teaspoon baking powder
½ teaspoon baking soda
½ teaspoon salt
5 tablespoons very cold unsalted butter, cut into pieces, or solid vegetable shortening
⅞ cup buttermilk
½ cup mashed, cooked sweet potatoes
1 tablespoon honey
1 egg beaten with 1 tablespoon water

1. Preheat the oven to 375°F and line a large baking sheet with parchment paper or nonstick baking mats (or use a nonstick baking sheet). Sift the dry ingredients together into a large bowl. Cut in the shortening until the mixture resembles rolled oats.

2. Make a well in the center of the mixture, add the buttermilk, sweet potatoes, and honey, and stir vigorously until the dough forms a ball. Knead lightly for about 30 seconds, until the dough just begins to look smooth.

3. On a floured surface, pat the dough out ¾-inch thick, making a 7-by-8-inch rectangle. Cut into 2-inch rounds, rerolling the scraps, and cutting out more biscuits. Transfer to the prepared pan, brush tops with egg wash, and bake for 10–12 minutes or until lightly browned.

Cast-Iron Skillet Yellow Cornbread with Maple Butter

Everyone knows that the best part of cornbread is the golden, buttery crust. A super-hot cast-iron skillet is the best way to create one.

I have a real thing for cast-iron pans: They hold the heat better than any other surface, the seasoning process makes them virtually nonstick, and they're cheaper than any fancy cookware set you can buy. I have them in a lot of sizes, including small 4-inch ones for making individual loaves. I'd use them for this recipe; you can also try making it in heavy muffin tins.

Serves 4–6

For the maple butter:
- 2 sticks (8 ounces) unsalted butter, at room temperature
- ½ cup pure maple syrup
- ¼ teaspoon ground cinnamon
- 1 teaspoon salt

For the cornbread:
- 3 tablespoons vegetable shortening
- 1¼ cups all-purpose flour
- ¾ cup yellow cornmeal
- 1 tablespoon baking powder
- 1 teaspoon salt
- 2 large eggs
- 2 tablespoons honey
- 1 cup milk
- 2 tablespoons melted unsalted butter

1. At least 4 hours before serving, make the maple butter: Combine all the ingredients in a medium bowl and mix together until smooth. Scrape the mixture into a bowl or ramekin, cover with plastic wrap, and refrigerate at least 4 hours or overnight.

2. Preheat the oven to 425°F and position the rack in the center of the oven. Place the shortening in an 8-inch cast-iron skillet and heat in the oven for 15 minutes.

3. Whisk together the flour, cornmeal, baking powder, and salt in a large bowl. Whisk together the eggs, honey, milk, and butter in a medium bowl. Add the wet ingredients to the dry ingredients and whisk until just combined. Remove the skillet from the oven and carefully pour the mixture into the skillet.

4. Bake for 20–25 minutes, until pale golden brown on top and a toothpick inserted into the center comes out clean. Cut into squares or wedges and serve warm, with maple butter.

Creamed Hominy with Cilantro

Entrées with Southern and Southwestern flavors are great with corn-based side dishes like spoonbread, cornbread, grits, and hominy. It's hard to master the differences if you're born outside the South, but I do know that it's all corn. I also know that I love the taste, especially with dishes like Roasted Pork Tenderloin with Sun-Dried Cranberry Stuffing or Cornmeal-Crusted Catfish with Grilled Red Onion Relish and Green Chile Tartar Sauce.

Corn used to be tougher and less sweet than today's breeds, so Native American cooks learned to treat it with powdered lime (as in limestone), making it more digestible. Whole kernels of this treated corn are called hominy; the ground kernels are called grits.

Serves 4

2 cups whole dried hominy, or 3 cups canned hominy, drained
2 tablespoons olive oil
1 large onion, finely diced
3 cloves garlic, finely chopped
2 cups heavy cream, plus extra as needed
1 tablespoon chipotle puree (page xiii)
  Kosher salt
1 tablespoon honey
¼ cup chopped cilantro

1. Cook the hominy (if using canned hominy, skip to step 3): At least 8 hours before cooking the dish, rinse the dried hominy, place in a medium bowl, and cover with cold water. Let soak at least 8 hours or overnight.

2. Drain the hominy and place in a medium saucepan. Add water to cover by at least 2 inches. Bring the water to a boil, reduce the heat to medium-low, and simmer, stirring occasionally, until the hominy is tender, at least 1 hour. Drain well.

3. Place the hominy in a food processor and pulse just until coarsely chopped. Heat the oil in a medium saucepan over medium heat. Add the onion and garlic and cook until soft. Add the hominy, the cream, and the chipotle puree, and simmer 10–12 minutes or until the hominy has absorbed the cream. If the mixture seems too dry, add more cream and continue cooking a few minutes longer. Season to taste with salt and honey. Remove from the heat and fold in the cilantro.

Fresh Creamed Corn with Sweet Red Peppers

Every August, after my daughter and I have eaten our fill of local Long Island corn on the cob (which takes several weeks of daily consumption), I make this irresistible dish. The pure sweetness of the corn is only enhanced by the red peppers and the summery addition of green basil.

Corn purists say that the only way to eat it really fresh is to cook it right in the field, to minimize the time between picking and cooking. Even the most dedicated, produce-loving chefs find that difficult to manage, but do cook your corn as soon after picking as possible.

Serves 6–8

3 tablespoons unsalted butter
1 small red onion, finely diced
1 large red bell pepper, finely diced
2 cloves garlic, finely chopped
12 ears fresh corn, kernels only
   (about 3 cups total)
   Salt and freshly ground pepper
1 cup heavy cream
2 tablespoons finely chopped fresh basil

Heat the butter in a medium saucepan over medium heat. Add the onion and pepper and cook, stirring, until soft. Add the garlic and cook for 1 minute more. Add the corn, season with salt and pepper, and cook for 5 minutes. Add the cream and cook until thickened, 5–7 minutes. Stir in the basil, season to taste with salt and pepper, and serve.

Roasted Corn on the Cob with Cotija Cheese and Fresh Lime Juice

Every August, I eat as much fresh corn as I possibly can, to get ready for the corn-free months ahead. This is my favorite way to cook it; roasting the corn in the husks concentrates the corn's sweetness. When you peel back the husks, the kernels give off the most incredible smell. Corn is traditionally cooked this way in the Southwest and in Mexico, where street vendors sell whole ears sprinkled with chile, salt, and lime.

Cotija is a Mexican cheese that can be very soft and mild, or firm and pretty sharp, like Parmigiano. Use any *cotija* that is hard enough to grate for this recipe; it may also be labeled *queso anejado,* or aged cheese.

Serves 4

8 ears fresh corn
1 cup *cotija* cheese, finely grated
2 tablespoons ancho chile powder
2 limes, cut in half

1. Preheat oven to 425°F. Prepare the corn for roasting by removing all the silk from the top and all but one layer of the husks (the husks will protect the kernels from drying out in the oven). Dip each ear in water, arrange on a baking sheet, and roast 20–25 minutes.

2. Strip off the husks and discard, return the corn to the baking sheet, and sprinkle with the cheese and ancho chile powder. Return to the oven and roast for 5 minutes more. Remove from the oven and squeeze the limes over the corn. Serve immediately.

Cornmeal-Fried Okra with Corn Relish

I learned to fry okra from a lady who calls herself "The Kitchen Witch" of Eastern Tennessee. I wouldn't be surprised if she did have some supernatural powers: Her fried okra was the cleanest, simplest, and crispest I've ever had. There's no getting around it: Okra usually has a certain slime factor. Her cooking method eliminates it completely, with or without magic.

Okra and corn stewed together is a Southern classic, but this is an even better way to use those ingredients. The juicy, aromatic corn salad mixed with crisp-fried okra slices is really fantastic.

Serves 4

For the okra:

Vegetable oil for frying

2 cups yellow cornmeal

Salt and freshly ground pepper

1½ pounds okra, trimmed and cut into
½-inch lengths

For the corn relish:

2 tablespoons corn oil or vegetable oil

1 large onion, finely diced

2 cloves garlic, finely chopped

1 red bell pepper, stem and seeds removed,
finely diced

4 plum tomatoes, finely diced

2 cups fresh corn kernels

Salt and freshly ground pepper

Hot sauce

1. Make the okra: Heat 2 inches of oil in a large, deep saucepan over medium-high heat to 370°F. Preheat the oven to 200°F.

2. Place the cornmeal in a bag and season with salt and pepper. Toss the okra in the bag until coated. Working in batches to avoid crowding the pan, fry the okra until golden brown, 3–4 minutes. Drain on paper towels. Transfer to a baking sheet and keep warm in the oven.

3. Make the relish: Heat the corn or vegetable oil in a medium skillet over high heat. Add the onion and cook, stirring, until soft. Add the garlic and red pepper and cook, stirring, for 2 minutes. Add the tomatoes and corn and cook an additional 2 minutes. Season with salt and pepper and hot sauce to taste. Gently fold in the okra and serve immediately.

Creamed Kale with Caramelized Baby Onions

Creamed spinach was pretty much the only vegetable they served at the steakhouses my parents took me to as a kid. Maybe that's why I loved those dinners so much!

This recipe combines two American classic sides—creamed spinach and creamed onions—and it's wonderful with roasts and steaks. Kale has a sturdier texture than spinach and won't get mushy. Plunging a vegetable quickly into ice water as soon as it's cooked is a trick that chefs call "shocking"; it stops the cooking and sets that bright green color.

Serves 6–8

For the onions:

6 tablespoons unsalted butter
40 pearl onions, peeled
  Salt and freshly ground pepper
2 tablespoons sugar
2 cups Chicken Stock (page xiv), or
  low-sodium canned stock or water

For the kale:

3 cups milk
2 pounds kale, center stalk removed, and cut
  into 1-inch ribbons
3 tablespoons unsalted butter
1 onion, finely chopped
3 tablespoons flour
  Pinch of nutmeg
  Salt and freshly ground pepper

1. Make the onions: Melt the butter in a medium saucepan over medium heat. Add the onions, season with salt and pepper, and cook, stirring occasionally, until the onions begin to brown, about 10 minutes.

2. During the last 5 minutes, sprinkle with the sugar and stir. Add the liquid and raise the heat to medium-high. Cook, stirring frequently, until the onions are glazed and the liquid almost completely evaporates, about 10 minutes. Set aside.

3. Make the kale: Pour the milk into a saucepan and heat over medium heat just until it boils. Turn off the heat and set aside.

4. Meanwhile, bring a medium pot of salted water to a boil. Add the kale and cook until tender, 10–15 minutes. Prepare a bowl of ice water. Drain the kale, plunge it into ice water, and drain again.

5. Heat the butter in a medium saucepan over medium heat. Add the onion and cook, stirring, until soft. Whisk in the flour and cook 3–4 minutes, just until cooked through but not at all brown (reduce the heat if necessary). Whisk in the warm milk and cook until thickened. Season with nutmeg and salt and pepper to taste. Combine the kale and onions in a large bowl and toss with the cream sauce.

Swiss Chard with
Red Onions and Serrano Chile Vinegar

I love Southern-style collard greens, cooked long and slow. Swiss chard is another hearty green in the cabbage family, but it cooks quickly, tastes great, and keeps its bright color.

I accent the green with crisp-tender pieces of sweet red onion, and sprinkle the plate with an addictive vinegar infused with serrano chiles. It reminds me of barbecue joints in North Carolina, where each table gets a bottle of spicy vinegar to punch up the flavor of the pulled pork.

Serves 4–6

2½ pounds Swiss chard
8 ounces slab bacon, diced
2 red onions, halved and thinly sliced
2 cloves garlic, thinly sliced
   Salt and freshly ground pepper
¼ cup Serrano Chile Vinegar (see below)

1. Tear the leaves of the chard off the thick stalks. Discard the stalks and coarsely chop the leaves.

2. Cook the bacon in a large skillet over medium heat until the pieces have browned and the fat has rendered. Remove the bacon with a slotted spoon, reserve it, and pour off all but 2–3 tablespoons fat from the pan. Add the onions and cook over medium-high heat, stirring, until soft. Add the garlic and cook for 1 minute more. Add the chard, season with salt and pepper, and stir to coat the leaves in the fat. When it starts to wilt, add the bacon to the pan and stir. Add the vinegar and cook 2 minutes more. Serve with additional vinegar on the side.

Serrano Chile Vinegar

4 serrano chiles, coarsely chopped
2 cups white wine vinegar
1 teaspoon kosher salt

Bring the chiles, vinegar, and salt to a boil in a medium nonreactive saucepan. Turn off the heat, pour into a bowl, cover, and let steep at least 2 hours or overnight at room temperature. Strain through a fine strainer into a bottle or jar.

Butter Bean and Sweet Onion Succotash

Here's an idea: The U.S. Congress should officially proclaim that those starchy, pale green beans I love will be called "butter beans" from now on. I bet most of the Northerners who reject lima beans would love butter beans, even though they are exactly the same thing. Butter beans sound so much more appetizing.

Whatever you call them, it just isn't a succotash without butter beans and corn. I add a little heavy cream to bind the mixture and keep it moist. Fresh parsley and hot sauce keep the flavors bright, and the crunch of fresh red onion livens up the texture.

Serves 4

For the beans:

1 pound shelled fresh butter beans (also known as lima beans), or use thawed frozen beans

1 tablespoon unsalted butter

1 tablespoon salt

For the succotash:

2 tablespoons unsalted butter

1 large sweet onion, such as Vidalia or Walla Walla, peeled and finely diced

½ red onion, peeled and finely diced

1 large red pepper, cored, seeded, and finely diced

2 cloves garlic, finely chopped

1 cup fresh corn kernels

½ cup heavy cream

Few dashes of hot sauce

Salt and freshly ground pepper

¼ cup finely chopped fresh flat-leaf parsley

1. Cook the beans: Place the fresh or thawed frozen beans, butter, and salt in a large saucepan and add water to barely cover. Cover the pot, bring to a boil, and cook over medium-high heat 8–10 minutes or until just tender. Drain the beans in a colander set over a bowl, reserving 1 cup of the cooking liquid.

2. Make the succotash: Melt the butter in a medium saucepan over medium-high heat. Add the onions and pepper and cook, stirring, until soft, 8–10 minutes. Add the garlic and cook for 1 minute. Add the corn and the reserved bean cooking liquid and cook until the corn is tender and the cooking liquid has evaporated. Stir in the beans, cream, and hot sauce, and cook until the mixture has absorbed some of the cream and the sauce is thick. Season to taste with salt and pepper and stir in the parsley.

Postcard from Lexington, Kentucky

The most beautiful sight in Lexington, Kentucky, has got to be all those gorgeous Thoroughbreds exercising in the grassy corrals around Keeneland, the local racetrack. But Kentucky country ham, Kentucky fried chicken, and Kentucky bourbon right out of the barrel all run a close second. Or maybe the most beautiful thing of all is a frosty mint julep in a pewter cup, overflowing with cracked ice and mint sprigs.

I figured that the place to get to the heart of Kentucky cooking had to be Keeneland, so I planned to join the racegoers, sipping juleps all day and spooning up burgoo, the classic Kentucky stew. Eddie Mars, Keeneland's chef, does make a mean burgoo; his version is a savory, comforting stew of beef, okra, tomatoes, onion, beans, corn, thyme (and a few other vegetables), slowly cooked together overnight. Nobody seems to use possum, squirrel, or rabbit in their burgoo anymore, although Eddie told me about an old recipe that starts with a hundred gallons of water and twelve squirrels. Burgoo's come a long way, baby.

You can get a great mint julep at Keeneland's Maker's Mark bar, totally authentic down to the shortened straw that makes you get your nose right down into the mint while you sip. But that was just the beginning of my bourbon odyssey. The afternoon I spent at the Labrot & Graham bourbon distillery was a great learning experience. Sure, I knew that bourbon was a spicy-sweet-smoky spirit that I loved, but what I didn't know was just how much dedication goes into making it so good.

The Thoroughbred trainers at Keeneland racetrack told me the same thing about Kentucky that the bourbon brewers did: They all say that the limestone-rich water that runs through the state is what makes their product (whether horses or bourbon) so good. Bourbon is the only spirit native to America, and almost all the bourbon in America is made in Kentucky, in one of the state's ten large distilleries (those are the legal ones).

Starting with crushed rye, barley, and corn (at least 51 percent corn, which makes it bourbon and not whiskey), 14,000 pounds of grain is combined with yeast and fresh, local water in a wooden vat. Pretty soon, the sugar in the corn starts to ferment, making the mixture bubble as furiously as the water in a Jacuzzi. But after seven days, the fermentation is over and the surface is as smooth as glass. At that point, the clear spirit is 157 proof, or almost 80 percent pure alcohol. Sane people don't drink it yet, but hey, they said I should try it for the green apple and cherry flavors. But between coughing and trying to keep my eyes from tearing, I couldn't taste much. That stuff is *strong.*

Later on, though, I couldn't stop tasting it. It sounds strange, but bourbon is aged in oak barrels that are actually *burned* before the raw spirit goes in. The interaction between the charred wood and the liquor is what gives bourbon its beautiful caramelized color and smooth, smoky flavor. That interaction goes on for five to eight years, until the Master Distiller decides that a particular barrel is ready to add its flavor to the mix. Most of the bourbon on the market is blended from many different barrels into a uniform product, but it's fun to taste the single-barrel ones if you can find them. And I'll definitely be using my Kentucky bourbon as a soak for vanilla beans, making a vanilla bourbon that's amazing in desserts and cocktails.

The corn that makes Kentucky bourbon so smooth and sweet also goes to feed the Kentucky hogs—and then, of course, it turns into Kentucky ham. I love the smoky-sweet flavor that makes good ham, but in New York, it seems easier for me to get Italian prosciutto or Spanish *jamón* than Southern country ham. Kentucky ham is always dry-cured, rubbed with either coarse salt or sugar (I liked the salted ones best). After curing, the ham is smoked, then hung up to age and dry out in the air. It can stay there for as little as six months and up to a year—the flavor keeps getting more intense and meaty (and the outside gets covered with an ugly, white mold). The end result, sliced thin and stuffed into split biscuits—either crisp, beaten ones or soft, flaky, country ones—makes one of the all-time great food combinations.

Kentucky seemed to be full of fun things to eat, like ham and biscuits, Kentucky Hot Brown sandwiches (a ham and turkey sandwich in a little casserole dish, baked with cheese sauce and bacon), and beer cheese, a savory mix of cheddar cheese, beer, mayonnaise, Worcestershire sauce, and hot sauce, which you eat on celery sticks.

I did have some more elegant meals, also based on real Kentucky traditions. Lamb fries (aka testicles) are a spring ritual; one chef took the baseball-sized glands and turned them into a dish of golden, crisp-fried slices that were creamy on the inside and as elegant as a French entrée of sweetbreads. They also fry up fresh, local morels in season: I was fascinated to learn that the big mushrooms are sometimes called "dry-land fish" in Kentucky. I left Kentucky feeling full and happy. Whether they're die-hard traditionalists who stick to burgoo and juleps, or easygoing types devoted to Hot Brown sandwiches and beer, Kentuckians are good people— and good cooks.

Desserts

Caramelized Apple-Blackberry Cobbler

Deep-Dish Apple Pie with Molasses

Pear Tart with Hazelnut–Brown Sugar Crust

Fresh Fig–Blackberry Shortcake with Maple Whipped Cream

Persimmon and Cinnamon Pudding

Banana Beignets with Orange-Caramel Sauce

Maple Custard with Gingersnaps

Pistachio Pralines

Warm Coconut-Filled Chocolate Cakes

Cinnamon-Ginger *Churros* with Milk Chocolate Dipping Sauce

Guava and Cheese Tarts

Sweet Potato and Allspice Pie with a Benne Seed Crust

Root Beer–Toasted Coconut Float

Caramel Ice Cream

Caramelized Apple-Blackberry Cobbler

Cobblers, crumbles, and crisps — I love them all. These homey treats, combinations of ripe, sweet fruit and pastry toppings, are some of the oldest tricks in the dessert book. Blackberries and apples are an untraditional but fantastic combination.

Serves 8

For the filling:

1 stick (8 tablespoons) unsalted butter, cut into tablespoons

15 firm Golden Delicious apples, peeled, cored, and sliced ¼-inch thick

1⅓ cups granulated sugar

2 cups blackberries

For the topping:

4 cups all-purpose flour

¾ cup granulated sugar

1 teaspoon salt

1 ½ teaspoons baking powder

½ teaspoon baking soda

1 teaspoon nutmeg

1 teaspoon ground ginger

2½ sticks (10 ounces) very cold unsalted butter, cut into small pieces

2 cups buttermilk

2 tablespoons turbinado (raw) sugar

1. Cook the apples: Melt 2 tablespoons of the butter in a large skillet over high heat. Add ¼ of the apples and cook, tossing, just until lightly browned. Add ⅓ cup of sugar and continue cooking, stirring often, until the sugar melts and turns brown and the apples are caramelized. Remove to a large, deep baking dish, at least 11 inches square. Spread the blackberries on top. Repeat the cooking process with the remaining butter, apples, and sugar, and spread on top of the blackberries.

2. Make the topping: Combine the flour, sugar, salt, baking powder, baking soda, nutmeg, and ginger in a large bowl. Add the butter and rub it into the flour mixture until the mixture resembles coarse crumbs. Add the buttermilk and mix just until combined. (Do not overmix.)

3. Preheat the oven to 350°F. Top the apples with large spoonfuls of batter, covering the surface. (There may be a little batter left over.) Sprinkle with raw sugar and bake until the top is golden brown and cooked through, 30–40 minutes. Serve warm.

Deep-Dish Apple Pie with Molasses

I wouldn't dare leave out a recipe for apple pie in a book of American cooking, so here is my absolute favorite recipe. The molasses and spices bring out the flavor of the apples.

It's funny how firmly we believe that apple pie is American—there isn't a single country in which apples are grown where you can't find a version of it. French *tarte aux pommes,* German *apfeltorte,* and of course plain old English apple pie were baked for centuries before the first American apple was picked!

Serves 6–8

For the pastry crust:

- 3 cups all-purpose flour
- 1 tablespoon granulated sugar
- 1 teaspoon salt
- 12 tablespoons (1½ sticks) cold unsalted butter, cut into small pieces
- ½ cup cold vegetable shortening, cut into small pieces
- 6–8 tablespoons ice water

For the filling:

- 8 large Granny Smith apples, peeled, cored, halved, and cut into ¼-inch-thick slices
- 2 tablespoons fresh lemon juice
- 2 tablespoons molasses
- ¼ cup light brown sugar
- ¾ cup granulated sugar
- 2 tablespoons cornstarch
- 2 teaspoons ground cinnamon
- ¼ teaspoon ground nutmeg
- 2 tablespoons cold unsalted butter, cut into small pieces
- 3 tablespoons milk
- 3 tablespoons molasses sugar or turbinado (raw) sugar

1. Make the pastry: Place the flour, sugar, and salt in the bowl of a food processor and pulse twice, just to combine. Add the butter and short-ening and pulse until the mixture resembles coarse crumbs. Add the water 1 tablespoon at a time, pulsing after each addition, until the dough just starts to hold together. Turn out the dough onto a lightly floured surface and gently form into a disk. Cover with plastic wrap and refrigerate at least 1 hour, or overnight.

2. Remove dough from the refrigerator and divide it in half. Roll out each half on a lightly floured surface into a 13-inch circle. Line a pie plate (9 inches across and at least 1½ inches deep) with one dough circle.

3. Toss the apples, lemon juice, molasses, sugar, cornstarch, cinnamon, and nutmeg together in a large bowl. Transfer the apple mixture into the prepared pie dish and dot the butter over the top of the filling. Place the remaining dough over the filling. With a small knife, trim the dough to make an even 1-inch overhang all the way around. Tuck the overhanging dough under, making a thick edge, and crimp the edges with a fork or your fingers. Refrigerate the pie for 15 minutes.

4. Meanwhile, preheat the oven to 400°F and position the oven rack in the lower third of the oven. Remove the pie from the refrigerator and place on a baking sheet. Using a knife, cut 6 vents in the top. Brush the top of the pie with the milk and sprinkle with the molasses sugar. Bake the pie for 20 minutes, then reduce the heat to 350°F and continue baking 25–30 minutes more, or until golden brown on top and the juices are bub-bling. Let rest 30 minutes before serving.

Pear Tart with Hazelnut–Brown Sugar Crust

Pears and hazelnuts taste wonderful together, probably because they flourish side by side in the Pacific Northwest. American cooks have really begun to appreciate the concept of *terroir*, the French rule about both wine and food that says, basically: "If it grows together, it goes together."

Oregon's Willamette Valley and Washington's Columbia River basin are two of the most fertile areas in America, and so many delicious fruits and berries grow there that it's almost overwhelming. Portland, Oregon, is located just where the Willamette and Columbia meet, and not surprisingly, it's a great food town. I had a memorable pear tart there, as simple and delicious as this one.

Serves 6–8

For the crust:

6 tablespoons cold unsalted butter

2 tablespoons granulated sugar

2 tablespoons light brown sugar

⅛ teaspoon salt

1 egg

1¼ cups all-purpose flour, sifted after measuring

⅓ cup finely ground hazelnuts

For the filling:

¼ cup apricot preserves

2 tablespoons apricot brandy or plain brandy

7 Anjou or Barlett pears, slightly underripe, peeled, cored, halved, and cut into ¼-inch-thick slices

2 tablespoons granulated sugar

2 tablespoons cold unsalted butter, cut into small pieces

1. Make the crust: In a mixer, cream the butter and sugar until light and fluffy. Add the salt and egg and mix until combined. Stir in the flour and hazelnuts with a wooden spoon just until combined. Form the dough into a disk, wrap in plastic wrap, and refrigerate at least 4 hours or overnight.

2. On a floured surface, roll out the dough into a 12-inch circle. Transfer to a 10-inch tart pan with a fluted removable rim and press the crust into the bottom and sides of the pan. Refrigerate 30 minutes.

3. Finish the tart: Preheat the oven to 375°F and place an oven rack in the lower third of the oven. Combine the preserves and brandy in a small saucepan and bring to a boil. Brush the bottom of the tart with some of the mixture. Arrange the pears in the crust, using the largest pieces around the rim of the tart, with the rounded edges up against the rim. Arrange another row of pears next to the first. Keep overlapping the slices to form a large rosette in the center. Tuck in any leftover slices, if desired.

4. Sprinkle the top of the tart with the sugar and dot with the butter. Bake 45–50 minutes. Remove from the oven and brush the top with the remaining glaze. Serve warm.

Fresh Fig–Blackberry Shortcake with Maple Whipped Cream

I love buttermilk biscuits, so a classic American shortcake has always been my favorite summer dessert. It's the combination of savory biscuits and sweet, fresh berries that gets me. Of course, you can use any seasonal berries you like. I find the texture of fresh figs totally irresistible, so I mix them in too; figs come into season at the end of the summer.

Serves 6

For the biscuits:

1¾ cups plus 1 tablespoon all-purpose flour

1½ tablespoons sugar

2 teaspoons baking powder

¼ teaspoon baking soda

¼ teaspoon salt

1 stick (8 tablespoons) very cold unsalted butter, cut into small pieces

½ cup buttermilk

3 tablespoons heavy cream

2 tablespoons turbinado (raw) sugar

For the fruit:

1 pint fresh ripe figs, quartered

1 pint fresh blackberries

½ cup granulated sugar

½ vanilla bean, split lengthwise and seeds scraped out with the tip of a sharp knife (or ½ teaspoon pure vanilla extract)

3 tablespoons Chambord (a berry liqueur) or crème de cassis

For the whipped cream:

1 cup cold heavy cream

½ vanilla bean, split lengthwise and seeds scraped out with the tip of a sharp knife (or ½ teaspoon pure vanilla extract)

3 tablespoons pure maple syrup

1. Make the biscuits: Preheat the oven to 350°F. Lightly grease a baking sheet. Combine the flour, sugar, baking powder, baking soda, and salt in a food processor and pulse a few times to combine. Add the butter and pulse just until the mixture resembles coarse crumbs. Add the buttermilk and pulse just until the mixture comes together. Remove the dough to a lightly floured work surface and use your hands to press it out into a square, about ¼-inch thick. Use a biscuit or cookie cutter (or a clean empty can) to cut out six 3-inch circles and place them on the prepared pan. Brush the tops with heavy cream and sprinkle with sugar. Bake until golden brown, 12–15 minutes. Remove to a baking rack and let cool.

2. Meanwhile, make the fruit mixture: Fold together all the ingredients in a bowl and let macerate for 30 minutes at room temperature.

3. When ready to serve, make the whipped cream: Place all the ingredients in a large bowl and whip to soft peaks. Slice the biscuits in half and place the bottom halves on serving plates. Divide the fruit on top. Top the fruit with a few large dollops of maple whipped cream. Gently place the top halves of the biscuits on the whipped cream and serve.

Persimmon and Cinnamon Pudding

Half the fun of being a chef is that you never know what's going to turn up in your kitchen. I remember when I tasted a persimmon for the first time, thanks to Janice Pakula, a sous-chef I worked with who made this comforting dessert. She knew that the key to enjoying the juicy-sweet flavor of persimmons is waiting until they're very, very ripe. An unripe persimmon can pucker your mouth faster than biting into a lemon, but a ripe one tastes like nectarines and quinces.

Wild persimmons are native to the Midwest, but it's the cultivated Asian *hachiya* persimmon that you see in markets in the fall. Our native persimmons are smaller and almost impossible to find outside their home turf of Indiana, Illinois, and Missouri.

Serves 4–6

6 very ripe *hachiya* (Asian) persimmons
1½ cups granulated sugar
½ cup light brown sugar
2 large eggs, lightly beaten
1½ cups milk
1½ cups flour
1 teaspoon baking powder
1 teaspoon ground cinnamon
½ teaspoon salt
½ cup heavy cream
2 tablespoons unsalted butter, melted
Whipped cream, vanilla ice cream, or cinnamon ice cream for serving

1. Preheat the oven to 350°F. Butter a baking dish, about 9 by 13 inches. Cut the persimmons in half and run them through a food mill into a bowl. Add the sugar and eggs to the persimmon pulp. Add the milk and stir until combined.

2. Sift together the flour, baking powder, cinnamon, and salt, and add to the milk mixture. Whisk until combined. Whisk in the heavy cream and melted butter and pour the mixture into the prepared dish. Bake until dark brown and a toothpick inserted into the center comes out clean, 55–60 minutes. Serve warm with whipped cream or ice cream.

Banana Beignets with Orange-Caramel Sauce

It doesn't matter to me what you call your fried dough: funnel cakes, *zeppoli,* beignets, doughnuts, fritters, or *churros*. I like them all. In New Orleans, beignets are for breakfast, with chicory coffee. These sesame-sprinkled ones are great for breakfast or dessert, especially when drizzled with a tangy, orange-infused caramel sauce.

It's important to whip the egg whites just before you fold them into the batter, so they don't deflate and lose all that air you whipped into them.

Serves 4–6

For the orange-caramel sauce:
1 cup granulated sugar
¼ cup water
½ cup freshly squeezed orange juice
¼ cup heavy cream

For the beignets:
¼ cup cornstarch
¼ cup all-purpose flour
Pinch of salt
3 tablespoons sesame seeds, toasted (page xiii)
1 egg, separated
½ cup beer
3 cups vegetable or canola oil
6 medium bananas
Confectioners' sugar for dusting

1. Make the sauce: Combine the sugar and water in a medium nonreactive saucepan over medium heat. Without stirring, bring the mixture to a boil and boil until dark amber in color, 10–12 minutes, swirling the pan occasionally to even out the color. Slowly pour in the orange juice and heavy cream and cook until smooth. Cook until the sauce is slightly thickened, 2–3 minutes. Set aside.

2. Make the beignets: Combine the cornstarch, flour, salt, and 2 tablespoons of the sesame seeds in a medium bowl. Make a small well in the center of the flour mixture. Drop the egg yolk into the well. Mix the egg yolk and dry ingredients together with a whisk, while slowly pouring in the beer. When the mixture is smooth (a few lumps are okay), cover and refrigerate for 30 minutes.

3. Heat the oil in a medium saucepan fitted with a deep-frying thermometer over medium heat to 365°F. When the batter is chilled, beat the egg white at medium-high speed until soft peaks form. Beat for a few more seconds, then fold the egg whites gently into the chilled mixture.

4. Peel the bananas and cut in half lengthwise. Cut each half into 3 equal pieces. When the oil is ready, drop the banana pieces 4 at a time into the batter. Coat completely with batter, then drop the pieces into the hot oil, working in batches to avoid crowding the pot. Fry for 1 minute, until golden brown, and remove from the oil with a slotted spoon. Drain on paper towels. Bring the oil back to 365°F before frying the next batch.

5. Sprinkle the beignets with confectioners' sugar and remaining sesame seeds. Serve immediately with Orange-Caramel Sauce (the sauce can be rewarmed in the microwave or over low heat, if you wish).

Maple Custard with Gingersnaps

Rich, cool, creamy homemade custard is something I just can't keep my spoon away from. I love the purely American flavor (sugar maples only grow in North America) of maple, and I use it often as a sweetener in savory dishes, to balance out the heat from chiles. This dessert shows off the maple flavor on its own, but you know I can't resist a little spice — so I serve it with peppery gingersnaps. The combination is crisp and creamy, spicy and smooth.

Serves 4

1 cup heavy cream
1 cup milk
½ vanilla bean, split lengthwise
2 whole eggs
3 egg yolks
1 cup maple syrup
1½ teaspoons maple extract
¼ cup bourbon
   Pinch of salt

1. Bring the cream, milk, and vanilla bean to a boil in a medium nonreactive saucepan. Remove from heat and let cool slightly.

2. Whisk together eggs, yolks, and maple syrup in a large bowl and slowly whisk in the warm milk. Strain through a fine strainer into a clean bowl. Ladle the custard into 6 ramekins or custard cups.

3. Preheat the oven to 325°F. Arrange the ramekins in a roasting pan and pour in hot tap water until it comes halfway up the sides of the ramekins. Bake until just set, 30–40 minutes. Let cool at room temperature, then cover and refrigerate at least 2 hours or overnight.

Gingersnaps

8 tablespoons (1 stick) cool unsalted butter
1¾ cups sugar
2 eggs
¼ cup molasses
¼ cup maple syrup
2½ cups bread flour
2 teaspoons baking soda
2 teaspoons ginger
½ teaspoon cinnamon
¼ teaspoon each, black pepper, cloves, allspice, and dry mustard

1. Preheat the oven to 350°F and line 2 cookie sheets with parchment paper or nonstick baking mats. In a mixer fitted with a paddle attachment, cream the butter and 1½ cups of the sugar until pale and fluffy. Add the eggs one at a time, mixing after each addition just until incorporated. Add the molasses and maple syrup and mix until combined. Sift together the flour, baking soda, 1 teaspoon of the ginger, cinnamon, black pepper, cloves, allspice, and dry mustard. Gradually add the dry ingredients to the wet ingredients and mix until combined.

2. Mix together the remaining ¼ cup of sugar and 1 teaspoon of ginger in a small bowl. Form the dough into ½-inch balls, roll in the ginger sugar, and place them 2 inches apart on the prepared baking sheet. Bake 8–10 minutes or until set and tops begin to crack. Remove to a baking rack and let cool for 10 minutes.

Pistachio Pralines

Cream, sugar, and nuts — how can you go wrong with pralines? They're easy to make, too. The French brought pralines to Louisiana, and made them with the buttery pecans they found growing there instead of traditional almonds. I've changed the recipe yet again, because I like pistachios best, for flavor and for the bright green color. The pralines can be eaten as is, or crumbled over ice cream.

Makes 18

1 cup firmly packed light brown sugar
1 cup granulated sugar
½ cup heavy cream
1 tablespoon finely chopped orange zest
2 tablespoons unsalted butter
1¼ cups shelled and toasted pistachio nuts (page xiii)

1. Combine both kinds of sugar, the cream, and the zest in a medium heavy saucepan fitted with a candy thermometer. Bring to a boil over medium heat, stirring constantly. When the temperature reaches 228°F, stir in the butter and pistachios. Continue cooking, stirring constantly, until the mixture reaches 236°F. Remove the pan from the heat and let cool for 5 minutes.

2. Line a large baking sheet with parchment paper or nonstick baking mats. Beat the mixture with a wooden spoon until the candy coats the pistachios well. Drop the pralines by tablespoons onto the prepared pan. Let cool. Store in an airtight container.

Warm Coconut-Filled Chocolate Cakes

If you thought dessert couldn't get any better than warm chocolate cake, think again. We drop a ball of frozen coconut *ganache*, a paste of chocolate and cream, into each one. As the cake bakes, the ganache melts into an oozing center of fragrant coconut. The result is unbelievable, and the best variation of German chocolate cake you can imagine. By the way, German chocolate cake is American, not German at all: "German" is a brand of chocolate.

Serves 6

For the filling:

9 ounces white chocolate, coarsely chopped
¾ cup unsweetened coconut milk
1 teaspoon coconut extract
¼ cup unsweetened coconut, toasted
(see page xiii)

For the cake:

1 cup sugar
¾ cup water
3 sticks (12 ounces) unsalted butter, cut into
large dice, plus extra for buttering molds
12 ounces semisweet or bittersweet chocolate,
chopped
5 whole eggs plus 5 egg yolks

1. Make the filling: Place the chopped white chocolate in a bowl. Bring the coconut milk to a simmer in a small saucepan. Pour the hot coconut milk over the chocolate, let sit for 1 minute to melt the chocolate, then whisk until smooth. Add the extract and fold in the coconut. Mold the mixture into six 1-inch balls. Place the balls on a baking sheet and freeze for at least 1 hour or, covered, overnight.

2. Make the cakes: Preheat the oven to 350°F. Thickly butter six 6-ounce ramekins. In a medium saucepan, combine the sugar, water, and butter. Bring to a boil. Remove from heat and add the chocolate, stirring until melted and smooth.

3. In a mixing bowl, combine the eggs and egg yolks and beat to mix well. Slowly add the chocolate mixture and mix well. Pour into the prepared molds. Place a coconut ball into the center of each mold and bake 8–10 minutes. Remove from oven and let stand a few minutes.

Cinnamon-Ginger *Churros* with Milk Chocolate Dipping Sauce

Churros, **crisp golden lengths of fried dough, are a favorite snack in border states like New Mexico and Texas. They're usually served with a cup of cocoa, made from the delicious Mexican chocolate that is flavored with cinnamon. I like** *churros* **as breakfast** *or* **as dessert, spiced with ginger and cinnamon and dunked into warm chocolate.**

Serves 4–6

For the *churros:*

2½ cups water
2 tablespoons unsalted butter
1 teaspoon salt
2 teaspoons ground ginger
2½ cups all-purpose flour
2 tablespoons dark rum
   Canola oil
1 cup granulated sugar mixed with
2 tablespoons ground cinnamon

For the sauce:

16 ounces good-quality milk chocolate, such as Lindt, coarsely chopped
1½ cups heavy cream

1. Make the dough: Bring the water, butter, and salt to a boil in a large saucepan. Reduce the heat to medium, add the ginger to the flour, and pour in the flour all at once. Stir with a wooden spoon until the mixture forms a fairly firm, elastic ball that comes away from the sides of the pan. Stir in the rum.

2. Transfer the mixture to the bowl of an electric mixer fitted with the paddle attachment. Beat the dough at medium speed for 1 minute. Transfer to a bowl (or just remove the mixer bowl from the stand) and cover loosely with foil. Let cool to room temperature.

3. Heat 2 inches of canola oil in a large skillet to 350°F. Line a baking sheet with parchment paper or nonstick baking mats. Insert a large (#820) star tip into a pastry bag and fill the bag with half the dough. Pipe 4-inch lengths of dough onto the baking sheet. Repeat with the remaining dough.

4. Make the sauce: Place the chocolate in a medium nonreactive bowl. Bring the cream to a simmer in a small saucepan. Pour the hot cream over the chocolate and let sit for 2 minutes, then whisk until smooth.

5. Just before serving, fry the *churros* in the oil, four at a time, 3–4 minutes, or until golden brown and cooked through. Remove the *churros* to a large plate lined with paper towels and dust generously with the cinnamon sugar. Pour the sauce into individual ramekins and serve warm with the *churros.*

Guava and Cheese Tarts

Café Versailles, one of Miami's oldest Cuban cafés, is my favorite spot for a guava-and-cream-cheese pastry and a *ching* or two (or three). *Ching* is the locals' name for the tiny shots of espresso coffee they drink—sometimes as many as fifty per day!

If you don't have tartlet pans, make the pastry rounds smaller and press them into nonstick muffin cups. Or just make one big tart!

Makes 8

For the pastry crust:

1¼ cups all-purpose flour
1 tablespoon granulated sugar
Pinch of salt
4 tablespoons cold unsalted butter, cut into small pieces
2 tablespoons cold vegetable shortening, cut into small pieces
4–6 tablespoons ice water
1 large egg, lightly beaten with 1 tablespoon water

For the filling:

½ cup cream cheese, softened
1 cup farmer's cheese, softened
⅔ cup granulated sugar
1 large egg, lightly beaten
1 tablespoon finely chopped orange zest
½ teaspoon ground cinnamon
1 teaspoon pure vanilla extract
Pinch of salt

For the topping:

⅔ cup guava paste (see Sources, page 231)
3 tablespoons freshly squeezed orange juice

1. Make the pastry: Place the flour, sugar, and salt in the bowl of a food processor and pulse twice, just to combine. Add the butter and shortening and pulse until the mixture resembles coarse crumbs. Add the water 1 tablespoon at a time, pulsing after each addition, until the dough just starts to hold together. Turn the dough out onto a lightly floured surface and gently form into a disk. Cover with plastic wrap and refrigerate at least 1 hour, or overnight.

2. Remove the dough from the refrigerator and let warm up for 5 minutes. On a lightly floured surface, using a floured rolling pin, roll the dough into a rectangle about ⅛-inch thick. Using a cookie cutter or rim of a thin glass, cut the dough into 3½-inch rounds. Gather the scraps into a ball, reroll them, and cut more rounds. Fit the dough rounds into ungreased 2½-inch tart pans, pressing them gently against the bottoms and sides. With the tines of a fork, gently prick the bottom of the crusts (don't break through the crust). Place the pans in the freezer and freeze for 15 minutes.

3. Meanwhile, preheat the oven to 375°F. Arrange the tart crusts on a baking sheet and brush the insides with the beaten egg mixture. Bake 15–20 minutes or until golden brown. Let cool on a baking rack for 10 minutes. Reduce the temperature of the oven to 350°F.

4. Make the cheese filling: Place the cheeses and sugar in a medium bowl and mix with a hand mixer until smooth. Add the egg, zest, cinnamon, vanilla, and salt, and mix until combined.

5. Make the guava topping: Whisk the ingredients together in a small bowl until combined.

6. Spoon the filling into the tart shells, dividing it evenly and filling each crust to within ¼ inch of the top. Spread about 1 tablespoon of the guava mixture over the top of each tart, arrange on a baking sheet, and bake for 20 minutes or until the filling is set and doesn't jiggle when lightly shaken. Cool to room temperature on a rack before serving.

Sweet Potato and Allspice Pie with a Benne Seed Crust

Sweet potato pie and benne seeds are Georgia classics, but I don't think anyone's put them together like this before. Sesame seeds were brought to this country by African captives, who called them *benne*, and considered the tiny seeds good luck. Benne wafers, buttery sesame cookies, are popular in Savannah; the cookie crust for this fluffy pie is a lot like them. Serve it with fresh, unsweetened whipped cream.

Serves 6–8

For the pastry crust:
14 whole graham crackers
2 tablespoons benne (sesame) seeds
1 tablespoon dark brown sugar
4 tablespoons unsalted butter, melted

For the filling:
2 sweet potatoes (about 1 pound total)
1½ cups light cream
3 large eggs
½ cup loosely packed dark brown sugar
¼ cup granulated sugar
1 teaspoon ground cinnamon
1 teaspoon allspice
¼ teaspoon nutmeg
Pinch of salt
Whipped cream for serving

1. Make the crust: Preheat the oven to 325°F. Break the graham crackers into pieces and place in a food processor with the benne seeds and brown sugar. Pulse until finely ground. Add the melted butter and pulse 2–3 times until the mixture just comes together. Press the mixture into the bottom and sides of a 9-inch pie plate. Bake until golden brown and set, 10–12 minutes. Remove from the oven and let cool.

2. Make the filling: Preheat the oven to 375°F. Prick the potatoes all over with a fork and place on a baking sheet. Bake until completely soft, 50–60 minutes. When cool enough to handle, slice the potatoes in half and scoop out the flesh. Place the flesh in a large bowl and add the remaining ingredients. Using a hand mixer, mix the ingredients until well mixed and smooth. Strain the mixture through a medium strainer into the prepared pie crust to remove any tough fibers.

3. Place the pie on a baking sheet and bake 40–45 minutes or until a knife inserted in the center comes out clean. Cool on a wire rack for 1 hour. Serve warm or cold with whipped cream.

Root Beer–Toasted Coconut Float

The all-American flavor of root beer is pretty much indescribable; we love it, but we don't really know what's in it. Originally, root beer was a real beer, fermented and a little bit alcoholic. It was flavored with native plants like sassafras and sarsaparilla, plus a combination of cherry, wintergreen, caramel, and ginger. Sounds weird—tastes great.

The spicy root-beer flavor is great with creamy coconut in this grown-up dessert float. The coconut ice cream is fantastic, but if you don't have an ice cream maker, you can just swirl 1½ cups of toasted coconut into softened vanilla ice cream. Freeze solid before serving.

Serves 4

For the coconut ice cream:

- 3 cups unsweetened flaked coconut
- 2 cups unsweetened coconut milk
- 12 large egg yolks
- 1 cup granulated sugar
- 2 tablespoons coconut extract
- 2 cups crème fraîche

To finish:

- 1 quart best-quality root beer, very cold
  Whipped cream (optional)
  Toasted coconut (optional)

1. At least a day before you plan to serve, start the ice cream: Heat the oven to 350°F. Spread the coconut on a baking sheet and toast, checking frequently after the first 5 minutes. Stir every 5 minutes for even browning. When the coconut smells toasty and looks slightly browned, after 10–20 minutes, remove immediately. Transfer 1½ cups of the toasted coconut to a medium bowl. Add the coconut milk, stir well, cover with plastic wrap, and refrigerate overnight. Set the remaining 1½ cups toasted coconut aside.

2. The next day, pour the coconut milk mixture through a strainer into a medium saucepan. Discard the coconut and bring the mixture to a simmer over low heat. Whisk the egg yolks and sugar together in a large bowl until pale and fluffy. Whisk in ¼ cup of the hot coconut milk, then repeat (this is to gradually raise the temperature of the eggs). Pour the egg mixture into the coconut mixture in the saucepan. Cook over low heat, stirring constantly with a wooden spoon, until thick enough to coat the back of the spoon. Half-fill a large bowl with ice water. Strain the mixture into a smaller bowl and rest it in the ice water. Let cool, stirring frequently. When cold, whisk in the extract, the crème fraîche, and the remaining toasted coconut. Process in an ice-cream machine according to the manufacturer's instructions. Scrape into a container and freeze.

3. To serve, place 3 scoops of coconut ice cream in a tall soda glass. Fill to the top with root beer. Top with a large dollop of whipped cream and more toasted coconut, if desired.

Caramel Ice Cream

My friend Katie Brown comes from a big family on Mackinac Island, a beautiful spot off Michigan's Upper Peninsula, where cars are forbidden and where she seems to know every last resident. As a city kid, I've always been fascinated by her Mackinac Island stories—and her many family recipes. Caramel ice cream is a Brown tradition; she even claims that there's an annual family-wide tasting, when every household makes up a batch! This delicious ice cream would be my entry.

Makes 1½ quarts

2 cups milk
4 cups heavy cream
12 egg yolks
2 cups sugar
2 tablespoons dark rum
¼ cup water

1. Bring the milk and 2 cups of the cream to a simmer in a medium saucepan. Combine the egg yolks and 1 cup sugar in a mixer fitted with a whisk attachment. Beat at medium-high speed until very thick and pale yellow, 3–5 minutes.

2. Whisking constantly, pour half of the warm milk mixture into the egg yolk mixture, whisking until blended. Stir the egg yolk mixture back into the remaining milk in the saucepan. Cook the mixture over medium heat, stirring constantly with a wooden spoon, until mixture is thick enough to coat the back of the spoon, about 10 minutes. Prepare a large bowl of ice water. Strain the custard into a medium bowl and rest the bowl in the ice water. Whisk in the rum and let cool.

3. Combine the remaining 1 cup sugar and the water in a medium nonreactive saucepan over medium heat. Without stirring, cook the mixture until dark amber in color, 10–12 minutes, gently swirling the pan occasionally to even out the color. Remove the pan from the heat. While stirring the caramel, carefully pour in the remaining 2 cups of cream, and keep stirring until completely combined. Let cool about 30 minutes and stir into the custard. Refrigerate for at least 2 hours, or overnight. Freeze in an ice-cream maker according to the manufacturer's instructions.

Postcard from Long Island, New York

Long Island, a long, thin piece of land lying right up against the Atlantic Coast of New York State, is an island with two distinct personalities. At one end are the big, busy NYC boroughs of Brooklyn and Queens, but drive east for an hour or so, as I do most summer weekends, and you'll see the scenery change to farms and vineyards — and then to sand dunes and clam joints. I know I'm there when I realize the honking I hear is coming from ducks, not taxis!

At its eastern end, Long Island forks, making two spits of land that embrace Peconic Bay in the middle. (It looks kind of like a lobster claw, in fact, which is appropriate, considering how many lobsters I eat out there every summer.) The North Fork is the home of working farms, vineyards, and a very old fishing tradition. The South Fork is home to the Hamptons, a collection of towns with beautiful beaches, good restaurants, and a lot of people having a really great time.

With its sandy soil, sea air, and long, hot summers, Long Island is perfectly equipped for growing grapes, potatoes, and ducks. In the last twenty years, North Fork wines have added to the region's luster — and the potato and duck farms are harder to find. In 1900, there were one hundred Long Island duck farms; today, there are just two. Duck is one of my favorite things to cook; like any meat with a good proportion of fat, it picks up flavors very well. And that layer of fat means that ducks, unlike chickens, for example, are well equipped to weather the Long Island winters, which can be long and harsh. I visited the Jurgielewicz family duck farm, which looked like duck heaven: elbow room galore, lots of ponds to splash in, and plenty of company.

I also love duck because its richness makes it delicious with the crisp wines I like. And that's just the kind of wine the Long Island vintners produce. Native American Concord grapes, which can't be used for wine (we make them into grape juice and jelly, though), have always grown on the Island. But winemaking on Long Island, using the European *Vitis vinifera* grapes, really didn't get started until the seventies. Now, twenty different vineyards, mostly on the North Fork, make Chardonnays, Merlots, Cabernet Sauvignons, Cabernet Francs, Pinot Blancs, and other food-friendly wines that get better all the time.

Long Island wines are great with the food at Nick and Toni's, a top-notch restaurant with a serious dedication to local produce. The owners and the chef take advantage of the South Fork's great climate, just like farmers have for three hundred years — they grow their own herbs, greens, tomatoes, potatoes, asparagus, and corn for the restaurant. And they know just the kind of food that the rich and powerful like: full of flavor, and low-fat (or at least pretending to be!).

Even more than fine restaurants, I think a beach community has to have great places to get fried clams, lobster, doughnuts, ice cream, and other summertime indulgences. My favorite neighborhood place for lunch is called just that — Lunch — and it's known far and wide for its unbelievable lobster rolls, creamy lobster salad stuffed into a toasted hot dog bun. I could eat one every day for the rest of my life. Then it would always be summer!

Thanksgiving

Cranberry Martinis

Roasted Turkey with Pomegranate–Black Pepper Glaze and Fresh Sage-Smoked Chile Gravy

Skillet Cornbread Stuffing with Mushrooms, Herbs, and Andouille Sausage

Fresh Cranberry–Fig Relish

Gratin of Green Beans with Roasted Garlic and Shallots

Mashed Potatoes with Scallions and Crème Fraîche

Sweet Potato and Plantain Puree with Maple and Cinnamon

Pumpkin Bread Pudding with Molasses Whipped Cream

Cranberry Martinis

To give a charge to your next Thanksgiving dinner, serve this easy but beautiful cock-tail. All it takes is a saucepan of simple syrup (water and sugar) steeped with cranber-ries and vodka. The vodka takes on a red tint and tang from the cranberries, and sweet-ness from the syrup. The result is like a Cosmopolitan, but Thanksgiving-themed and easier to make.

Serves 8

2 cups sugar
1 cup water
2 cups fresh or thawed frozen cranberries
   A fifth (about 1 liter) of vodka
   Cranberries
   Lime wedges

1. At least three days before serving, bring the sugar and water to a boil in a medium saucepan and cook, swirling the pan occasionally, until the sugar is completely melted and the mixture is slightly thickened. Remove from the heat, stir in the cranberries, and let sit at room temperature for 2 hours. Pour the vodka into a large bowl and add the cooled cranberries. Let sit for at least 2 days, stirring occasionally. Strain the vodka into a bottle and chill overnight.

2. To serve, fill chilled martini glasses with the vodka. Add a few cranberries to each glass and garnish with a lime wedge.

Roasted Turkey with Pomegranate–Black Pepper Glaze and Fresh Sage-Smoked Chile Gravy

I believe that Thanksgiving dinner should have all the traditional elements, so I just add a few flavor twists to make the meal even better. For example, aromatic fresh sage is the classic herb for Thanksgiving stuffing and gravy: I think it's great combined with the smokiness of chipotle chiles.

A roasted turkey should always have a glossy brown skin, but it can be tough getting it that way without overcooking the flesh. I like to brush the bird at the end of the cooking with a brown glaze of pomegranate molasses, a common ingredient in Middle Eastern cooking. (It's not really molasses, just pomegranate juice reduced until thick and syrupy.) The juicy, sweet-sour flavor always reminded me of cranberries, so it makes perfect sense in Thanksgiving recipes.

Serves 6–8

For the turkey:

1 fresh turkey, about 16 pounds
1 stick (8 tablespoons) unsalted butter, softened
  Salt and freshly ground pepper
3 cups Chicken Stock (page xiv), or
    low-sodium canned stock
  Pomegranate–Black Pepper Glaze (see below)

For the gravy:

1 large onion, finely chopped
1 large carrot, peeled and finely chopped
2 stalks celery, finely chopped
3 cloves garlic, finely chopped
1 cup dry white wine
3 tablespoons flour
  Pan drippings
3 cups Chicken Stock (page xiv)
1 tablespoon chipotle puree (page xiii)
2 tablespoons finely chopped fresh sage
  Salt and freshly ground pepper

1. Cook the turkey: Preheat the oven to 450°F. Remove the neck, heart, gizzard, and so on from inside the turkey. Rinse the bird thoroughly inside and out with cold water and pat dry. Rub the entire surface with the butter and season the bird outside and in the cavity with salt and pepper.

2. Truss the turkey and place breast-up on a rack in a large roasting pan. Roast for about 45 minutes, until brown, basting every 15 minutes with stock. Reduce the temperature to 350°F and continue roasting for another 1¼ hours (continue basting every 15 minutes) or until an instant-read thermometer inserted in the thigh registers 180°F. For the last 20 minutes of roasting, *instead of basting with stock,* brush the entire surface of the turkey with 1 cup of the pomegranate glaze. Do not baste again; the glaze will form a crust. When the turkey is cooked through, remove from the oven and brush with the remaining glaze. Let rest at least 15 minutes before carving.

3. Make the gravy: Strain the drippings from the roasting pan into a medium saucepan and degrease the roasting pan, removing any visible fat from the surface with a spoon. Place the empty roasting pan (don't clean it) over two burners on top of the stove and turn the heat to medium-high. Add the onion, carrots, celery, and garlic to the pan and cook, stirring, until golden brown. Add the wine and cook, scraping the bottom of the pan, until completely reduced. Add the flour and cook, stirring constantly, 3–4 minutes, or until lightly golden brown. Add the degreased pan drippings, stock, and chipotle puree, and simmer until the sauce thickens and no longer tastes at all floury. Season to taste with salt. Strain the sauce into a bowl and stir in the sage.

4. To serve, cut down along each breast and remove it whole. Cut the breasts into slices, as you would slice a loaf of bread. Cut the thigh meat into chunks. Place the breast slices on a large serving platter and arrange the thigh meat and the legs on top. Pass the gravy in a pitcher or sauce-boat at the table.

Pomegranate–Black Pepper Glaze

1½ cups pomegranate molasses (see Sources, page 231)

3 tablespoons Dijon mustard

3 tablespoons prepared horseradish, drained

2 tablespoons coarsely ground black pepper
  Salt to taste

Whisk the ingredients together in a medium bowl.

Skillet Cornbread Stuffing with Mushrooms, Herbs, and Andouille Sausage

Here's the best way to make sure you have enough stuffing: Don't limit yourself to what you can stuff into the bird. An unstuffed bird cooks faster and more evenly—so I prefer to make a fabulous moist, spicy stuffing and bake it on the side until golden and crusty.

Cornbread and andouille, a smoky spiced sausage from Louisiana, are a great combination, and the fresh sage picks up on the flavor in the gravy. Using day-old cornbread means that it's dry enough to absorb the moisture and seasonings without getting mushy.

Serves 6–8

¾ pound andouille sausage or another spicy sausage, diced

3 tablespoons olive oil

1½ pounds assorted wild mushrooms (such as cremini, shiitake, and oyster), coarsely chopped

Salt and freshly ground pepper

2 red onions, finely diced

1 large carrot, finely diced

1 stalk celery, finely diced

3 cloves garlic, finely chopped

1 cup dry white wine

1 recipe Cast-Iron Skillet Yellow Cornbread (page 167), cut into cubes and dried out overnight

2 large eggs, lightly beaten

2–3 cups Chicken Stock (page xiv), or low-sodium canned stock

2 tablespoons chopped fresh sage

¼ cup chopped fresh parsley

1. Preheat the oven to 375°F. Heat a large ovenproof skillet over high heat until smoking. Add the sausage and cook, stirring, until golden brown. Remove with a slotted spoon and drain on a plate lined with paper towels.

2. Add 1 tablespoon of olive oil to the pan and heat over high heat. Add the mushrooms, season with salt and pepper, and cook, stirring, until lightly browned. Transfer the mushrooms to a plate.

3. Add 2 tablespoons of oil to the pan, add the onions, carrot, and celery, and cook, stirring, until soft, 5–7 minutes. Add the garlic and cook for 1 minute more. Add the wine and cook until completely reduced. Return the sausage and mushrooms to the pan and stir to combine. Transfer from the heat and let cool slightly.

4. Preheat the oven to 350°F. Place the cubed corn bread in a large bowl, add the sausage-mushroom mixture, the eggs, 2 cups of the stock, and the herbs. Mix well and add more stock if the mixture seems too dry. It should be fairly wet. Season with salt and pepper and return the mixture to the skillet. Bake in the oven 25–30 minutes, or until golden brown and firm.

Fresh Cranberry–Fig Relish

Tangy cranberry relish is a Thanksgiving classic, and you've got to make it fresh—it's the easiest holiday recipe there is. Cranberries and sugar are the basic ingredients, but fresh orange and ginger, plus onions and garlic, make it even better. I love the texture of figs here, but they can be omitted. Don't omit any of the sugar, though; cranberries aren't nearly as sweet as they look. They are packed with natural pectin, which makes the sauce jell as it cools.

Serves 6–8

3 tablespoons unsalted butter
1 large onion, finely diced
2 cloves garlic, finely chopped
3 tablespoons grated fresh gingerroot
2 cups orange juice
½ cup light brown sugar
1 pound cranberries
6 fresh or dried figs, cut into ¼-inch dice
1 tablespoon freshly grated orange zest

Melt the butter in a medium saucepan over medium-high heat. Add the onion, garlic, and ginger, and cook, stirring, until soft. Add the orange juice and brown sugar and cook until boiling. Add half of the cranberries and cook, stirring, until they pop. Add the remaining cranberries and cook for 5 minutes more. Remove from the heat and stir in the figs and zest. Let cool and serve at room temperature.

Gratin of Green Beans with Roasted Garlic and Shallots

This delicious side dish is my cleaned-up version of a classic green bean casserole. I keep the beans simple and fresh, then cover them with a layer of caramelized, concentrated onion flavor in the shape of roasted garlic cloves and shallots. A bubbling blanket of nutty Parmesan cheese on top binds it all together.

Serves 6–8

1½ pounds *haricots verts* (small French green beans) or thin, tender green beans, cut in half if very long

1½ sticks (12 tablespoons) unsalted butter

1 head roasted garlic (page xiii), cloves squeezed out and coarsely chopped

¾ cup freshly grated Parmesan cheese

4 shallots, roasted and thinly sliced (page xiii)
   Salt and freshly ground pepper

1. Bring a large pot of salted water to a boil, add the green beans, and blanch until just cooked through, about 2 minutes for very thin beans. Drain in a colander and rinse with cold water until cooled. Drain well and transfer to a medium baking dish.

2. Preheat the broiler. Melt the butter in a medium skillet over high heat. Add the garlic and shallots and cook, stirring, until the butter begins to brown. Pour the mixture over the green beans and mix well. Season to taste with salt and pepper and sprinkle the cheese evenly over the top. Place under the broiler and broil until the cheese is melted and golden brown. Let sit at room temperature for 5 minutes before serving.

Mashed Potatoes with Scallions and Crème Fraîche

It's just not Thanksgiving for me without mashed potatoes — a dish I'm always thankful for. This smooth puree is swirled with veins of tangy crème fraîche and studded with thin slices of scallion. It's rich, luxurious, and easy to make.

Mascarpone is a soft, fresh Italian cheese that is a little like our cream cheese; crème fraîche is a French product that resembles sour cream. If you can't find either one, use a combination of cream cheese and sour cream, beaten together until smooth.

Serves 6–8

5   pounds baking potatoes, such as Idaho or Russet, peeled and quartered
1   stick (8 tablespoons) unsalted butter, at room temperature
1   cup heavy cream
1   cup milk
1   cup crème fraîche or mascarpone
½   cup thinly sliced scallions
    Salt and freshly ground pepper

Boil the potatoes in salted water until soft. Drain well and return them to the pot. Place the pot over low heat, add the butter, heavy cream, milk, and crème fraîche and mash until smooth and heated through. Fold in the scallions and season to taste with salt and pepper.

Sweet Potato and Plantain Puree with Maple and Cinnamon

I can never decide between sweet potatoes and mashed potatoes for Thanksgiving dinner, so I just make both. The flavor of sweet potatoes make a great backdrop for two of my favorite aromatics: maple and cinnamon.

To give the sweet potatoes a smoother texture when mashed, I add a few sweet, ripe plantains to the mix. Look for plantains with skins that are almost completely black, with just a few spots of yellow.

Serves 6–8

5 large sweet potatoes, scrubbed
2 very ripe plantains
1 stick (8 tablespoons) unsalted butter, cut into 4 pieces
  Salt
2 teaspoons ground cinnamon
¼ cup plus 2 tablespoons maple syrup
¾ cup heavy cream

1. Preheat the oven to 375°F. Place the potatoes and plantains on a large baking sheet and roast until the potatoes are soft and the plantains are completely black, 50–60 minutes.

2. As soon as they are cool enough to handle, slice each potato in half lengthwise, scoop out the flesh, and place it in a large food processor. Peel the plantains and add the flesh to the sweet potatoes. Add the butter, salt, cinnamon, and ¼ cup maple syrup, and process until smooth. Add the cream and pulse until combined.

3. When ready to serve, preheat the oven to 350°F. Place the puree in a medium baking dish and bake for 10 minutes to heat through. Remove from the oven, drizzle the top with the remaining 2 tablespoons of maple syrup, and serve.

Pumpkin Bread Pudding with Molasses Whipped Cream

This wonderful recipe is the love child of pumpkin pie and bread pudding. Instead of a plain pie crust and dense pumpkin filling, this recipe gives you a gently spiced pumpkin custard, a scattering of rum-soaked raisins, and bites of tender bread. Softly whipped cream adds a hint of toasty molasses flavor.

If you like, you can bake this in individual ramekins for an even more golden crust.

Serves 6–8

For the pudding:

- ¾ cup raisins
- 1 cup dark rum
- Unsalted butter
- 5 eggs
- 3 egg yolks
- ¾ cup dark brown sugar
- ½ teaspoon ground nutmeg
- 1 teaspoon cinnamon
- ¼ teaspoon ground cloves
- ¼ teaspoon ground ginger
- ¼ teaspoon salt
- ¾ cup canned pumpkin puree (not preseasoned pumpkin pie filling)
- 2 cups heavy cream
- 1¾ cups whole milk
- 1 vanilla bean, split lengthwise, seeds scraped out with the tip of a sharp knife
- 1 large or 2 small loaves challah or brioche, cut into bite-size cubes and dried out overnight

For the whipped cream:

- 1½ cups very cold heavy cream
- 3 tablespoons molasses
- 2 teaspoons pure vanilla extract

1. Make the pudding: Place the raisins and rum in a small saucepan and bring to a boil over high heat. Remove from the heat and set aside to let the raisins plump for 30 minutes. Drain the raisins and set aside. Discard the rum.

2. Preheat the oven to 350°F and butter a 2-quart baking dish. In a large bowl, whisk together the whole eggs, egg yolks, and brown sugar until smooth. Add the spices, salt, pumpkin, cream, milk, raisins, and vanilla seeds, and whisk until smooth. Add the bread and stir gently to coat. Let sit for 10 minutes to let the bread soak. Scrape the mixture into the prepared pan. Set the baking dish into a larger deep pan and place on the center rack of the oven. Pour hot water into the larger pan until it comes halfway up the sides of the smaller one. Bake 50–60 minutes or until the pudding is almost completely set (it should still move a little in the middle when you shake the pan). Remove and let cool for 30 minutes before serving.

3. Make the whipped cream: Place all the ingredients in a large bowl and whip to soft peaks. Serve the pudding warm with the whipped cream.

Postcard from Vidalia, Georgia

Vidalia onions aren't just the most famous onions in the world; I think they may be the only famous onions in the world. But you can't really understand what a big deal Vidalia onions are until you've been to Vidalia, Georgia.

Vidalia onion country surrounds the pretty town of Vidalia, making a fifty-mile circle around it. What sets their product apart from the millions of tons of onions that grow in the rest of the country is the soil; their patch of ground is unusually low in sulfur (I didn't test it, but that's what the farmers told me). The onions are definitely the sweetest I've ever tasted, and the only ones that are so mild you can bite into them like an apple.

Over the last seventy years or so, farmer R. T. Stanley and others have figured out just how to irrigate and fertilize their onions to make them the best. But the weather has to cooperate. Stanley says, "When I'm growing them, I'm praying for it to rain; when I'm harvesting them, I'm praying for it not to rain." When the fresh onions come out of the ground, starting in April, they have green tops and soft skin. The sun helps them firm up and take on that dry, golden, papery shell. The farmers call this "curing," and when that's done, the onions go to market. But only between mid-April and Thanksgiving: That's how long one year's harvest lasts.

The only thing that's better than the onions in Vidalia is the people. They're great cooks, and *friendly*. Everybody wanted to help fix my Northern accent so that I could say the name of the town right. To set the record straight, it's "Vah-*day*-lia." I think.

The best meal I ever had in Vidalia was made by four different local cooks. For my appetizer, I went over to Ruth Underwood's house. Every year, Vidalia hosts a festival to celebrate the onion harvest, and Ruth is a four-time champion in the food competition. Her baked onion dip—chopped Vidalia onion, cheese, mayo, and garlic salt, baked together until rich and brown—is just the kind of dish I'll indulge in on a cold Sunday afternoon. And I loved her onion marmalade; the onions cooked way down until the natural sugars are brown and caramelized, then mixed with cayenne and vinegar for some spark.

For my supper, I lined up at Vidalia's best buffet, the Chatters café. In addition to fantastic fried chicken, biscuits, and pie, Kathy Mann introduced me to real Southern specialties you just don't see where I live—like turnip tops, butter beans, fried whole catfish, and fried fatback. I said yes to everything, washed it all down with cold glasses of sweet tea, and moved on to my next stop: dessert.

Marcia Suber and Anita Estroff are Vidalia's mistresses of classic Southern desserts. Marcia told me, "Every buffet line in Georgia has a banana pudding or a sweet potato souffle at the end of it," so I asked them to show me both. It was like cooking class with your favorite kooky aunts as teachers: Having a good time is just as important to them as being good cooks. I liked their attitude, and I also fell in love with the way those Southern ladies say my name: "Bobbeh." Most important though, their rich, creamy desserts were delicious.

If you missed the Vidalia onion harvest this year, you can start looking out for the new crop the farmers are working on: Vidalia carrots, just as sweet and juicy as the onions. You know I can't wait.

The
Fourth of
July

Frozen Watermelon Martinis

Slow-Barbecued Texas Brisket with Bourbon Barbecue Sauce

Grilled Lobster Tails with Tomato-Cilantro Vinaigrette

Lobster Claw and Potato Salad with Horseradish-Mustard Dressing

Crunchy Three-Cabbage Slaw

Toasted Coconut Custard Pie with a Brûlée Crust

Frozen Watermelon Martinis

Refreshing, intoxicating, and patriotic, this slushy drink is a great kickoff for a Fourth of July event. Watermelon is popular around the world (it was brought to our country from Africa), but on the Fourth, it's an all-American must.

Serves 8

5   cups watermelon pieces, seeds removed
½   cup sugar
½   cup water
2   tablespoons fresh lemon juice
1¼ cups vodka
2   ounces melon liqueur (optional)
8   lemon twists, for garnish

1. In a food processor, puree the watermelon until very smooth, about 4–5 minutes. Pour the pureed watermelon into two empty ice cube trays and freeze for at least 4 hours. Freeze martini glasses for serving.

2. Bring the sugar and water to a boil in a small saucepan and cook until the sugar has completely dissolved. Let cool.

3. When ready to serve, combine the frozen watermelon cubes, ¼ cup simple syrup, lemon juice, vodka, and liqueur in a blender and blend until smooth. Taste for sweetness and add more simple syrup if necessary. Pour into glasses and garnish each with a lemon twist.

Slow-Barbecued Texas Brisket with Bourbon Barbecue Sauce

There's nothing more American than Texas barbecue. A sandwich of thin-sliced barbecued brisket on a soft roll (with a dab of smoky barbecue sauce and a mound of coleslaw) might just make your guests stand up and sing "The Star-Spangled Banner"!

A sure sign of quality Texas barbecue is the "smoke ring," a reddish-brown outer layer the meat develops during the Texas treatment: a dry spice rub and a super-slow cooking method. It takes a long time, but the flavor makes it absolutely worth it! It's best to let the meat "relax" off the heat for a while to become tender before carving it, then slice and reheat it before serving.

Serves 6–8

For the spice rub:

- 3 tablespoons ancho chile powder
- 1 teaspoon chile de arbol powder or another pure chile powder
- 2 teaspoons cumin
- 1 tablespoon kosher salt
- 1 teaspoon freshly ground black pepper
- 2 tablespoons dark brown sugar
- 2 tablespoons finely chopped fresh garlic

For the brisket:

- 1 whole beef brisket, about 5 pounds
  Salt
  Bourbon Barbecue Sauce (see below)

1. Make the spice rub: Combine all the ingredients in a bowl.

2. Make the brisket: Preheat a grill to high. Rub the brisket with the spice rub. Place the brisket on the grill and brown on one side. Reduce the heat to low. Brush the top with Bourbon Barbecue Sauce and turn the brisket over.

3. Close the cover of the grill and slowly barbecue the brisket until tender, about 4 hours, basting with barbecue sauce every 30 minutes. *(You can also cook the meat, loosely wrapped in foil, in a 225°F oven, about 1 hour per pound. Baste every 30 minutes.)* Remove the brisket from the grill, brush generously with barbecue sauce, let rest for 15 minutes, and slice thinly against the grain. Serve with remaining sauce.

Bourbon Barbecue Sauce

- 2 tablespoons canola oil
- 2 red onions, finely diced
- 4 cloves garlic, finely chopped
- 2 tablespoons ancho chile power
- 1 tablespoon pasilla chile powder or another pure chile powder
- 2 teaspoons chile de arbol powder or another pure chile powder
- 1 large can (32 ounces) plum tomatoes plus juices, pureed
- 1 cup water
- 2 tablespoons chipotle puree (page xiii)
- ¼ cup each ketchup, Dijon mustard, molasses, honey, and dark brown sugar
- ½ cup red wine vinegar
  Salt and freshly ground pepper
- 2 cups bourbon

Heat the oil in a large saucepan over medium-high heat. Add the onions and cook, stirring, until soft. Add the garlic and cook 2 minutes more. Add the chile powders and cook 5 minutes more. Add the tomatoes, water, chipotle puree, ketchup, mustard, molasses, honey, brown sugar, and vinegar, and season with salt and pepper. Cook the sauce until thickened, 25–30 minutes. Add the bourbon, bring to a boil, and cook 10 additional minutes, to allow the alcohol to burn off. Taste for salt and pepper and set aside.

Grilled Lobster Tails with Tomato-Cilantro Vinaigrette

A casual backyard barbecue is my favorite way to celebrate the Fourth. And big, sweet Maine lobsters, which are in season in the summer, make me feel a lot more patriotic than burgers and hot dogs. So that's what I serve alongside the brisket sandwiches. Boiling the lobsters makes the meat tender — the quick grilling just adds the smoky flavor I love. Then I hit them with a herbaceous vinaigrette right as they come off the grill; the heat releases all the aromas and flavors.

Serves 8

Eight 2-pound live lobsters
Olive oil
Salt and freshly ground pepper
Tomato-Cilantro Vinaigrette (see below)

1. Bring a large pot of salted water to a boil. Add the lobsters to the pot, cover, and boil 10–12 minutes, or just until bright red. Remove the lobsters from the water, let cool slightly, and twist off the tails. Twist off the claws and set aside for the potato salad recipe.

2. When ready to serve, preheat a grill to high. Brush the flesh side of the lobster with olive oil and season with salt and pepper. Grill the lobster, flesh side down, 1–2 minutes or until browned and hot. Remove from the grill, drizzle immediately with Tomato-Cilantro Vinaigrette, and serve.

Tomato-Cilantro Vinaigrette

4 plum tomatoes, halved, seeded, and coarsely chopped
¼ cup white wine vinegar
1 small shallot, finely chopped
¼ cup chopped cilantro
2 teaspoons honey
  Salt and freshly ground pepper
¾ cup olive oil

Place the tomatoes, vinegar, shallot, cilantro, and honey in a blender, season with salt and pepper, and blend until smooth, about 2 minutes. With the motor running, slowly add the oil until emulsified. Season to taste with salt and pepper.

Lobster Claw and Potato Salad with Horseradish-Mustard Dressing

You'll never think about potato salad the same way after tasting this. This outrageously good mixture brings rich lobster meat, tender starchy potatoes, and crisp scallions together in a creamy mayonnaise dressing sparked with mustard and horseradish. You can't imagine how delicious it is — just make it!

Serves 6–8

4 pounds unpeeled Yukon Gold potatoes
16 lobster claws, meat only, diced or shredded (see previous recipe)
1 cup good-quality mayonnaise
¼ cup whole grain mustard
3 tablespoons prepared horseradish, drained
3 tablespoons white wine vinegar
3 cloves garlic, finely chopped
  Salt and freshly ground pepper
6 scallions, white and pale green parts only, thinly sliced
2 tablespoons chopped fresh tarragon

1. Place the potatoes in a large pot and cover with cold salted water. Bring to a boil and cook until just done, about 10 minutes. Drain. As soon as the potatoes are cool enough to handle, cut into ½-inch dice. Combine the potatoes and lobster in a large bowl.

2. Meanwhile, whisk together the mayonnaise, mustard, horseradish, vinegar, and garlic in a medium bowl and season to taste with salt and pepper. Add the mayonnaise mixture to the warm potato-lobster mixture and stir gently until combined. Fold in the scallions and tarragon and season to taste with salt and pepper.

Crunchy Three-Cabbage Slaw

You've got to have both coleslaw and potato salad to make it an all-American cookout on the Fourth. A creamy potato salad like my Lobster Claw and Potato Salad with Horseradish-Mustard Dressing calls for a crisp, tangy coleslaw like this colorful one, packed with crunchy sweet peppers and three different cabbages. The vinaigrette serves to tenderize the salad as well as flavor it.

Serves 6–8

½ small head green cabbage, shredded
½ small head red cabbage, shredded
½ small head Napa cabbage, shredded
2 carrots, shredded
1 red onion, halved and thinly sliced
1 yellow bell pepper, halved, seeded, and cut into thin strips
1 orange bell pepper, halved, seeded, and cut into thin strips
2 jalapeño peppers, seeded and finely diced
½ cup cider vinegar
1 tablespoon Dijon mustard
2 teaspoons dry mustard
2 teaspoons sugar
⅓ cup vegetable oil
    Salt and freshly ground pepper

Toss together the cabbage, carrots, onion, bell peppers, and jalapeño peppers in a large bowl. Whisk together the vinegar, mustards, and sugar in a medium bowl and season with salt and pepper. Slowly whisk in the oil until emulsified. Pour the dressing over the vegetables and toss to coat. Season to taste with salt and pepper. Let sit at room temperature at least 15 minutes before serving.

Toasted Coconut Custard Pie with a Brûlée Crust

Coconut cream pie was my favorite childhood dessert, and I still love to make it. The last time I did, that smooth white filling just looked so inviting: I couldn't resist putting a crunchy crust on top of it. A quick sprinkling of raw sugar and a minute or two under the broiler, and I had a brand new pie, a delicious combination of coconut cream pie and crème brûlée.

Serves 6–8

For the crust:

1½ cups all-purpose flour

1 tablespoon sugar

½ teaspoon salt

6 tablespoons cold unsalted butter, cut into small pieces

¼ cup cold vegetable shortening, cut into small pieces

4–6 tablespoons ice water

For the filling:

3 cups unsweetened coconut

2 cups milk

¾ cup sugar

4 large eggs

2 teaspoons pure vanilla extract

3 tablespoons turbinado (raw) sugar

1. Make the pastry: Place the flour, sugar, and salt in the bowl of a food processor and pulse twice, just to combine. Add the butter and shortening and pulse until the mixture resembles coarse crumbs. Add the water 1 tablespoon at a time, pulsing after each addition, until the dough just starts to hold together. Turn the dough out onto a lightly floured surface and gently form into a disk. Cover with plastic wrap and refrigerate at least 1 hour, or overnight.

2. On a floured work surface, roll the dough out into an 11-inch circle. Transfer into a 9-inch pie plate (preferably glass). Flute the rim of the crust and prick the bottom with the tines of a fork. Refrigerate until ready to use.

3. Toast the coconut: Preheat the oven to 350°F and set a rack at the middle level. Spread 1 cup of the coconut evenly on a sheet pan. Toast the coconut until golden brown, 6–8 minutes total, stirring once.

4. Make the filling: In a medium saucepan over low heat, heat the milk until bubbles appear around the edges. Add the remaining untoasted coconut. Remove from the heat and let cool completely. Pour the mixture through a fine strainer into a bowl, pressing on the coconut to extract as much moisture as possible.

5. Reheat the oven to 350°F. Whisk together the eggs and sugar in a medium bowl, then whisk in the milk, the toasted coconut, and the vanilla extract. Pour the mixture into the prepared pie

shell, place the pie on a baking sheet, and bake 35–45 minutes, or until the filling is set, but not overcooked. The center of the pie should still jiggle when gently shaken. Let cool on a rack, then refrigerate, covered, at least 4 hours.

6. Just before serving, preheat the broiler (or fire up a kitchen torch). Sprinkle the top of the pie evenly with the sugar. Broil until the sugar has melted, 1–2 minutes. Remove and let the sugar cool before serving.

Postcard from Northern California

If you're a shellfish fiend like me, any trip to California is a good excuse for a detour to the Dungeness crab stands on Fisherman's Wharf in San Francisco. With all due respect to the watermen of Chesapeake Bay and their blue crabs, the incredible size of Dungeness crabs (they are found only in the Pacific) makes them totally irresistible. But I never thought my passion for Dungeness crabs would almost kill me! Dungeness crabs used to be plentiful in San Francisco Bay, but these days the fishermen have to go farther and farther out as the season progresses. Which explains why last year I found myself out to sea, well past the Golden Gate bridge, in a tiny boat in a very big storm. To recover from three hours in pounding swells, I headed right back to Fisherman's Wharf to refresh myself with some cioppino and sourdough bread, one of America's great food combinations.

Cioppino is an old favorite of mine and a San Francisco classic, a savory Italian-American combination of tomatoes, garlic, red pepper flakes, and as much shellfish and fish as the pot will hold. The seafood restaurants along the Wharf all make cioppino pretty much the same way: The key ingredient is the roe and fat from the crabs, which is used to enrich and flavor the delicious tomato broth. Each restaurant also runs an outdoor stand on the Wharf, where they sell oysters, cooked Pacific lobsters (they lack the big front claws of Atlantic lobsters), and whole Dungeness crabs that you can eat by the water.

Also on the Wharf is San Francisco's oldest and best baker of sourdough bread, Boudin's, where the starter dates all the way back to 1849. Boudin's bread is perfect: chewy, crisp, and tangy without being aggressively sour. Some say that it's the foggy, salty air of the Bay Area that makes the sourdough bread there so good: Sourdough starter feeds on the wild yeasts in the air, and has to be exposed to them often. Sourdough is so important in the West (a nickname for people who live in Alaska is "sourdoughs") because the early settlers and gold miners relied on it completely for baking bread. Unlike yeast, sourdough starter can replenish itself forever and never dies as long as it stays warm and is fed a little flour occasionally. Some old sourdoughs used to wear their starters in pouches around their necks to keep them warm and healthy!

The last time I had lunch on the Wharf happened to be the day before the Chinese New Year, so I headed over to Chinatown to watch the preparations. San Francisco's Chinatown is the oldest in the country and still observes the traditions, like a big noisy parade (the dragons, firecrackers, and drums are supposed to scare off evil spirits for a whole year). Chinese New Year banquets include plenty of foods that are red (the color of good luck) and that resemble gold coins (think golden-baked cookies or fried round dumplings), to ensure a prosperous new year. I could hardly keep up with all the symbolism, but the vegetables and shellfish were as sparkling fresh and plentiful as ever.

Later that day, I drove up to Sonoma, a county so dedicated to producing fine Mediterranean ingredients that it's like a miniature Provence. Lamb, goat cheese, olive oil, microgreens (even tinier than baby greens), foie gras, chanterelle mushrooms, and of course wine are all being raised, made, and collected by the dedicated (you might even say obsessed) artisans of Sonoma County.

Olives have been grown in California since the days of the Spanish missionaries, but now the business of making olive oil is really taking off in Sonoma. I visited a spanking new olive press, shared by many growers, where they all bring their olives to be cold-pressed into extra-virgin olive oil. The California producers are making small batches of oil from specific kinds of olives, so you can buy oil that is all Picholine or Manzanillo, each one with different flavor qualities. I tried out seven different ones, trying to imitate my guide as she showed me how to taste the oil by taking a sip and then sucking in air "to make it run over your back teeth." Aside from making a lot of slurpy noises, this method helps you appreciate the oil's natural sweetness (at the front of your mouth) and then its pepperiness (in the back of your throat). I was interested that they use dark blue glass for the tasting cups: The usual story is that greener oils taste more peppery and gold oils more smooth, but these experts said that's actually not true. They tell you to taste, not to look.

My guide to the world of California mushrooms was professional forager Charmoon Richardson (he told me that his name came to him while meditating twenty-five years ago). Chanterelles and morels are wild mushrooms that grow in many of the damper regions of the United States, but no one knows exactly why or how—and they've never been successfully cultivated. From years of foraging, Charmoon can look at a grove of trees and be pretty sure whether it holds a stash of mushrooms or not. In Sonoma, the chanterelles can grow as big as a dinner plate—or a Dungeness crab.

Sources

For duck breasts and other game:

D'Artagnan, Inc.
www.dartagnan.com
Phone: 800-327-8246
Fax: 973-465-1870

For chiles and other Southwestern ingredients:

The Kitchen Market
Phone: 888-468-4433

For chiles, corn husks for making tamales, pomegranate molasses, coconut milk, and other international ingredients:

www.ethnicgrocer.com
Phone: 800-523-1961

Or:

Dean & Deluca
www.deananddeluca.com
Phone: 800-221-7714
Fax: 800-781-4050

For all Latin/Mexican/Caribbean ingredients, including guava paste:

Latin Grocer, Inc.
www.latingrocer.com
Phone: 877-477-2323

Index

sandwich on toasted garlic bread with cheddar, tomato-olive relish, and skillet fries, 37
spice-rubbed ribeyes with pinto bean relish, 138
stock:
chicken, xiv
shrimp, xiv
vegetable, 8
striped bass, slow fire-roasted, with fresh mint and
tomato relish, 98
stuffings:
skillet cornbread, with mushrooms, herbs, and
andouille sausage, 208
sun-dried cranberry, 144
succotash, butter bean and sweet onion, 174
sweet potato(es):
and allspice pie with benne seed crust, 195
biscuit crust, smoked chicken and caramelized vegetable pot pie with, 120
biscuits, 166
-chicken hash with poached eggs and green chile hollandaise, 32
and clam chowder, New England, 12
lemon-glazed, 165
and plantain puree with maple and cinnamon, 212
-Vidalia onion salad, 146
whipped, 156
Swiss chard:
black-eyed pea risotto with smoked bacon and, 87
with red onions and serrano chile vinegar, 173

tacos:
BBQ pork loin, roasted Red Bliss potatoes, and
tomatillo-red pepper relish, 40
New Mexico-style soft, with hacked chicken and salsa
verde, 39
tamales:
red bean, with roasted tomato salsa, 78-79
wild rice, with sage butter, 66-68
tarts:
guava and cheese, 194
pear, with hazelnut-brown sugar crust, 183
Thanksgiving, 202-13
cranberry martinis, 204
fresh cranberry-fig relish, 209
gratin of green beans with roasted garlic and shallots,
210
mashed potatoes with scallions and crème fraîche,
211
pumpkin bread pudding with molasses whipped
cream, 213
roasted turkey with pomegranate-black pepper glaze
and fresh sage-smoked chile gravy, 205-6
skillet cornbread stuffing with mushrooms, herbs, and
andouille sausage, 208
sweet potato and plantain puree with maple and cinnamon, 212

tomatillo:
chilaquiles with scrambled eggs, 31
-clementine sauce, 128
-red pepper relish, 40
tomato(es):
-cilantro vinaigrette, 222
and fresh mint relish, 98
Jersey, and Vidalia onion salad with blue ranch dressing, 48
-olive relish, 37
-red chile sauce, 30
roasted, 18
roasted, broth, 92
roasted, salsa, 79
sauce, 84
summer, and spring onion soup, cold, with grilled
scallops, 9
yellow, crispy soft-shell crab salad with green
garlic vinaigrette and, 50
tortillas, fried, 58
tostones, plantain, grilled shrimp with avocado cocktail
sauce on, 62
trout, pan-fried rainbow, with pecans and brown
butter, 99
turkey, roasted, with pomegranate-black pepper glaze
and fresh sage-smoked chile gravy, 205-6

vegetable(s):
caramelized, and smoked chicken pot pie with sweet
potato biscuit crust, 120
stock, 8
see also sides; specific vegetables
venison:
-black bean chili with green chile crema and white
cornbread, 154-55
pan-roasted, with spicy cranberry-Mexican
cinnamon sauce and whipped sweet potatoes, 156
vinaigrettes:
aged sherry, 53
black olive, 86
green garlic, 50
shallot, 49
spicy orange, 46
tomato-cilantro, 222
warm lemon-crispy caper, 94
vinegar, serrano chile, 173

watermelon martinis, frozen, 218
whipped cream:
maple, 184
molasses, 213
wild rice:
risotto, 130
tamales with sage butter, 66-68
waffles, shrimp and littleneck clam curry with candied mango butter on, 106-8